D1600563

Romantic Literature, Race, and Colonial Encounter

Nineteenth-Century Major Lives and Letters
Series Editor: Marilyn Gaull

The nineteenth century invented major figures: gifted, productive, and influential writers and artists in English, European, and American public life who captured and expressed what Hazlitt called "The Spirit of the Age." Their achievements summarize, reflect, and shape the cultural traditions they inherited and influence the quality of life that followed. Before radio, film, and journalism deflected the energies of authors and audiences alike, literary forms such as popular verse, song lyrics, biographies, memoirs, letters, novels, reviews, essays, children's books, and drama generated a golden age of letters incomparable in Western history. *Nineteenth-Century Major Lives and Letters* presents a series of original biographical, critical, and scholarly studies of major figures evoking their energies, achievements, and their impact on the character of this age. Projects to be included range from works on Blake to Hardy, Erasmus Darwin to Charles Darwin, Wordsworth to Yeats, Coleridge and J. S. Mill, Joanna Baillie, Jane Austen, Sir Walter Scott, Byron, Shelley, Keats to Dickens, Tennyson, George Eliot, Browning, Hopkins, Lewis Carroll, Rudyard Kipling, and their contemporaries. The series editor is Marilyn Gaull, PhD from Indiana University. She has served on the faculty at Temple University, New York University, and is now Research Professor at the Editorial Institute at Boston University. She brings to the series decades of experience as editor of books on nineteenth century literature and culture. She is the founder and editor of *The Wordsworth Circle*, author of *English Romanticism: The Human Context*, publishes editions, essays, and reviews in numerous journals and lectures internationally on British Romanticism, folklore, and narrative theory.

PUBLISHED BY PALGRAVE:
Shelley's German Afterlives, by Susanne Schmid
Romantic Literature, Race, and Colonial Encounter, by Peter J. Kitson

FORTHCOMING TITLES:
Coleridge, the Bible, and Religion, by Jeffrey W. Barbeau
Byron: Heritage and Legacy, edited by Cheryl A. Wilson
The Long and Winding Road from Blake to the Beatles, by Matthew Schneider
Reading the Sphinx: Ancient Egypt in 19th Century Literary Culture, by Lynn Parramore

Romantic Literature, Race, and Colonial Encounter

Peter J. Kitson

palgrave
macmillan

First published in 2007 by
PALGRAVE MACMILLAN™
175 Fifth Avenue, New York, N.Y. 10010 and
Houndmills, Basingstoke, Hampshire, England RG21 6XS
Companies and representatives throughout the world.

PALGRAVE MACMILLAN is the global academic imprint of the Palgrave Macmillan division of St. Martin's Press, LLC and of Palgrave Macmillan Ltd. Macmillan® is a registered trademark in the United States, United Kingdom and other countries. Palgrave is a registered trademark in the European Union and other countries.

ISBN-13: 978–1–4039–7645–1
ISBN-10: 1–4039–7645–7

Library of Congress Cataloging-in-Publication Data

Kitson, Peter J.
   Romantic literature, race, and colonial encounter / Peter J. Kitson.
     p. cm.—(Nineteenth-century major lives & letters)
   Includes bibliographical references (p.) and index.
   ISBN 1–4039–7645–7
     1. English literature—18th century—History and criticism.
   2. Race in literature. 3. English literature—19th century—History and criticism. 4. Colonies in literature. 5. Imperialism in literature. 6. Politics and literature—Great Britain—Colonies. 7. Great Britain—Colonies—History—18th century. 8. Great Britain—Colonies—History—19th century. 9. Romanticism—Great Britain. I. Title.

PR448.R33K58 2007
820.9'3552—dc22   2007010409

A catalogue record for this book is available from the British Library.

Design by Newgen Imaging Systems (P) Ltd., Chennai, India.

First edition: December 2007

10 9 8 7 6 5 4 3 2 1

Printed in the United States of America.

Transferred to Digital Printing in 2008

*This book is dedicated both to the
memory of my father Wilfrid Kitson
and my mother Winifrid Kitson*

CONTENTS

ACKNOWLEDGMENTS

I would like to thank the following libraries and their staff: the British Library, the National Library of Scotland, the Wellcome Institute for the History of Medicine, the National Maritime Museum and the Library of Congress. I would also like to thank Simon Chaplin, the Senior Curator of the Hunterian Museum at the Royal College of Surgeons for his invaluable help and advice about John Hunter's notions of human difference.

This project has been generously funded by grants from the Arts and Humanities Research Council (UK) which provided me with the time to complete and finalize this work. I owe a special debt of gratitude to the British Academy for a series of grants for allowing me to undertake research on individual chapters of this study.

I would also like to thank the following people for their support and advice. My especial thanks go to Debbie Lee, Tim Fulford, Sharon Ruston, Marilyn Gaull, and Nicholas Roe, without whose generous and patient advice this book might never have been written. I also want to thank Peter, Bonnie, and Madge Williams for their support throughout the period of the writing of this book.

A part of chapter 1 appeared in Nicholas Roe's collection *Samuel Taylor Coleridge and the Sciences of Life* (Oxford University Press, 2001) and an earlier version of chapter 4 was published in Timothy Morton's collection *Cultures of Taste/Theories of Appetite: Eating Romanticism* (Palgrave Macmillan, 2004).

Introduction

Since the 1990s, there has been a proliferation of studies that focus on Britain and Europe from the early modern period onward that are concerned with questions of identity, whether involving gender, class, nation, religion, politics, empire, colonialism, and, possibly the most ambiguous term of all, "race." Srinivas Aravamudan has recently drawn our attention to the contribution of "Xenophobia, colonialism, orientalism and racism" to the "constitution of national identity" (10). This is certainly true of the eighteenth and early nineteenth centuries as literary texts and cultural artifacts are placed in the context of what is described, in a recent collection of essays, as *The Global Eighteenth Century*. Its editor, Felicity A. Nussbaum, claims that the collection "resituates eighteenth-century studies within a spatially and conceptually expanded paradigm." The contributors analyze "the European encounter with other populations throughout the world and offer ways to think critically about the imperative of that colonial project" (1). Similarly, another recent and influential collection of essays seeks to chart the terrain of a "new imperial history" discussing the problems of identity, modernity and difference in the long eighteenth century (Wilson 2003). My study works with similar notions of the relationships between literature and culture generally, although its focus and emphasis is more securely on the last decades of the eighteenth century and the early decades of the nineteenth. It is also more narrowly concerned with a specific idea or body of ideas and the ways that those ideas are delineated, applied, absorbed, contested, and problematized: the idea of race.

The work is, I believe, timely because it addresses issues current in literary and historical study. Recent studies of the British Empire, such as Linda Colley's *Captives* (2003), have stressed the anxieties and uncertainties surrounding colonial and imperial advancement. A number of other studies have emphasized British conceptions of weakness and doubt when confronted by Islamic others (notably Ottomans and Barbary Corsairs from Morocco, Algiers, and Tunisia) in the period before 1850. Scholars and writers have addressed aspects of colonialism, race, and human variety in the eighteenth and nineteenth centuries. My work is especially indebted to recent writing by Srinivas Aravamudan, Hannah Augstein, Robert Bernasconi, Alan Bewell, Patrick Brantlinger, Tim Fulford, Jonathan Lamb, Suvir Kaul, Nigel Leask, Felicity Nussbaum, Debbie Lee, Alan Richardson, Nicholas Thomas, Roxann Wheeler, Saree Makdisi, Robert Young, and Marcus Wood. This substantial body of critical work, which is rapidly growing, is recasting studies of the eighteenth and early nineteenth centuries in a global context in which identity and difference are created from an often bewildering range of historical processes and discourses, of which race is one of the most important.

This is not to say that race is the most significant discourse of difference in the Romantic period. By and large I would argue that probably it is not and that those stalwarts of identity formation, religion, class, gender, and nation remained powerful. After 1850, there is a much stronger case for regarding race as the primary and crucial category that Europeans used to understand their relationships with other people. Studying the race idea in the Romantic period allows us to speculate about how race became so important. Linda Colley has shown how Protestantism provided an ideology by which Britain was able to forge a powerful sense of identity in the eighteenth century (Colley 1994). Protestant evangelicism remained a potent force in defining national identities in the nineteenth century, especially with the activities of the London Missionary Society and the beginnings of that great wave of Protestant missionary activity that was to sweep all parts of the world. The London Missionary Society began its existence in 1794 in a coffee house in London (Lovett 1: 3–116). The society was an expression of the "Evangelical Revival" that dominated the early nineteenth century; it was not a government-sponsored endeavor, but a society organized by Baptists, Independents, and other nonconformists. The Evangelical crusade of Christianizing the world had begun. In 1796 the South Seas were targeted, followed by operations to Africa in 1799 and Ceylon in 1804 (missionaries were banned in India until 1813). The last great objective of the Society, however, was the biggest prize of all, the Celestial Empire of China. Missionary accounts provided for the West much information about peoples newly discovered or rediscovered. Although their model for understanding other peoples and cultures was one based on a familial concept of humanity, their writing was frequently imbricated with racial thought, often in contradiction to the leading tenets of their theology. Race can also cut across other divisions, especially those of class and nation as, in the period under discussion, ideas of race and nation seldom overlapped but grouped peoples in configurations different from those that prevailed after the nineteenth-century dominance of the ideology of the nation-state. In the early stages of the formulations of their typologies, the key theorists of human variety also tend to homogenize large numbers of peoples and the main category for describing British and European remained J.F. Blumenbach's "Caucasian," or one of the major variations upon it. In some iterations, nations can contain more than one race, the Franks and the Gauls in France, for instance. Races can also include many nations. Racial typologies, like other forms of categorization, may also have a descriptive function that does not necessarily imply hierarchy. This study also attempts to describe how racial thought becomes saturated with assumptions relating to the different moral, intellectual, and aesthetic values attributed to different kinds of human beings. Scholars working in this field are much indebted to the pioneering studies of Londa Schiebinger (1994), and more recently, David Bindman (2002).

The "Race" issue—the origins of the "Race" idea and its growth, articulation, and continued pervasiveness—is one that preoccupies a great deal of contemporary literary and cultural criticism. One of the main reasons for this is that, in the words of Robert J. C. Young, "the nightmare of the ideologies and categories of racism continue to repeat upon the living" (28). Historians of race have noted that there is a congruence between the development of a systematized sense of human difference in the natural sciences and the period we roughly designate as Romantic, if not earlier. George Mosse boldly claims that "Eighteenth-century Europe was the cradle of modern racism" (1). In his seminal study of the idea of race, Ivan Hannaford also argues for its comparatively modern pedigree. Classical Greek and early modern texts divide peoples into political categories, such as Greeks and Barbarians (formally those not speaking Greek), rather than biological groupings. Hannaford argues that the idea of race is "fundamentally an Enlightenment notion used within the structure of legitimate intellectual inquiry to explain complex human arrangements, such as caste and tribe, that are based on historical presuppositions and dispositions totally antipathetic to both politics qua politics and to race" (6). David Lloyd shows that Enlightenment and Romantic natural philosophers established a paradigm of difference that was no longer an arbitrary mark or a cultural distinction, but rather consisted in and of natural signs written on the body itself (62–69). By the early nineteenth century, then, what increasingly served to distinguish one people from another was not their religion, their degree of "civilization," their customs or their beliefs, but rather their anatomy and external appearance. These scholars attempt to track a particular strand of thought that becomes the dominant mode of racial thinking in the nineteenth century. As Bulmer and Solomos comment, "Whatever the longer-term history of images of the 'other' in various societies and historical periods it does seem clear that only in the late eighteenth century and early nineteenth century does the term 'race' come to refer to supposedly discrete categories of people defined according to their physical characteristics" (8). This is not, of course, simply to maintain that pre–nineteenth-century thinking is necessarily innocent of racial thought and that Romantic transcendentalism, disguising racist thought in the garb of an aesthetic and idealist philosophy, is the real villain of the story, but that, for whatever reason, thinkers of the Enlightenment and Romantic periods sought to provide accounts of human difference in which the physical and biological were increasingly more important than they were in earlier periods. Their motivations for doing so are mixed and complex, and their working methods saturated with assumptions and prejudices of which they were mostly unaware, or could not be aware. It is also an assumption of this study that the race idea, in the majority of cases in this period, is not obviously, or even consciously, fabricated to account for such historical and material events and processes as colonialism and slavery.[1]

In her major and comprehensive study of eighteenth-century categories of human difference in British culture, Roxann Wheeler has convincingly argued that a kind of paradigm shift, one that signals a move from an interest in cultural to physical or bodily markers, occurs toward the end of the century in ideas about the differences between peoples and cultures:

> In eighteenth-century Britain, the ideology of human variety broadly changed from being articulated primarily through religious difference, which included such things as political governance and civil life, to being articulated primarily through scientific categories derived from natural history that featured external characteristics of the human body—color, facial features, and hair texture. At the end of the century, the contours of racial ideology were more established than a century before, a solidification that accompanied the more important role of race and racism in the intellectual pursuits and structures of everyday life in Britain. The transference from a cultural emphasis to a bodily emphasis was imperfect, of course, and occurred at various paces in different realms that used racial ideology as a reference point. (Wheeler 2000, 291)[2]

Wheeler argues that it is not until the third quarter of the eighteenth century (roughly the time at which this study begins) that skin color emerges as "the most important component of racial identity" in a range of scientific and other texts (9). Wheeler's revisionary account of race thinking in the eighteenth century, however, also counsels against limiting racist culture entirely to the realm of natural science and its physical typologies of difference, demonstrating how the notion of four-stage social development derived from the Enlightenment cultural anthropology of Adam Smith, Adam Ferguson, John Millar, Lord Kames, and others was also imbricated with racist assumptions. Informed by the cultural anthropology of Nicholas Thomas and others, Wheeler's work demonstrates how difference was not confined to the issue of white and black complexions.[3] Nussbaum has similarly problematized our notion of race in the long eighteenth century in her wide-ranging discussions of poems, drama, fictions, autobiographies, and visual representations. Nussbaum substantially agrees with Wheeler that prior to the last decades of the century, representations of racial difference were cross-hatched with representations of gender, masculinity, and national identity. During the period, sexual and racial identities, in the modern sense of the word, were beginning to emerge, but were marked with ambivalence, contradiction, and confusions (*Limits of the Human* 2003, 1–20). Kathleen Wilson has similarly argued that traditional notions of difference and identity in the eighteenth century "religion, history, community" could be "just as pernicious and essentializing, and create symbolic barriers as impassable as any scientific or biological ones, in the early modern period and today." Such "cultural articulations of race posted as 'natural' could be just as essentializing as the most reductionist physiological theory." Wilson is concerned to establish how the "alchemy of national identity" is formed or constructed from both "cultural ideas about race" and "racialized notions of nation" (2003, 12).

All those working on race issues in the eighteenth century and after are indebted to both Wheeler's and Nussbaum's pioneering and scholarly discussions of the relationships between ideas of human difference and literary texts. My own study substantially agrees with their insights, but, being focused on the later decades of the eighteenth and early decades of the nineteenth centuries, is more concerned with the significance of the biological and the various other models of race deriving from this source. By the end of the Romantic period, the biological understanding of race was clearly becoming the dominant paradigmatic explanation of human difference. Though there was still enormous confusion as to what the races were, how many there were, where they originated from, and how their difference was occasioned, all these confusions became less foggy in the world of European empire.

"Race" is a very slippery term used in several different ways in the eighteenth and early nineteenth centuries and later in our own times. As Bulmer and Solomos comment, "[T]he very notion of *race* has no fixed and unchanging meaning" and "from a historical view it is clear from research on the usages of the notion of race over the past two centuries that it has taken on various forms in different national contexts" (7). Robert Young has convincingly and brilliantly shown that the texts of racial theory are not homogenous and stable but "contradictory, disruptive and already deconstructed" (27). Yet one of the major debates about the use of the term concerns the importance one attaches to the biological and somatic aspects of its thinking. According to most scholars, racism in the modern sense did not exist as a way of thinking before the Enlightenment, as there were no developed sciences of biology, comparative anatomy, and anthropology. Nor were there any genetic hereditary principles to support it. Margaret T. Hodgen, for instance, argues that, in the early modern period "any effort to distinguish among the 'races' of mankind on either anatomical, physiological, or cultural grounds was relatively negligible" (213).[4] Robert Bernasconi claims that "the invention of the concept of race...took place sometime after the introduction of the broad division of peoples on the basis of colour, nationality, and other inherited characteristics that could not be overcome subsequently, as religious differences could be overcome by conversion." Earlier historical oppression, persecution, or extermination of subordinate peoples may have been "racist" in the looser sense of the term, but it was not "sustained by a scientific concept of race" (2001, 11).

Others, however, have argued that biological determinism is only one historical phase, or one articulation of a racist grammar that dates back to as early as the sixteenth century. This can be seen in the prevalence of a Christian semiotics that associate black with evil and sinfulness, and whiteness with purity, as well as in a pervasive ethnocentrism derived from the material process of colonialism and settlement from Columbus onward.[5] An exemplary critic of this kind, David Theo Goldberg, has argued that the term "race" with its concomitant category "racist thinking," emerged in the sixteenth century as a central invention of European modernity. Goldberg uses the term to describe a process of "group differentiation" by which Western society promoted and developed general standards, which were then universalized. He tracks this naturalization of the Eurocentric vision up to modernity's formulations of moral personhood and subjectivity. All racism at its core is thus a mechanism for promoting exclusions and inclusions (1993, 1–84; 1990, xvi–xxiii).[6] Similarly Torres, Mirón, and Xavier Inda conclude that "race" is a "fluid, unfixed concept which signifies differently depending on the social and historical contexts in which 'it' is articulated" (7). Again, Wheeler warns that "it is imperative to define eighteenth-century race and racism in ways that are not based in biology or determinism" and that we should understand that the primary vehicle for eighteenth-century racism was the conviction that "people in remote parts of Europe and Asia were inferior because they had not become commercial people as quickly or as easily as Europeans" (2000, 300). Wheeler, like Goldberg, wants to retain the notions of race and racism, but wishes to use them in the more general sense of a justification for group dominance over other subject groups, although she is more culture-specific in her analysis. Such notions recall the earlier and brilliant postcolonial insight of Albert Memmi that one becomes racist with "the deployment of a difference to denigrate the other, to the end of gaining privilege or benefit through that stigmatization" and that "the focus on biological difference…is not the essential aspect of racism." According to Memmi, "Racism does not limit itself to biology or economics or psychology or metaphysics: *it attacks along many fronts and in many forms*, deploying whatever is at hand, and even what is not, inventing when the need arises" (37–38, 78, 92).

This book attempts to discuss various aspects of the race idea in the late eighteenth and early nineteenth centuries. It does not try to provide an intellectual and cultural history of the depiction of other cultures and regions, such as the Near East and the Indian subcontinent, which are not discussed in any great detail because of the extensive body of writing already in existence. Chapter 1 sets out the intellectual background, defining and describing the rise of the race idea in the classificatory systems of the Enlightenment and Romantic thought. Although there were earlier progenitors of the notion that physical characteristics are hereditary and that they signify certain intellectual, moral, or, aesthetic hierarchies, it is in what we commonly call the Romantic period that such ideas become more fully established in the natural sciences and were applied to other forms of cultural writing. This chapter attempts to articulate the growth and development of the idea and the major debates that surround it and then discusses the cases of the two Romantic writers most aware of contemporary racial thought: S.T. Coleridge and Thomas De Quincey. Chapter 2 concerns the field of the natural sciences, but focuses more specifically on the new Romantic science of comparative anatomy. Not all, but a great many of the theorists of human difference in the late eighteenth and early nineteenth centuries were practicing comparative anatomists. This chapter shows how the science of comparative anatomy was, from its inception, a racial science concerned with the determination of the relationship of humanity to the rest of the natural world, and with the further speculation of the differences between humans and the causes of those differences. The chapter concludes with a reading of the most famous literary comparative anatomist of the period, Victor Frankenstein, and what the debates may mean for the ways in which we might elucidate the theories of race espoused or implied by Mary Shelley's novel.

Chapter 3 addresses the major debate on the relationship between ideas about race and the debate on the transatlantic slave trade. Historians of slavery and race have for long argued about the priority of racial thought to the institution of slavery with some arguing that black slavery was a consequence of an already deep-seated European racism, while others claiming that racism was produced by slavery. Although prejudice against those with darker skins has been present prior to the establishment of plantation slavery, I argue that the race idea postdates the practice. There are biological arguments for slavery in the debate but they are seldom used by the planters themselves, and are more obvious in the abolitionist writing that seeks to refute them. This chapter discusses the views of natural philosophers about slavery and attempts to articulate the race theory of abolitionist writing. Chapter 4 discusses the impact of writing about the South Seas on the development of race theory. More than any other theater of discovery, Oceania influenced contemporary theories of difference. The peoples discovered to the West by Bougainville, Cook, and others forced theorists of human variety, notably Kant and Blumenbach, to revise their theories to take into account the existence of peoples with markedly differing physical features who lived in relatively close proximity. Race theory competed here most obviously with an Enlightenment stadial theory of human progress from savagery, through barbarism to civilization and liberty, as well as with Protestant missionary writing, both of which manifested different methodologies for understanding human difference in Oceania.

Chapters 5 and 6 move the focus of the study to the "Far East," specifically the Qing Empire and its surrounding peoples. These two chapters address the interpenetration of the race idea with contemporary notions of orientalism and the alleged recurrent stereotyping of Asian peoples. Chapter 5 focuses on a wide range of representations of China and her peoples in the late eighteenth and early nineteenth centuries. The discourses are not limited to natural science, but cover economic, political, diplomatic and, missionary areas too. Notoriously, the Qing Empire was transformed in this period from one of the most admired and esteemed non-European polity to a despised, degenerate, and collapsing edifice. Chapter 5, in particular, outlines the crucial importance of the Macartney Embassy of 1792–94 that generated a substantial discussion about the status of the Qing Empire. Chapter 6 extends this analysis to take account of the racial doppelganger of the Chinese, the Tartar, and argues that this category of human was constructed over a substantial period of time as a kind of "in-between" race, between the three great empires of Central Eurasia: the Qing, the Romanov, and the Ottoman. The chapter concludes with a discussion of Thomas De Quincey's extraordinary essay, "The Revolt of the Kalmuck Tartars" (1834).

Chapter 1

The Race Idea and the Romantics: Coleridge and De Quincey

Defining "Race"

The focus of this first chapter has been narrowed to consider the importance of one of the languages of racism from the mid-eighteenth century to the early nineteenth century, that is, "classic racism," the "racism of ideology" or "scientific racism." This involves the affirmation in scientific and literary discourses that humanity can be divided into certain distinct groupings on the basis of common physical (and often moral and intellectual) characteristics that were regarded as hereditary. This is not to be taken as an argument that "racism" did not exist before biological racism was articulated and developed, nor that it disappeared when that form of belief began to lose credibility, particularly after the atrocities of German National Socialism. The rationale for focusing my discussion in this way is determined by the growing importance of the race idea in the period under discussion, as, increasingly, the leading, though never the exclusive, paradigm for discussing human variety. It may well be that this is a discussion of the surface language or one of the idioms of racism and not the deep structure or grammar of the ideology that David Theo Goldberg attempts to delineate in his work. Nevertheless, by juxtaposing an understanding of this idiom in a number of areas, we may also gain some understanding of how the deep structure of racism, the underlying bass notes of the symphony, reveals itself in its leitmotif. This is not to say that thinking of race in biological terms is the only form of racism that should be considered; clearly it is not. In the chapters which follow a number of differing models of human variety are explored; however even those other models often partake, consciously or otherwise, of essentialist conceptions of race, even when they may be hostile, resistant, or out of sympathy with biologically determined models of human behavior and difference. When one surveys the range of writings on this subject one is often left with more of a sense of confusion and ambiguity than any clear and straightforward articulation of racial thinking.

The texts discussed in this chapter, and elsewhere in this book, are troubling and disturbing pieces of writing. Some might argue that it would have been better if texts such as Edward Long's discussion of "Negroes" in his *History of Jamaica* (1774) and Charles White's *Account of the Regular Gradation in Man* (1799) never saw the light of day again; so virulent are these two authors' comments on and assumptions about the status of African and other peoples. Many of the writers discussed in this book were also surgeons and anatomists who obsessively measured their black and other racial subjects, dissected their corpses, and frequently collected their genitalia—both male and female—as well as their crania as specimens for anatomical illustration and display. Indeed some might concur with the Rev. Richard Watson when he argued in 1824 that the real enemy of racial equality were scientists per se, "the minute philosophers, who take the gauge of intellectual capacity from the disposition of the bones of the head, and link mortality and the contour of the countenance" (Quoted in Curtin 242). However this would certainly be mistaken. Science itself as an activity could, in theory, be neutral and the intentions of eighteenth-century natural philosophers were seldom to falsify their research to arrive at predetermined conclusions, no matter how much their assumptions might lead to practices weighted to prove their prejudices. However, in the current climate of opinion in which we interrogate our linguistic, cultural, and aesthetic assumptions for signs of the ways in which they might be complicit with, or resistant to, later bodies of racist thought, it is important that we investigate how such texts may have pioneered the ways in which later generations classified, characterized, and then stereotyped the peoples of the world.

Romanticism as an aesthetic system has frequently been accused of complicity in this racist project because of the ways in which its adherents privileged notions of nation and "race." According to Martin Bernal "Romanticism" was one of the major forces that led to the overthrow of the generally accepted notion that Greek civilization was indebted for its ideas and achievements to the Afro-Asiatic civilization of Ancient Egypt. Bernal argues that the Romantic concern with ethnicity, the local and the particular as expressed in an admiration for the vigorous, virtuous, and primitive folk (especially in J.G. Herder and James MacPherson, but also Wordsworth), led to the belief that as the landscape and climate of Europe were better than those of other continents, Europeans must be superior (198–223). More recently, Laura Doyle has argued that Romantic period texts demonstrate what Hannah Arendt referred to as "race–thinking before racism" a movement "in Western aesthetics from classicism to nativism to racialism" (15–39). Such a progress, it is claimed, leads to the subsequent mid-nineteenth-century pronouncements such as that of the nineteenth-century British anatomist Dr. Robert Knox (of Burke and Hare fame) that "Race is everything: literature, science, art in a word, civilization, is traceable solely to the race to which the individual or nations belong" (7).

David Bindman has explored this subject in the realm of eighteenth-century visual arts, especially German aesthetic theory, in great scholarly detail, demonstrating how the idea of race in the eighteenth century both shaped and was shaped by the contemporary aesthetic theories. He concludes that "the essential elements of nineteenth- and twentieth-century racial aesthetics were present in the eighteenth century, but these elements were usually separated from each other by a number of antitheses that were somehow resolved in the nineteenth century" (2002, 11–21, 225). In the field of popular culture, H.L. Malchow has surveyed Gothic writing from the Romantic period and beyond noting how the "creation of a popular vocabulary in the late eighteenth and nineteenth centuries" served to represent racial and cultural difference "as unnatural—a 'racial gothic' discourse that employed certain striking metaphoric images to filter and give meaning to a flood of information from abroad" (2–3). Patrick Brantlinger applied nineteenth-century racial theorizing, both Darwinian and pre-Darwinian, to the subject of the contemporary extinction of so-called primitive and savage races, establishing in a series of literary and scientific texts how race theories underwrote genocidal practices and founded a culture of scientific mourning for the peoples who disappeared around the globe, from North American Indians to Tasmanian Aboriginals (2003). All these scholars and critics, to whom my work is much indebted, accept that race thinking became more scientific in the late eighteenth and early nineteenth centuries and that its impact was not confined to scientific texts. Rather they argue that there was an interrelationship between aesthetic, literary, cultural, and scientific discourses which mutually shaped all. This study attempts to build on such insights and scholarship and to move the focus to such areas of debate, as Oceania and the Far East, which have received less attention in recent writing, thus adding detail to the overall and expanding panorama. By the early nineteenth century, what came to distinguish one people from another in all kinds of discourses from the visual arts to popular literature was not their religion, their degree of "civilization," their customs or their beliefs, but rather their anatomy and external appearance.

It is crucial, however, to understand what is understood in the period by that very slippery term "race." Michael Banton and others have shown in some detail how the use of the word "race" has changed over time, especially in the context of British and European societies (1–6). There are at least three main uses of the term in the late eighteenth and early nineteenth centuries, two of which are closely related. First there is the sense of race as denoting the lineage of a person. In 1570 John Foxe, in an early usage of the term, referred to "the race and stocke of Abraham" (Banton 2; Augstein, *James Cowles Prichard's Anthropology*, 1999, 69). Ivan Hannaford argues that in the early modern period in England "to belong to a race was to belong to a noble family with a various ancestry and a profession of public service and virtue" (175). Prior to the early nineteenth century, as Nicholas Hudson has shown, the word is used interchangeably with terms such as "nation," "tribe," and "peoples" (247–64). Used in this sense the term is historical and diachronic, describing familial descent or lineage and not physical features or appearance. Second the term is also used to characterize physical types. This use of the word, deriving from the Enlightenment classificatory system of Linnaeus (and others) relates to a series of attempts to classify and categorize collections of individuals in terms of physical appearance, skin color, hair texture, anatomical form, and other physical features. These classificatory systems were fueled by the great increase in scientific data that resulted from the voyages of exploration in the latter half of the eighteenth century, especially the three great voyages of Captain James Cook (1769–75), who circumnavigated the globe, encountering new varieties of human beings (Pratt 15–37). In such systems, the word "race" is used synchronically to describe external appearance and not descent, stock, or lineage. In most natural philosophers of the time, the word tends to be used synonymously with "variety," to describe a variation within the human family of races. The third usage of the term also describes physical characteristics but as types (in a quasi-Platonic sense) and not as varieties. This use of the word as employed, for instance, by Robert Knox in the 1840s is synonymous with the notion of "species": a permanent type of living form which does not normally interbreed with others of different species, or if it does, produces only infertile offspring, as in the case of the horse and the donkey (Buffon's test for defining species). The British anthropologist, James Cowles Prichard regretted the ambivalence surrounding the term when he wrote in 1836:

> Races are properly successions of individuals propagated from any given stock; and the term should always be used without any involved meaning that such a progeny or stock has always possessed a particular character. The real import of the term has often been overlooked, and the word race has been used as if it implied a distinction in the physical character of a whole series of individuals. By writers on anthropology, who adopt this term, it is often tacitly assumed that such distinctions were primordial, and that their successive transmission has been unbroken. If such were the fact, a race so characterised would be a species in the strict meaning of the word, and it ought to be so termed. (Prichard 1836–47, 2:109; Augstein, *James Cowles Prichard's Anthropology*, 1999, 71)

In the Enlightenment and Romantic periods the term "race" is used in widely different senses, ranging from a nominalist and relativist understanding of the concept to a usage which denotes a form of biological determinism, intellectually consistent with the later excesses of German National Socialist thought. The semantics of the issue are further problematized by the difficulties of translation, where words which should correctly be translated into English as "variety" might end up as "species" or "race." Thomas Bendyshe, Blumenbach's nineteenth-century English translator, generally used the Kantian term "Race" ("Rasse") for Blumenbach's Latin "varietate" and both terms have different inflections and meanings in the period. Most contemporary writers on the issue tend to dispense with the term altogether as essentially meaningless and often pernicious; though it is still frequently used in a nonbiological way in the social sciences.[1]

ORIGINS OF THE RACE IDEA

Modern racial thinking, it is generally claimed, begins with Enlightenment attempts to classify the natural world. Certainly race as a physical and biological concept begins to assume a new importance from this time onwards, accreting a critical mass as it rolls through into the nineteenth century, but it is not the only way of viewing humanity, nor is there a consensus among its adherents on any one model. In his *Arca Noae, sive historia imperium* of 1666, Georgius Hornius identified the progeny of Noah's three sons with their skin color; the Japhetites were white, the Semites yellow, and the Hamites, black (Poliakov 143). Most critics, however, have identified the work of the French traveler François Bernier as possibly the first commentator to group the various peoples he encountered on his travels into physically discrete groups in his essay, "A new division of the earth according to the different species or races of men" of 1684.[2] Bernier proposed four or five "espèce ou races" on the basis of geography, color, and physical characteristics: European, African, Asian, and Lapps. Bernier is unclear as to whether the North American Indians form a separate grouping or whether they should be classed with the European and finally inclined to the latter view. For Bernier such peoples were marked by permanent and hereditable physical characteristics, such as the blackness of the African's skin. Much of the essay is concerned with the beauty of the women of Bernier's racial groupings. He allows that beauty may be found everywhere, even "among the blacks of Africa," though he finds the women of the Indies most alluring. He also repeats the established wisdom that Georgia and Circassia provide "an infinity of very handsome women, as well as very handsome men" (3–4).

Bernier's observations were brief, sketchy, and hardly systematic. It was left to the Swedish naturalist Linnaeus to provide the clearest and most influential categorization of humanity into racial groups of the eighteenth century. Linnaeus sought to provide a classificatory system for the natural world, including humanity. He was not the first to attempt this. The natural philosopher and anatomist John Ray had already attempted to situate creatures in their family groupings according to a range of physical characteristics in such works as *The Wisdom of God Manifested in the Works of the Creation* (1690) but his system was unclear and maintained many traditional categorizations (Banton 2; David Knight 52–57). Linnaeus, however, identified one physical feature with which to classify creatures according to their genus, species, and variety. The tenth edition of his *Systemae naturae* (1758) divided the genus *Homo* into two species, one diurnal (with six varieties) and one nocturnal. The single nocturnal species of humanity was *Homo troglodytes* (or *Homo nocturnus*). The former had six diurnal varieties: *ferus* (four-footed, mute, and hairy); *americanus* (red, choleric, erect); *europaeus* (white, ruddy, muscular); *asiaticus* (yellow, melancholic, inflexible); *afer* (black, phlegmatic, indulgent); and *monstrosus* (several deviant forms). The basic four varieties of

American, European, Asiatic, and African were modeled on the four elements (earth, air, fire, and water) and the four corners of the world created by the four rivers of Eden (Eze, *Race and Enlightenment* 1997, 13–14).[3] In the division between men and the apes there was doubt on which side of the line "Pygmies," "Hottentots," and orang-utans belonged, and, indeed, no clear understanding about what these terms actually signified.[4]

Linnaeus's system was essentially an adaptation of the Great Chain of Being, which demonstrated gradation in nature and which was static and unable to account for change, although it did rob man of his special place at the centre of God's creation (John Ray had previously separated humanity from the animals). The notion of gradation postulates that all natural forms, from the lowest to the highest, are arranged in a graded series which ascends by imperceptible degrees. Each natural form was immutable and as created by God (though Linnaeus would later allow elements of transmutation in his theory). Linnaeus's static account of human variety began a trend of racial thinking that would lead to such theories as those of Robert Knox concerning the primacy of fixed racial types. Linnaeus's classificatory orders for humanity and the rest of natural creation were criticized at the time for their arbitrariness and essentialism. Lord Kames claimed that Linnaeus's classification of the animal world into classes and orders, "resembles the classing of books in a library by size, or by binding, without regard to the contents: it may serve as a sort of dictionary; but to no other purpose.... How whimsical it is to class together animals that nature has widely separated, a man for example and a bat."[5]

Linnaeus's espousal of the concept of gradation in nature found confirmation with the "discovery" of the "facial angle" by the Dutch anatomist Pieter Camper. Camper was best known for his contributions to the field of natural history and his celebrated dissections of orangutans, elephants, birds and many other animals. He was also an artist and a sculptor and he combined his dedication to natural history with an interest in the arts, an interest strongly informed by neoclassical aesthetics. He intended to provide helpful guidelines for correct anatomical drawings and as a model for artists (the works were translated into English in 1794). His audience however often understood that he had devised a scale of gradation for the creatures of the animal realm: greater perfection and intelligence were mirrored in an increasingly less receding forehead and jawline. The ideal and typical profile of Greek statuary defined the greatest degree of beauty and intellectual potency. Camper was, unusually for his time, a relativist in aesthetics but the neoclassical preferences of his audience determined a belief that the wider the angle, the more beautiful the subject, thus introducing a hierarchy of gradation into what was no more than an arbitrary measurement. According to Camper, the facial angle grew wider as one progressed from apes through to Africans, Tartars (or Calmucks), Indians, to Europeans, and then to the heroic statues of classical Greece.

The story of the influence of Camper's facial angle and its variants is told in chapter 2 of this book, in particular, its impact on the British surgeon and anatomist John Hunter and on that of the Manchester surgeon and obstetrician, Charles White. White argued in a series of lectures at the Manchester Literary and Philosophical Society from 1795 onward (published in 1799) that "everyone who has made natural History an object of study, must have been led occasionally to contemplate the beautiful gradation that subsists amongst created beings, from the highest to the lowest. From man down to the smallest reptile...Nature exhibits to our view an immense chain of beings" (White 1). He drew upon the comparative anatomical works of the German Samuel Thomas von Sömmerring, as well as those of Hunter and the writings of Lavater and the polygenist theories of the Jamaican writer Edward Long. White also used his own measurements of African people who lived, or visited, Manchester and Liverpool. From these researches he concluded that the Negro "seems to approach nearer to the brute creation than any other of the human species" and that "various species of men were originally created." White's racial prejudices were also informed by his aesthetic preferences. The European was the most advanced but also the most "beautiful of the human race." His panegyric to the European emphasizes the majestic beard of the male and the breasts of the female:

> Where shall we find, unless in the European...that nobly arched head...the perpendicular face, the prominent nose, and round projecting chin? Where that variety of features, and fulness of expression; those long, flowing, graceful ringlets; that majestic beard, those rosy cheeks and coral lips? In what other quarter of the globe shall we find the blush that overspreads the soft features of the beautiful women of Europe, that emblem of modesty, of delicate feelings, and of sense?...Where except on the bosom of the European woman, two such plump and snowy white hemispheres, tipt with vermillion? (135)

Notions of gradation from Linnaeus to White stressed the fixity of the natural world and were consistent with the views that there were in reality several species of humanity that preserved their physical and moral features over substantial periods of time. The debate about whether or not humanity was one species with a common origin or several species with multiple origins was an important one for the eighteenth and nineteenth centuries prior to Darwin. Theorists generally held one of two opposing theories, though the difference in their application is commonly much exaggerated.[6] First, that humanity was one family, and that variety occurred from an originary race. This was known as the monogenist hypothesis. In the writings of natural historians such as the Comte de Buffon and J.F. Blumenbach, this process occurred through environmental and climatic pressures and was the result of a process usually described as "degeneration," whereby races or varieties degenerated from an originary European ancestor. This theory was easily compatible with scripture and it was the view subscribed to by the majority in the period. Monogenists, however, seldom, if ever, dispensed with the principle of racial hierarchy itself; both Buffon and Blumenbach held that the European race was both the primary and more beautiful variety than its subsequent degenerations (though for Blumenbach, unlike Buffon, degeneration could lead to increasingly beautiful animals). Monogenesis remained the orthodox scientific account of the period. Alternatively human difference could be accounted for by the theory of separate origins or creations, what was known as the polygenist hypothesis. Adherents of this view argued that human difference appeared so marked and permanent that it could only be explained by a series of separate creations not mentioned in scripture (if scripture was to be considered at all). Those holding this view were often Christians but they could also be materialists and skeptical. Both positions, monogenist and polygenist, must be discussed under the heading of scientific racism, though the former did not need to be expressed in Christian terms and the latter was often formulated, however ingeniously, to reconcile it with the dictates of scripture.

Though a hypothesis promoted by Paracelsus and Giordano Bruno, the belief in polygenesis is usually traced back to Isaac La Peyrère's hypothesis, in *Prae-Adamitae* (1655), that the story of Adam only applied to the Jews and that there had been other and earlier creations (Popkin 1987; Poliakov 175–82). The idea was encouraged by the discovery of the peoples of the new world made known to the West. As Norris Saakwa-Mante shows the British surgeon John Atkins employed the hypothesis in the 1730s to develop a racial account of physiology and disease (28–57). The most notable, indeed, infamous, spokesman for the polygenist account of separate species before Charles White was Edward Long, a bureaucrat and judge in Jamaica for twelve years. Although not a champion of the plantocratic cause, Long's *History of Jamaica* (1774) argued that the African, or "Negro" constituted a separate species from that of the White kind of humanity. Long was an eccentric and unsystematic commentator who frequently contradicted himself, especially when it came to discussing human variety, and biological essentialism was not the only model he adopted.[7] The Negro is thus an intermediate group between humanity and the higher apes, in particular the orangutan. Long thus divided the genus *Homo* into three distinct species: European and similar races, the "Negroes" and the "orangoutangs." He thus provided an allegedly scientific and empirical racial theory, which he used to support notions of black inferiority as a justification for the institution of slavery:

> When we reflect on...their dissimilarity to the rest of mankind, must we not conclude, that they are a different species of the same *genus?*...Nor do [orang-utans] seem at all inferior in the same intellectual faculties to many of the Negroe race; with some of whom, it is credible that have the most intimate connexion and consanguinity. The amorous intercourse between them may be frequent...and it is certain, that both races agree perfectly well in the lasciviousness of disposition. (Long 1774, 2: 356, 370)

The Polygenist view was supported by a number of prominent thinkers in the eighteenth century including Voltaire, Kames, and George, and, in the nineteenth century by Jean-Baptiste-George-Marie Bory de Saint Vincent, Julien-Joseph Virey, Louis-Antoine Desmoulins, Johan Baptist von Spix, and Carl Friedrich Philip von Martius. Kames, argued that "the colour of the Negroes...affords a strong presumption of their being a different species from the Whites." Though he admits that an inferiority in their understanding is due more likely to their "condition" than their origin, Kames suggested that creations post-Babel and postdiluvian may have occurred (Kitson *Theories of Race* 1999, 58–59). Desmoulins, in his *Histoire naturelle des races humaine* (1826), went so far as to argue for the existence of about sixteen different human species (Augstein, *Race* 1996, 133–34, 127–40). Though Desmoulins was profligate in his polygenesis, most of his fellow-believers tended to argue for two or three kinds of human species. In his later years, Goethe also flirted with the idea that humans had separate origins (Poliakov 133–34). It was Julien-Joseph Virey, the originator of our notions of biorhythms, who proved to be one of the most influential polygenists in France. His *Histoire naturelle du genre humain* (Year

IX [1800–1801]) divided humans into the fair and white and the dark and black. Writing during the revolutionary period of French military expansion, Virey claimed that Africans were possessed of black brains and black blood and repeated Long's fantasy that they copulated with the apes. Virey asked:

> What would our world be without the Europeans? Powerful nations, a proud and indomitable race, immortal genius in the arts and the sciences, a happy civilization.... The European called by his high destiny to rule the world, which he knows how to illumine with his intelligence and subdue with his courage, is the highest expression of man and at the head of the human race. The others, a wretched horde of barbarians, are, so to say, no more than its embryo. (Quoted in Poliakov 180–81)[8]

Despite its often distinguished following, polygenesis remained very much the minority position in the period under discussion. Though it was probably more influential than many historians have cared to admit. In chapter 3 of this book I argue that, despite the views of numerous historians of slavery, polygenesis was not an influential justification for the institution or the transatlantic trade in slaves. In the later part of the nineteenth century it was used more influentially by the "American School" of anthropology of Samuel George Morton, Josiah Nott, George Gliddon, and Louis Agassiz in the United States to justify slavery, but its rejection of the scriptural basis of the story of the origin of man meant that its currency was always somewhat limited to those who were of a skeptical, materialist, or antireligious frame of mind (hence its correlation with the revolutionary science of France).[9] With the growing influence of polygenist theories of separate human origins in the mid- to late nineteenth century, Robert J.C. Young has argued that after about 1840 or so, the "question of species, and therefore of hybridity, was always placed at the centre of the discussions" related to race. This kind of race thinking was opposed to an Enlightenment ideal of "Universality, Sameness and equality" (6–19). Young is right to claim that polygenesis as a belief was not as prevalent in the late eighteenth and early nineteenth century as it was after the 1840s, yet he underestimates the extent to which the belief appealed to Enlightenment scientists and thinkers, such as Voltaire, Virey, and the French ideologues. Young also exaggerates the distinction between monogenist and polygenist racist thinking, as both were capable from their inception of extreme racist application before Darwin's severe monogenist hypothesis of the descent of humanity established itself as the paradigmatic scientific explanation for human origins.[10] As Darwin himself would point out, once the "principle of evolution is generally accepted...the monogenists and the polygenists will die a silent and unobserved death" (Darwin 280). Sadly the death of the monogenist-polygenist debate led to the increased belief in biological determinism and ideas of racial superiority not less, to which Darwinism greatly contributed.[11]

Monogenist thinkers tended to take their bearings from a more dynamic view of nature. Linnaeus's French contemporary, and great rival, Georges-Louis Leclerc, Comte de Buffon embarked on this direction in his great *Histoire naturelle* (1749–1804).[12] Buffon rejected what he believed to be the Linnaean view of classification of animals according to a number of shared physical characteristics, preferring, instead, to locate species in the processes of animal reproduction. Species are thus defined as "the constant succession of similar individuals that reproduce."[13] The idea of species makes no sense outside of reproductive continuity. Buffon wrote very little about "race," occasionally referring to the white and black race (Roger and Bonnefoi 177). He argued (following John Ray) that species could be defined by their fertility and that the offspring of the mating of different species, if they occurred at all, were infertile. Thus humanity was one species. Buffon argued in his essay of 1766, "De la degeneration des animaux" that species themselves altered, or degenerated, according to physical and environmental factors though each generation of species continued to repeat the original form of its kind. He insisted that there was only one origin for all human peoples and he provided a geographical and cultural distribution of the races, accounting for difference in terms of degeneration from an original through biological, climatic, and environmental causes. As for skin pigmentation, Buffon argued for the especial importance of climate (heat and cold); in this he followed Montesquieu though he went much further in attributing physical characteristics to its influence. As humans moved from their geographic places of origin in Europe, they degenerated, and were most degenerate in the New World and Africa.[14] Such a process of degeneration was, for Buffon, always a process of degradation. It was not a process of transmutation that produced new and viable life forms. The orangutan might thus be the most degenerate of men, one step beyond the "Hottentot" who received the brunt of Buffon's scorn. Buffon's aesthetic notions were Eurocentric and neoclassical. He assumed the first humans were the most beautiful and that "the most beautiful people in the world" dwelt "between the 40th and 50th degree of latitude" (1792, 4: 350; Augstein, "Land of the Bible," 1999, 63). The peoples judged as the "most ugly and the most deformed" by Buffon were the Calmucks or Mongolians (202; Meijer 163).

The primary determinants of difference for Buffon were skin color and stature. He divided humanity into six varieties: Americans, Africans (Ethiopians), Chinese (South Asian), Tartar, Laplander (Lapp or Polar), and European. Not surprisingly Europe produced "the most handsome and the most beautiful people in the world." (1792, 4: 350)[15] Buffon argued for what he called the "analogical method" by which parallels were to be drawn between human and animal physiology by drawing on the experiences and observations of professional livestock breeders (Augstein 1996, xv–xvi). However, he did not believe in strict groupings and argued for the existence of many transitional peoples. He also believed (unlike Kant) that the process of degeneration was reversible and that if Africans and Tartars returned to their original homeland (actually in northwest Asia between forty and fifty-five degrees latitude), they would slowly revert to the primary and proper human form. Buffon's notion that races could degenerate into savagery through the agency of climatic forces was one that was adopted by the Dutch canon Cornelius de Pauw. De Pauw's *Recherches philosophiques sur les Américains, ou Mémoires intéressants pour servir a l'Histoire de l'Espèce humaine* (1768) argued that the Amerindians were degenerate, weak, impotent, dumb, and generally inferior to the Europeans. De Pauw's arguments were to be very influential, especially on German thinking about racial difference (Zantop, *Colonial Fantasies* 1997, 47–65). Buffon's ideas were also disseminated in Britain though Oliver Goldsmith's popular *History of the Earth and Animated Nature* (1774) (Lynskey 33–57).

Buffon's dynamic of environmental change was seminal although his thought was often modified. The enigmatic mechanisms by which environments might occasion organic change, however, were far from clear. Two fundamental questions about the fact of difference concerning the nature of those things which defined it and what caused it remained unanswered. Buffon and later Blumenbach proposed the hypothesis of degeneration caused by climatic and environmental factors. This was probably the consensus, contested and uncertain as it was. Samuel Stanhope Smith, for instance, whose work is discussed in chapter 3 argued that blackness was caused not only by such factors as extreme heat and cold, but also by the state of savagery; thus the more civilized a people, the fairer they became. This process, he claimed, he witnessed among those slaves who were domesticated on the plantations of good masters (Smith 1965, 152–53).

Some thinkers, however, argued for the importance of heredity over environment. Pierre Louis Moreau de Maupertius's *Venus physique* (1745) rejected previous notions that the characteristics of humans and animals were contained in preformed germs arguing that both parents contributed to the physical characteristics of their offspring.[16] Maupertius applied this idea to the origin and formation of human races, claiming that an individual's physical characteristics were formed by both parents and could be perpetuated as permanent. A black skin could have occurred by a quirk or accident in the reproductive process. Evidence for this was available in the numerous examples of black Africans producing white offspring (actually albinos) (Maupertius 75–77, 81). Such pigmentation would then be preserved by isolation. Maupertius also postulated that the climate of the tropics might have caused a black skin, which then became permanent through heritability. The corollary of Maupertius's views was that no species was permanent or fixed and that new characteristics might occur, which could then be passed on as permanent through the process of heredity. In his *Système de la nature* (1751), Maupertius went on to argue that new species of humanity might be formed through the incremental buildup of minor physical changes accumulated by the process of heredity. He seemed to believe that, though the small foot of the Chinese woman is achieved by human art, the practice may aid in producing smaller feet through heredity (Maupertuis 74). Maupertius is thus one of the very first to articulate the modern conception of the race idea. By and large, his work demonstrates an Enlightenment universalism and relativism:

> Had the first white men who saw black men, encountered them in forests, they might not have called them men. But in turn, those found in large cities, governed by wise queens who caused the arts and sciences to flourish at a time when all other people were still barbarians might not have wished to accept the whites as brothers. (65)

Though committed to a relativist approach, whereby the "difference between whiteness and blackness...is but a slight thing in nature" (76–77), Maupertius's discussions are informed by strong aesthetic and Eurocentric thinking: Africans "are distinguished by their color as well as their facial features. The nose is broad and flat, the lips are thick, and there is wool instead of hair, all of which seems to indicate a new species of man." Maupertius, like Long and Linnaeus, even included the tailed men of Borneo or the orangutan, among the varieties of humanity, asking "should that classification which we have not made dependent on the color white or black be made according to the number of vertebrae?" (65). Maupertius's aesthetic preferences are clear in his description of African features as ugly and his panegyric to the beauty of the mixed features of European women (67).

THE RACE IDEA TAKES SHAPE: KANT TO HEGEL

Immanuel Kant proposed a similar answer to Maupertius as to the enigma of how human variety occurred. He also was influenced by Buffon's more dynamic vision of natural history, yet rejected the view that species and genera were meaningless, and that only individuals were significant.[17] He had been impressed by Linnaeus's attempt to provide a physical taxonomy of humanity. Kant's pre-*Critique* anthropological writings and their relationship to his more abstract philosophical and aesthetic texts have become part of a heated debate about their complicity in the creation of the modern idea of race. Robert Bernasconi, Emmanuel Chukwudi Eze, and David Bindman have launched a compelling critique of Kant's work, identifying him as a key figure in the construction of racial and racist ideologies, whereas Sankar Muthu has mounted a sophisticated defense of Kant and other Enlightenment thinkers, who postulate that humans are cultural agents about whom judgments of inferiority and superiority are inappropriate.[18] Kant argued that the ancestral human stock had been endowed with latent powers that could be empowered or triggered by alterations in the environment. His essay "Über die verschiedenen Racen de Menschen" ("On the Different Human Races") of 1775 claimed that there were four distinct varieties of the human species, each possessed of a specific natural disposition and identified primarily by the color of their skin, the primary marker of race. [19] Kant follows Linnaeus in arguing for four races, though he is unsure whether the recent explorations of Oceania have discovered a fifth race of humanity to Europeans. Kant defines "race" in the following words:

> Among the deviations, that is, the hereditary similarities that we find in animals that belong to a single line of the descent are those called races. Races are deviations that are constantly preserved over many generations and come about as a consequence of migration (dislocation to other regions) or through interbreeding with other deviations of the same line of descent, which always produces half-breed offspring. (9)

Each of the varieties or races derived from an ideal, original, "stem genus" that corresponded to the white European variety with its blond or red hair, white skin, and blue eyes. Kant distinguished between "races" and "varieties" in the animal kingdom, the former maintaining their physical characteristics over protracted generations and producing hybrids when breeding with other deviations from the same stock, and the latter consistently maintaining their differences and not producing hybrids. Thus Negroes and Europeans are different races, though blond and brunette men and women are different varieties of human being.

Kant divided humanity into four races: White, Negro, Mongolian or Kalmuck, and Hindu. Again physical characteristics were the primary determinants of difference and these were determined by the generative force dormant in the organism, but activated by environmental change along certain naturally predisposed lines. Kant argued that "a special seed or natural predisposition is to be found in organic creation," which will become activated by a change in external factors, but once activated (like the creation of a black skin) will then become permanent (13–20). Human beings were originally created to populate the entire earth, and therefore they must contain "many seeds and natural predispositions" to be activated by changes in external circumstances affecting the reproductive process. Kant's notion of "purposive causes" in nature, applicable to the processes of human variety, would prove to be attractive to Romantic writers, such as Coleridge and De Quincey, as well as natural historians such as Blumenbach (14). For instance, those humans who moved into the Arctic region, Kant argued, needed a smaller build with a more rapid circulation of the blood to cope with the extreme cold. The "Kalmuck facial form, marked by its beardless chin, snarled nose, thin lips, squinting eyes, flat face, and the red brown color with black hair" resulted from the coldness and brightness of the light of the snow. The Negro type was the inevitable response to a hot climate, which produced a race with turned up noses, tumid lips, unpleasant smells, woolly hair, and a lazy, soft, and dawdling temperament (16–17). Once such characteristics have been developed and become part of the reproductive process, they become permanent, even should people migrate to lands with different environments. As with Linnaeus and Buffon, aesthetic and moral qualities appeared to have an affinity with the purely physical. The blackness of the Negro skin was occasioned by the profusion of iron particles in the blood which for Kant also "explains why all Negroes stink." Not surprisingly, Kant finds that the most fortunate "combination of influences of both the cold and hot regions" lies between thirty-one and fifty-two degrees latitude, in Europe. Here the "greatest riches of the earth's creation are found" and this is where humans diverge least from their original form (19). Like Buffon and others, Kant argued that "Humanity exists in its greatest perfection in the white race" (Schiebinger 1990, 387).

Kant identified nations and races according to their differing aesthetic and moral sensibilities in his essay *Observations on the Feeling of the Beautiful and the Sublime* (1764) in which he argued for a hierarchy of response with the German at the summit and the African at the bottom: the "Negroes of Africa have no feeling that rises above the trifling." Echoing David Hume's notorious statement in a footnote of 1753 to his essay "Of National Characteristics," Kant stated that Africans had never produced "anything great in art or science." In response to the report of an apparently witty rejoinder from a black carpenter, Kant affirmed that "this fellow was quite black from head to foot, a clear proof that what he said was stupid" (Eze, *Race and Enlightenment* 1997, 53–57; Bindman 2002, 70–88; Immerwahr 481–86). Kant's theories have led Robert Bernasconi to identify him as the first proponent of the modern conception of race finding "within his philosophy expressions of a virulent and theoretically based racism, at a time when scientific racism was still in its infancy" (2002, 145).

Kant's contribution to the debate was challenged in its own time by J.G. von Herder and, more obliquely, by J.F. Blumenbach amongst others. Herder's *Ideen zu einer Philosophie der Geschichte der Menscheit* (Reflections on the Philosophy of the History of Mankind) of 1784 rejected the classification of humanity into races according to physical characteristics, such as skin color (Muthu 21–46; Bindman 2002, 151–89). More than this, Herder was much more sympathetic to the cultural primitivism that characterized much of the representation in this period of African people, affirming a cultural pluralism that precluded the kind of European supremacist thinking that was endemic to Kant's work. For Herder, each culture contained its own unique and valuable truth: "Since whiteness is a mark of degeneracy in many animals near the pole, the negro has as much right to term his savage robbers albinoes and white devils...as we have to deem him the emblem of evil, and a descendant of Ham, branded by his father's curse" (Eze, *Race and Enlightenment* 1997, 71, 75–78). Herder's anthropological speculations are themselves not entirely free of his own cultural preferences and assumptions; he also insisted that the African is predisposed to a greater degree of sensuality than the European (Zantop, *Colonial Fantasies* 1997, 74–76; Bindman 2002, 163–73).

The contribution of the German Enlightenment to the nascent theories of human variety is only now just beginning to be explored. As Suzanne Zantop points out, this group "codified a notion of racial difference that linked observations of the physical properties of specific peoples to conjectures about their intellectual, moral, and aesthetic value as compared to Europeans and, among Europeans, Germans" (*Colonial Fantasies* 1997, 68, 66–80). In addition to the cultural explorations of the theories of Kant and Herder, the science of comparative anatomy developed in the classroom and lecture theaters of the German universities, most notably those of Göttingen. Germany's leading anatomist of the period was Samuel Thomas von Sömmering. Utilizing the bodies of several unhappy and unfortunate Africans who had been settled in a colony near Kassel set up by Duke Frederick II of Hessen-Kassel, Sömmering prepared his treatise *Über die körperliche Verschiedenheit des Mohren vom Europäer* (Concerning the physical difference between the Moor and the Europeans) of 1784. The book was expanded one year later as *Über die körperliche Verschiedenheit des Negers vom Europäer* and it survived as one of the basic texts on the African physique well into the nineteenth century (Schiebinger 1990, 387). Sömmering made detailed anatomical comparisons between the cadavers of Africans and European and the "ape tribe," but his notions and conclusions were full of the kinds of prejudice and careless assumptions that riddle the texts of the period. Accepting the hypothesis of Camper's facial line, Sömmering commented on how nature in constructing the "Negro's skull" seemed to have "reversed the proportions of her favorite model" (White cxl–cxlv). He presents detailed measurements of the skulls and skeletons of African and Europeans. It became clear to Sömmering that the most significant categories of difference in the period were those of sex and race and both were to be established by anatomical studies.

There is a substantial body of German and French writing relating to the differences of race and gender in the late eighteenth and early nineteenth centuries that is still largely unexplored. Christian Ernst Wünsch, a professor at Frankfort am der Order argued in his *Unterhaltungen über den Menschen* (Leipzig, 1796) that "Rasse" provided the biological underpinning for a national, cultural identity and that the formation of the skull was *the* key indicator of physical, mental, and moral superiority. The Göttingen professor of philosophy Christoph Meiners, in his *Grundriss der Geschichte der Menschheit* (Outline of the History of Mankind) 1786, elaborated, from the researches of Sömmering, Blumenbach, and Herder, a Manichaean distinction between the white and dark races in which the supremacy of the white European is clear. It was Meiners, rather than Blumenbach, who Germanized racial theory and whose work became proleptic of later modern biological (especially Nazi) racism (Zantop, *Colonial Fantasies* 1997, 81–87; Bindman 2002, 219–21; Poliakov 178–80). With the work of Meiners in Germany, and later that of Dr. Robert Knox in Britain, we can see the conflation between national and racial characteristics that was to become the hallmark of nineteenth-century racial discourse. In a series of articles that appeared in 1792 in *Göttingsche historishes Magazin* and *Neues Göttingiches Magazin*, Meiners constructed his basic opposition between the beautiful white Caucasian peoples and their multiple dark others. His two basic races were "Caucasian" and the "Mongol"; these included Asians, Africans, and Americans (Zantop, "Beautiful, the Ugly, and the German" 1997, 23, 21–35; Rupp-Eisendriech 131–83). Meiners listed among his naturally inferior groups of peoples, Africans, women, servants, criminals, and Jews. He sought to demonstrate the proposition that "the Negroes must be as limited in understanding and inferior in good nature as they are ugly" (Zantop, "The Beautiful, the Ugly and the German," 1997). For Meiners the "white" race (and its pure blood) was clearly superior and, even if all humanity had been at one time descended from the same stock, the races were essentially separate now. Meiners, like Long and others, clearly used racial theory as a justification for slavery and the slave trade. He asks rhetorically, whether "such insensitive, excitable and phlegmatic, dumb and evil-minded people as the Negroes should be given such rights and such liberty?" (Zantop, *Colonial Fantasies* 1997, 85). Furthermore Meiners refined his European race to construct a German race, based on the purity of its blood and possessed of superior biological, moral, and intellectual attributes.

Easily the most influential writer of the period on the subject of human difference for the Romantic period was the German natural historian and friend of Sömmering, Johann Friedrich Blumenbach. Appointed to a chair of Medicine in 1776, Blumenbach is often regarded as the founder of the science of physical anthropology and it was to this area of natural history that his interests gravitated. In his *De Generis Humani Varitate Nativa* (On the Variety of the Human Species) (1775) Blumenbach rejected the notion of gradation in nature. He also rejected Kant's use of a priori categories and any attempt to classify humans into races by skin color alone. He believed that comparative anatomy and the comparative study of physiology would enable the natural philosopher to draw the final dividing line between specific and variational distinctions, firmly placing African people with the rest of humanity and clearly separating humanity from the ape kind. Blumenbach revised Linnaeus's classification of man as one mammal among others by introducing the further distinctions of biped and bimanous and quadrupeds and quadrumanous, authoritatively removing humanity from any conflation with the ape kind.

Having accomplished the separation of the order of man from those of the animals, Blumenbach then turned to the issue of difference between humans. He believed that mankind was one species and that variety or racial difference occurred through a process of degeneration. For Blumenbach "degeneration" did not signify (as it did for Buffon) deterioration but, instead, deviation from an original form. In the natural world the process of degeneration often led to more beautiful and improved varieties. This deviation resulted from external and environmental forces such as climate, diet, and mode of life that acted upon the "formative fluid" of life (a notion he picked up from Kant). Blumenbach defined racial difference in a bodily sense, relating it to skin color, hair texture and color, skull form, and anatomical details generally, including other parts of the body such as ears, breasts, feet, and so on. His aim was to get beyond the superficial exterior differences, such as skin color. He dismissed the "facial line" of Camper so beloved to Sömmering and White, in favor of an accumulated series of such differences. Following Linnaeus and Kant, Blumenbach suggested the existence of first four and then, in the second edition of his *De Generis* of 1781, five principal varieties of humanity: the Caucasian, Mongolian, Ethiopian, American, and Malayan. The fifth variety, the Malayan, was added to include the peoples of Oceania, recently made known to Europeans by explorers such as Cook and evidenced in the Tahitian and other skulls Blumenbach received from Joseph Banks.[20]

In 1795 Blumenbach notoriously first used the term "Caucasian," which he found in the travel writings of Jean Chardin and the racial writings of Christoph Meiners, to describe the Indo-European people and produced the extraordinarily influential fivefold racial typology that would haunt anthropological studies until recent times. He believed that it was probable that after the Deluge, civilization had begun again in the Caucasus where Noah's ark came to rest.[21] In many ways this was an unfortunate consequence of his thought, as Blumenbach was actually (like Buffon) an opponent of fixed physical racial types and he did not regard the races or varieties of humanity as sharply distinct, viewing the transition from one to another as a gradual and almost imperceptible sequence and emphasizing the extreme diversity that was found within his races. However, notions of hierarchy surfaced quite notably in his work. Like Buffon and Kant, he theorized that the first or primeval race was white as it was "very easy for that to degenerate into brown, but very much more difficult for dark to become white" (269) and that the furthest deviations from this originary norm were the Ethiopian and the Mongolian, with the American and Malay as intermediate races (Junker 498–501). Unlike Kant, however, Blumenbach held that this physical typology did not influence moral or intellectual capacities. But he did reintroduce a note of aesthetic preference similar to that struck by Camper when he described the Caucasian as "the most beautiful race of men" (269).[22] In his later *Beyträge zur Naturgeschichte* (Contributions to Natural History) (1806), Blumenbach tried to redress the balance by stressing the achievements of individual black writers, "good authors, poets, philosophers, and correspondents of the Paris Academy" and paid tribute to the "perfectibility and original capacity for scientific culture" of the Negro (312). So unusually positive were Blumenbach's estimations of the achievements of African people that Philip Curtin, rather overenthusiastically, regards his work as a "positive and scientific anti-racism" (47).

More troubling, however, was Blumenbach's fetishistic collection of physical data, namely, the eighty-odd skulls he possessed (later augmented) that formed the basis of his physiological research. Many of those were supplied for him by the British natural historian, Sir Joseph Banks (Fulford, Lee, and Kitson 127–48). Although his work was genuinely not narrowly based on skull formation, it was this aspect which seems to have caught the imagination of his contemporaries and successors. Blumenbach's "Golgotha" as he called it became an important source of empirical data as well as something of a curiosity. The young S.T. Coleridge, himself heavily influenced by the work of the German natural philosopher, saw the collection in 1798 when he studied at Göttingen. This fascination with the skull as the primary and permanent marker of racial difference was exploited by the American anatomist Samuel George Morton in his *Crania Americana* (1839) and *Crania Aegyptica* (1844) both of which contained detailed measurements of the various skull sizes of the different races, allegedly providing for the first time a precise scientific measurement of racial difference (Young 128–29; S.J. Gould 1981, 50–69). Nevertheless despite his liberal intentions, Blumenbach had been voyaging in dangerous and stormy waters and it is not easy to exonerate him from the abuses that later racialists carried out when building upon his work.

Later German philosophers and followers of Kant also promulgated racial attitudes as part of their work. Most notably the exponents of the *Naturphilosophie*, which exerted such a powerful influence over Coleridge, discussed human difference in the context of their larger philosophical ambitions. Such thinkers saw natural phenomenon as a visible symbol or working out of a universal idea. Gottlieb Fichte ascribed a Germanic origin to all Europeans (excepting the Slavs) and argued for an original race or "Urvolk." Non-Germanic white peoples were relegated to an inferior status. Another key writer of the German *Naturphilosophie*, Lorenz Oken, argued that there were four races; a luminous, human white race, a terrestrial and simian black race, a Mongol race symbolized by air, and an Amerindian race symbolized by water (Poliakov 240–41). Similarly Hegel's philosophical system was applied to human races. He accepted the Indo-Aryan origin of humanity and claimed that non-European peoples were less human than the European because they were not fully aware of themselves as conscious and historical beings. Africa was beyond the realm of world history, which had originated in Asia and developed to self-consciousness in Europe:

> All our observations of African man show him as living in a state of savagery and barbarism, and he remains in this state to the present day. The negro is an example of animal man in all his savagery and lawlessness. (Hegel 177)

German idealist philosophy carried with it models of human difference and variety that were, in essence, biologically essentialist and possessed of the race idea in their varying manifestations. Once an idealist paradigm was applied to world history and the origins and development of human civilizations, such speculations were more or less inevitable and brought with them notions of progressive and static peoples, engaged within or resistant to the development of the world spirit as it works itself out through history.

The Race Idea is Established

Blumenbach's work and his stress on the unity of humanity greatly influenced successive writers on race in the period, including both William Lawrence and James Cowles Prichard in Britain, Samuel Stanhope Smith in America, and, more ambiguously, Georges Cuvier in France. All these writers held the monogenist line against those such as Voltaire, Long, Kames, George Forster, and White. Smith specifically opposed Kames and White, arguing for an environmental and climatic solution to the problem of racial diversity. For Blumenbach, Smith, Cuvier, and Prichard the monogenist hypothesis was attractive because it provided an account that was consistent with the biblical story of the Creation and the dispersal of Noah's sons after the Flood. They were also influenced by racial thinking, whether derived from scientific or other prejudices. Smith believed that blackness was a sign of savagery as well as an effect of climate and he prophesied that, in the temperate climate of the new Republic of the United States, civiliza-tion would blanch and soften the features of the Negro until he or she approximated to the white settler; indeed he perceived this process to be occurring in the bodies of slaves on the plantation estates kept by kind and benevolent masters (Samuel Stanhope Smith 1965).[23]

The surgeon and anatomist William Lawrence rejected the biblical account of the Creation and the Flood and his work was more narrowly biological and zoological in scope than that of his contemporaries when it came to classifying the animal world. Lawrence's interest in human difference and variety was long-standing. He had read a paper at age twenty on the varieties of the human species to the Abernethian Society at St. Bartholomew's Hospital (Wells 351). In 1807 he trans-lated Blumenbach's *Handbuch der vergleichenden Anatomie* (1805) as *A Short System of Comparative Anatomy* (1807). Lawrence wished to make precise zoological comparisons between men and animals, and between the different human varieties. Although believing in the essential unity of mankind, he regarded "the highly civilized nations of Europe" as racially superior to "a troop of filthy Hottentots" and, indeed, "the whole of the more or less barbarous tribes that cover the entire continent of Africa" (Lawrence 1823, 209). His work is deeply racist, closer in tone to the dismissive comments of Kant and Hume than to the praise of Blumenbach for the achievements of black people. Lawrence was a family friend of the Shelleys and his relation-ship to them is discussed in chapter 2 of this book. With Lawrence and Prichard we are moving to a scientific worldview which is becom-ing recognizably modern. Following the work of the early Prichard, Lawrence argued that generation and heredity were the sources of racial formation and not environment. Using the analogy of ani-mal husbandry he noticed how "the greatest differences are pro-duced when man regulates the sexual intercourse of animals" (226). Where Blumenbach and Smith argued that degeneration came about through the processes of domestication in animals and civilization in humans, Prichard and Lawrence edged more closely to an awareness of the processes of sexual selection, though neither was a Darwinian evolutionist (Mudford 430–36). Although dismissive of Prichard's hypothesis of an originary black race, Lawrence proposed that racial variation was the result of spontaneous alteration, perpetuated by isolation and breeding, along the same lines as animal variation.

Comparative anatomy and physiology were not the only contexts in which to discuss human variety. Another major tradition of understanding human variety is represented by the work of Johann Reinhold Forster, Sir William Jones and James Cowles Prichard. Forster's approach to the phenomenon of physical diversity in the South Seas was Blumenbachian, but he also employed a study of the mores and beliefs of the South Sea Islanders to complement his researches. Jones was the most distinguished Oriental scholar of his time. His interests were more concerned with linguistic and mythological matters. His study of Sanskrit and of other languages led him to suspect that there must have existed an originary language prior to Sanskrit and the languages of Europe from which they all derived. Similarly Jones's study of mythological systems and cultures led him to conclude that there was a common source for the beliefs of Ancient India and Classical Greece. Jones's method of tracing racial groupings back through customs, manners, and languages rather than by identifying common physical characteristics was an alternative to the zoological approach. Jones's ideas about China and Tartary will be discussed in chapters five and six of this book.

This project was also adopted by James Cowles Prichard who combined a study of the natural history of "man" with an investigation of his mores. With Prichard we approach a kind of study that is notably closer to our modern understanding of ethnology than physical anthropology, although the terms were confused in the period (Stocking 369–90; Rainger 51–70). Prichard was a man of his age. As H.F. Augstein, in her authoritative study of his work, comments, Prichard's "research programme...was intended to use science to prove religion as it was laid down in the Scriptures" (*Prichard's Anthropology* 1999, xii). He ceaselessly attempted to reconcile the scriptural account of the world with the results of his massive collection of ethnological data, insisting with increasing force, that the "history of languages was the key to the history of the human species" (xv). Originally accepting the notions of his "venerable friend" Blumenbach concerning the unity of mankind and the process of degeneration, he stood the Caucasian hypothesis on its head by arguing, in the first edition of his *Researches into the Physical History of Man* (1813), that the original primary race was black, as there were well-documented reports of black parents occasionally producing white offspring, but no reliable demonstrations of climatic conditions producing black offspring from white parents (Augstein, *Prichard's Anthropology* 1999, xv, 15). Although still equating blackness with the primitive and savage, Prichard's hypothesis was radical for its time.

In the first version of *Researches* Prichard replaced the Buffon-Blumenbach principle of environmentalism with that of heredity. Congenital hereditary variations might be diffused through an inbreeding population, leading to the propagation of a new race. Thus he maintained that human variety occurred through the accidental eruption of new variations in humankind. Dispensing with Blumenbach's typology of race, which he found arbitrary and unconvincing, he preferred instead to combine the scientific theories of human variety with the linguistic studies of Sir William Jones and the Asiatick Society. Among his other works are substantial and erudite volumes arguing for the similarity of the Celtic language and mythology to Asiatic languages. For Prichard, race was never a rigid category and he stressed the variability of group nations and tribes. In the second edition of his slightly altered title *Researches into the Physical History of Mankind* (1826), he denied that there was such a thing as the Negro race, more or less abandoning the concept of race altogether: "[I]t is by no means evident that all those nations who resemble each other in the shape of their skulls, or by any other peculiarity are of one race, or more nearly allied by kindred to each other than to tribes who differ from them in some particulars" (Prichard 1826, 1: 238, 237–39). In terms of variety he thus became a nominalist, denying biological essentialism (Augstein, *Prichard's Anthropology* 1999, 105–22). The biological argument remained for him largely analogical and he argued that it was necessary to trace the affinities of different nations in terms of language, religion, political institutions, and manners. Associated with the evangelical wing of the church he believed passionately in the truth of the Creation story, the unity of man, and the truth of the original Christian dispensation, of which all other religions were corruptions. He regarded all mythology as a corruption of an original and primitive monotheist, Trinitarian divine revelation, preserved by the Hebrews after the Flood. The aim of his scientific work was to trace, on the basis of linguistic and cultural similarities, the origin of mankind to a single family that had been dispersed over the face of the earth after the Flood. To this end he produced substantial volumes from 1813 accumulating a mass of ethnological data from scientific and travel accounts. In the last version of his anthropological work *The Natural History of Mankind* (1843) he distinguished between what he regarded as the three great families of man, deriving from scripture: the Semitic (Syrio-Arabian), the Japhetic (Indo-European), and the Hamitic (African).

CUVIER AND THE RACE IDEA

In the same way that Prichard dominated British anthropological and ethnological work in Britain, Georges Cuvier, the "Napoleon" of early nineteenth-century French science dominated the area in France. He composed the first truly complete work in the history of comparative anatomy, the *Leçons d'anatomie comparé* (1800–05) and produced one of the great works of natural history, the *Règne animal* (1817, 1829–30).[24] Like Prichard he preferred a typology of race based upon the biblical account of Noah's three sons, but he differed from him in stressing the basic permanency of racial type as a sharply defined and morphologically stable unit. Cuvier divided the races up into Caucasian, Mongolian, and Ethiopian, arguing that the Ethiopian had never progressed from barbarism, and that the Mongolian had remained stable, and only the Caucasian was progressive. He accepted that the Caucasian race survived the Flood in the high mountains and originated from Mount Caucasus. He then subdivided this great race into two major branches, the "Aramæans and Syrians" and the "Indians and Germans." In so doing, Cuvier was emphasizing the growing division of peoples into Aryan and Semitic that would engender such tragic consequences in the twentieth century. Such a distinction was quite alien to the anthropology of Blumenbach and his followers. Cuvier's second race, the Mongolians, originated from a separate high tract of land, Mount Atlai, north of the Gobi desert. His third race, the "Nègres," survived the catastrophe of the Flood on another spot, possibly Mount Atlas (Cuvier 1834, 64–65, 69–72). In assuming that postdiluvian humans had three separate places of origin, instead of one, Cuvier roused suspicions that he was, in fact, a crypto-polygenist. The *Leçons* also reemphasized the notion of gradation in race theory by applying a more complex version of Camper's "facial line," the "cephalic index," which, while being determined by more measurements, had the same result in demonstrating the inferiority of the Ethiopian and Mongolian races (Cuvier 1802, 2: 9).[25]

Cuvier was famously responsible for dissecting and popularizing the case of Saartjie Baartman or Sarah Bartmann, the "Hottentot Venus" on her death in 1815. Saartjie Baartman had arrived in London in 1810 and immediately been displayed as a curiosity, after which she was also exhibited in Paris. On the ladder of human development the "Hottentot" (Khoikhoi) vied with the Australian aborigine or, sometimes, the Kalmuck for the honor of occupying the lowest rung in the European rating. Her gender also relegated her to a lower status than the males of her people. Cuvier's monograph on Baartman's dissection, published in the *Mémoires du muséum d'histoire naturelle* for 1817, upholds this consensus. It comments on a number of Saartjie's features, including her small skull, her pouting lips, but especially her buttocks, and genitalia. Saartjie possessed the accumulation of fat in her buttocks, known as the condition *steatopygia*, and the famous, so-called *sinus pudoris* or "Hottentot Apron": a hypertrophy of the labia and nymphae caused by the manipulation of the genitalia and serving as a sign of beauty among certain tribes. These features were used (by Voltaire and others) to argue that the "Hottentot" was physically remote from the European and closer to the primates. Cuvier removed Baartman's genitalia and presented the specimen to Musée de l'homme.[26] This particular case of Saartjie Bartmann and her French dissector speaks redolently to us of early nineteenth-century attitudes to race and gender (Fee 415–33; Schiebinger 1990, 387–405). In Cuvier and others, we have the basis for the later nineteenth-century theorists of polygenism, or the existence of separate races. Cuvier's thinking was conditioned by a teleological conception of biological types, which based its classificatory methods on the acquisition of precise measurements of skeletal and especially cranial structures and regarded cranial differences as correlative of mental abilities.

With the growth of comparative anatomy and the increasing tendency of nineteenth-century writers on race to follow the route of physical anthropology rather than the cultural ethnography of the later Prichard, we see the end of the eighteenth-century tradition of the noble savage, especially as applied to the African slave, a trope so beloved by the abolitionist poets (Sypher; Boulukos 2007). The tenor of nineteenth-century writing was increasingly set by the works of Long, Meiners, and White. Informed by the atrocities of the slave revolution in Saint Domingue and resting on the allegedly scientific basis of numerous physical measurements, this body of writing increasingly came to speak for the fears of those concerned to justify and explain the aggressive colonialism of their day.[27] The race idea in its numerous manifestations was clearly influential in their day, replacing older ways of regarding difference in terms of civilization and savagery or in terms of religion versus nationality with an allegedly scientific set of hierarchies inscribed upon the body—hierarchies that were themselves swept away by the savage monogenist hypothesis of Darwinian natural selection. This cultural and scientific racism obviously filtered down to all levels of society.

RACE AND ROMANTICISM: THE
CASE OF COLERIDGE

Writers of the Romantic period, by and large, with a few notable exceptions, did not directly engage with these works of natural philosophy and their speculations concerning the variety of man in any systematic way. Nevertheless, the race idea impinged on much of their work, concerned as it often was with other cultures and societies. Most were acquainted with the main works of natural philosophy. The influence of Buffon and Samuel Stanhope Smith, for instance, was especially pervasive on the Godwin and Shelley Circle. Mary Wollstonecraft reviewed both Buffon's and Smith's works for Joseph Johnson's *Analytical Review* in 1788 (*Works* 7 50-55, 293-300, 411).[28] Such writers and thinkers were also aware of the works of William Lawrence, and critics have speculated on the implications of his work for Percy and Mary Shelley's writings. It is possible that the poet and artist William Blake knew the work of Camper. In *The Marriage of Heaven and Hell,* the Jews are told to leave off counting gold and the African is apostrophized: "O African, black African! (Go, winged thought, widen his forehead!")" (Blake 123). David Bindman has associated this parenthetical aside, equating mental and spiritual capacity with physical form, with the works of Camper and Lavater on the racial attributes of skull formation (Bindman, "Blake's Vision of Slavery," 373–79).

It is the writing of William that may be most typical of some of the more visceral racial attitudes of late nineteenth century. Cobbett began as a supporter of the slave trade, which he believed was necessary for British commerce, supported by scripture, and justified by what he saw as the racial inferiority of Africans. He also absorbed the argument that the slaves in the plantation system of the West Indies were better off than the British working classes and the concern for their welfare shown by prominent British evangelicals and abolitionists was misplaced. Cobbett was unnerved by the slave revolts in the West Indies, the use of black soldiers in the British army in the colonies, and the growing general fashion for what he termed "Negromania." His comments on these and other matters are xenophobic outbursts, fraught with the kind of sexual and social anxieties, reminiscent of those of Edward Long in the 1770s, especially concerning the mixing of the bloods in miscegenation, an obsession which was to endlessly reappear in nineteenth-century discussions of race. In Marcus Wood's terms, Cobbett was "a lively racist, an anti-Semite, Francophobe and primitive Negrophobe" (2002 152).

For Cobbett, "negroes are a bloody minded race: they are made and marked for servitude and subjection: it is the purpose which they were obviously intended for, and every day affords us fresh proof" (1804, cols 125–26). After 1808 or so Cobbett relented from some of his more extreme views and abandoned the use of sugar, coffee, and rum. This opposition to slavery, however, brought little moderation to his notions of African people and their racial status. Cobbett's view of race is of hierarchy and difference on a natural scale of animality and one where the mixing of the races is a subject for disgust and dread. Cobbett's "negroes" are defined in terms of their bestiality, savagery, color, and smell.

> Certainly the negroes are of a *different sort* from the Whites. An almost complete absence of the reasoning faculties, a sort of dog-like grin, and a *ya-ya-ya* laugh, when spoken to, may be, for anything I know, marks of *superiority;* and indeed, we should be disposed to adopt this opinion, if we were to draw our conclusions from the choice which has, in some countries, been made of white men to be invested with power; for, they come very near to Negroes in all respects except colour of skin and smell of carcass. I am, therefore, not presumptuous enough to take upon me to assert, that the Blacks, are not the *superior* beings; but, I deny all *equality*. They are a *different* race; and for Whites to mix with them is not a bit less odious than the mixing with those creatures which, unjustly apparently, we call beasts. (Cobbett 1821, col 147)[29]

Cobbett's offensively racist paranoia—it is hard to describe it otherwise—is underpinned by the writings of Long and White and sets up relations of difference between peoples that might as well form themselves into a full-fledged polygenist account of race. However if we want to discover in Romantic period writing an awareness of the race idea itself, then it is to those ideological doppelgangers of the Romantic period, S.T. Coleridge and Thomas De Quincey, that we must turn. Although Coleridge does not appear to have had a coherent systematic theory of race throughout his intellectual career, he appears to move within the major Christian scientific views of the period, beginning as an Enlightenment Universalist, accepting Blumenbach's hypothesis after his stay at Göttingen, and then modifying this hypothesis much in the manner of Prichard, with whose work he was surprisingly unfamiliar.[30] Ultimately it was his interest in the *Naturphilosophie* with its laws of polarity that determined the direction his thought was to take and to mark out its trajectory away from Prichard's liberal, Christian ethnology.[31]

Coleridge's earlier works such as the "Bristol Lectures" of 1795 include comments on other nations but they are not yet formulated in terms of scientific theory. In the "Lecture on the Slave Trade" of 1795 he represents the Africans as "innocent and happy—the peaceful inhabitants of a fertile soil, they cultivate their fields in common and reap the crop as the common property of all." He argues that the African has by virtue of his pastoral existence "an acuteness of intellect...which the mechanic whom the division of Labour condemns to one simple operation is precluded from obtaining" (1974, 240). Coleridge's picture here is ethnocentric in representing African life as a primitive idyll close to his own pantisocratic ideals but the representation is not scientifically racist. This holds true also for his description in the *Conciones ad Populum* (1795) of the savage North American Indians who massacred the settlers of Wyoming in 1778 under the command of the British army. The "savage Indians" were invited by English generals to "banquet on blood." Coleridge comments how these "Drinkers of human Blood, and the Feasters on human Flesh were seen in horrid circles, counting their scalps and anticipating their gains" (*Lectures 1795,* 56–57). Here the American Indian, "human Tygers" are seen in terms of a pre-Enlightenment distinction of savage and civilized. Neither the Africans nor the Indians are regarded as racial types but as peoples at an earlier stage of civilization. The marks of difference between the African and Indian on the one side and the European on the other are those of religion and civilization, distinctions problematized by the anti-Christian and barbaric behavior of the slave traders, the English generals, and those at home who upheld their conduct. In his review of Thomas Clarkson's *History of the Abolition of the Slave Trade* for the *Edinburgh Review* of 1808, Coleridge desynonymized the words "savage" and "barbarian," applying the savage to the American, Peruvian, and Mexican peoples and the word "barbarian": to the Africans. The Africans were thus distinguished from the European in that they were at an earlier state of development and without civilization. All that was required was that the Europeans would bring civilization to them. The Americans had or had possessed it in the past and lost it (1995, I: 241–42). Again we can see this as ethnocentric as well as containing an incipient defense of colonialism, but not a full-fledged biological racial theory.

Coleridge's notions of science and natural history altered however when he went to study in Germany in 1798. He was "an assiduous attendant" at Blumenbach's lectures on physiology and natural history and saw his "Golgotha" or collection of skulls (1957–73, 3: 4047). Coleridge came to regard Blumenbach's physiology as a theistic alternative to the scientific materialism of French thought and he was captivated by Blumenbach's notion of a formative force or vital principle divinely implanted and developing in response to external stimuli (Levere 205–12). He gave Blumenbach's work fresh thought under the stimulus of his friendship with J.H. Green for whom he appears to have prepared a series of notes to be used by the surgeon in his annual course of lectures at the Royal College of Surgeons in 1828. These notes and speculations interestingly revise Blumenbach's work along the lines that Prichard was simultaneously pursuing. In addition to accepting Blumenbach's hypothesis of the formative force, he concurred with the monogenist notion of there being one species of humanity radically different from all other animals. This species was variegated along Blumenbachian lines into five distinct races, determined by degeneration from a primary race. The difference between races was thus one of degree. For Coleridge "variety" held a meaning different from that of "race" (the words had been more or less interchangeable for Blumenbach) and related to "minor, more fugitive and accidental differences" (1995, 2: 1388–90). Here he suggests that the concept of "race" is a semantic necessity and not an absolute category: "What are differences of Kind as opposed to differences of degree—& who is to be judge what difference in degree is equivalent to a difference in Kind" (1389).

Coleridge was obviously opposed to polygenist thinking. In 1827 he annotated Louis-Antoine Desmoulins's *Histoire naturelle des races humanines* (1826), which put forward a polygenist classification of man into sixteen distinct species, then divided these into races or subspecies. As a materialist, Desmoulins rejected the scriptural account of the genesis of man. He also detected racial difference in the European group itself, conflating ideas of nation and race. Coleridge's response was characteristic in identifying and demonizing a French materialist natural philosophy opposed to scripture: "This work is quintessential French—and Desmoulins's the pure & *intense* Frenchman. No other nation could have produced the author of this work." Coleridge objected that Desmoulins had banished God and Providence from the system. His challenge to Desmoulins was to show "any instance of five or six aboriginal Species in the whole Catalogue of the Mammalia so slightly distinguished from each other or passing so imperceptibly into each other, as in this 5 or 6 ~~Species~~ Races of Man." That is, he viewed the differences between humans as so slight in comparison with difference in the animal kingdom that they could not reasonably be classed as distinct species. Coleridge's arguments were not objective;

his heartfelt imperative was to maintain in natural philosophy, the symbolic truth of "the necessary idea" of the narrative of the dispersal of Noah's sons: Shem, Ham and Japhet which prevented him from countenancing explanations which accounted for human difference in terms of separate species (1980–84, 2: 176–77).

Coleridge wished to place man at the summit or "ultimate intent" of organic creation (1995, 2: 1397), incorporating the attributes of lower beings as he rises above them. This leads him to revise Blumenbach in a more disturbing way. Where Blumenbach had preferred the Caucasian race on grounds merely aesthetic, Coleridge wishes to see the Caucasian or Indo-European race as the summit of organic development: "To Prof. Blumenbach we owe the enumeration of the races now generally adopted into the Caucasian as the center[,] the Mongolian, the Malay, the American & the African." With the Caucasian we "find the moral beauty, the cui bono or final cause of the Fact—that the Human Species consists of ONE *historic Race*, and of *several* others" (1402). From this "Historic Race" all the other races (including the present Europeans) have degenerated down to "the wretched state of the Boschesman in the wilds of Caffari or the New Hollanders" (1401). Here degeneration is used in Buffon's pejorative rather than Blumenbach's more neutral sense. Nature, however, allows a "re-unitive process" and the "Historic race" thus acts on the others as "a central Sun relatively to the Planets, communicating Light, heat . . . ameliorating them even where it leaves them in their peculiar orbit" (1402). The disappointing conduct of the central race, however, has proved it to be degenerate; Coleridge instances the destruction of the New World by Spanish colonists as evidence for this belief. So too are certain climates uninhabitable without physical degeneration brought about by the "animalizing changes of moral degeneracy." As an example of this he cites "the black pigment in the rete mucsus of the Negro" (1404). Thus, unlike Blumenbach, Coleridge argues that cultural and moral behavior has a formative physical effect. The claim of the present central race to primacy is a right conferred only negatively "by the less degree" of its "degeneracy" and "positively by the direction" in which it is moving (1406). Like Prichard, Coleridge wishes to dismiss what he calls the "Ourang utan Hypothesis" of human development, by postulating a fall from original purity to contemporary debasement, rather than some form of protoevolutionary descent from the primates. For Coleridge, the true "natural state" of every animal is not its present degraded state but that "in which the tendency of the animal to perfect itself according to its species meets with most aids & fewest obstacles"

(1413). In so arguing, Coleridge had gone beyond the parameters of Blumenbach's theory in the cause of his own version of the German *Naturphilosophie*. He wished to integrate human natural and social history into his systematic study of the inner constitution of nature and its laws and development, after about 1815.[32]

Blumenbach's typology of mankind remained attractive to Coleridge because it could be used to reconcile the Mosaic account of human history with the principles of polar logic. Like Prichard he wished to reconcile the facts of natural history with the ideas contained in scripture.[33] Unlike Prichard, who eventually dispensed altogether with the notion of race as essentialist, Coleridge hung on to the fivefold division because it presented an uncanny similarity with aspects of his *Naturphilosophie*. In a Notebook entry of June 1819, he attempted to "explain the origination and geographical position of Blumenbach's five Races...on one side and the Mosaic Triad, Shem, Ham and Japet" on the other (4: 4548). In 1828 he annotated Green's copy of a German translation of Blumenbach's *De Generis*, along these lines. In the marginal notes, Coleridge satirizes those "Systematizers of Natural Hystery" who have relied on gradations in natural history to construct a system. Nature is not bound through continuity in space and the object of the true system is "to discover and bring together before the mind the...principal objects which nature effects in the process of elevating matter into organization and *manifest* vitality...to compel the elementary stuffs to reveal their interior Being, and their finer affinities, is an evident end in the organizing process." In so doing, Coleridge veers away from Blumenbach. He does not reject Blumenbach's classificatory "Pentad of Races" (although Blumenbach arranged his varieties along a linear dimension, not in the form of a pentad), but attributes to it no more than "the merit of being the most convenient Division hitherto proposed." Like Prichard, Coleridge wishes to attach to it what he calls "its historical Staple-ring:" the Mosaic account of human diversity (1980–84, 1: 536–39). This division, also preferred by Prichard, was threefold and derived from Noah's three sons. In Notebook 36, Coleridge while approving of the "classical neatness" of Blumenbach's distinction in "respect of countenance and bodily form" yet criticized it for not distinguishing "in respect of intellectual faculties, and moral predisposition" (1980–84, 1: 541n).

Blumenbach's fivefold division of races suited Coleridge's own most widely used model for describing the system of nature, the Pentad. In this adaptation, the "Prothesis" is Noah; the "'Historic Race of Shem' is the positive pole (the religious)"; the "Antithesis or Negative

Pole is Japhet (the scientific)"; and the "Hammonic" is "the point of Indifference (the symbolic)." The curse of Noah upon the race of Ham begins the process of degeneration that is marked by physical and moral degeneration. From this process Coleridge deduced his "Generous" or historic race, which possessed the qualities by which the genus is formed and characterized, and which is derived from intermarriages between the descendants of Shem, Japhet, and Ham. The synthesis is the Celtic people. The "Degenerous" race, the opposite of the historic race, consists of the "Negro" and the products of intermarriage between the Mongolian, the American, and the Malay. Coleridge's central or generous race, however, was not an anticipation of Knoxian or other Anglo-Saxon supremicists, but a people composed of the "Jews, Syrians, Chaldeans, Arabians, Persians, Greeks, Italians, German, Swedish, Norwegian, Danish, English and Scotch" (1957–73, 4: 4548). He argued that this scheme had the advantage over that of Blumenbach of being founded on history. An entry in Notebook 26 for around 1827 demonstrates how he had adopted the terms of his "old and dear friend BLUMENBACH" but how he now prefers to substitute for them his own scheme of Shem, Japhet, and Ham. His own version of Pentad is framed to express degeneracy, with the "Caucasian race" as the "Prothesis" and "least degenerate" as opposed to the model of progressive development as described by "Dr Pritchard from the Negro, or [Lorenz] Oken, from the Oran, to the European." As Trevor Levere shrewdly comments, "The logical pentad, married to biblical exegesis, had given Coleridge the key to anthropology.[34]

Thus, if we are to evaluate and understand Coleridge's notions of human difference and his contribution to the race idea, it is necessary to put them into the context of early nineteenth-century theories of the natural world. Such theories were provisional and hesitant, prior to the later certainties of Darwinian evolution. As Robert Young points out we come to these "texts of racial theory," "contradictory, disruptive and already deconstructed" (29). Coleridge's view of race changed much during his lifetime and there is as much justice in claiming his earlier, pre-Enlightenment views (if we so term them) of race as typically Romantic as his later, more disturbing notions of the "historic" race. We can also see how his ideas were determined by the imperatives of his dynamic theories of nature and his belief in a Judaeo-Christian pattern of fall and redemption that would allow the "Historic" race to reunite the present diversity of mankind, as Christ redeemed the individual. Other ways of explaining human diversity were, however, available and it is interesting to speculate how Coleridge's might have progressed had he lived longer. Would he have followed the ethnographical path of Prichard, abandoning a physical anthropology that moved increasingly in the direction of Robert Knox's polygenist and materialist speculations, and tenaciously retaining his Christian synthesis of nature and history? It seems unlikely he could ever have embraced the "Oran utan hypothesis" of human development that he so bitterly opposed wherever it was promulgated.

THOMAS DE QUINCEY'S IDEAS OF RACE

Like Coleridge, Thomas De Quincey associated himself with racial theorists in both his personal life and his intellectual leanings. In early life, he encountered his fellow Mancunian, the anatomist, surgeon, and polygenist theorist of humanity, Charles White. In his "Autobiography," De Quincey tells of how when his sister Elizabeth died, aged nine, White was one of the two physicians to attend on her, the other being Dr. John Percival. De Quincey writes very little about the role of Percival but he records how White "pronounced her head to be the finest in its development of any he had ever seen—an assertion which, to my own knowledge he repeated in after years, and with enthusiasm" (19: 8n, 19). Elizabeth died of hydrocephalus, a condition which led to the expansion of the forehead, and which White associated with the obtuse facial angle of ideal Greek statuary. The enlargement of her forehead gave Elizabeth, De Quincey comments, "an air of intellectual grandeur." De Quincey refers to White as "the most distinguished surgeon at that time in the North of England" and as someone who "had published a work on human craniology, supported by measurements of heads elected from all varieties of the human species." De Quincey was fully aware of the racial import of White's work; the surgeon had "by one whole generation run before the phrenologists and craniologists—having already measured innumerable skulls amongst the omnigenous seafaring population of Liverpool, illustrating all the races of men" (8n, 257). In his "Sketches of Life and Manners" (1834), De Quincey describes White's *Account* as "a large book to prove that the human being was connected by a regular series of links with the brute; i.e. that the transition from the African skull to that of the ape, in some species or other, was not more abrupt than from the European to the African" (10: 10, 11). De Quincey's obsessive fixation with White's equally obsessive fixation with the skulls of his sister and others, combined with his rather disturbing memory of White's aesthetic "enthusiasm" about his sister's distended forehead recalls White's association of racial hierarchy with an erotics of physical beauty. The importance of Elizabeth's death in the formation of De Quincey's extraordinary psychopathology and its interrelationship with his later racial hatreds and obsessions have been powerfully and brilliantly evoked in John Barrell's *The Infection of Thomas De Quincey* (1991). Barrell suggests that after her death, Elizabeth's skull may have been dissected by Percival and White (who no doubt would have liked to have the specimen for his own collection) and that the recollection or imagined fantasy of her ruined and bandaged skull may be the primary referent informing the symbolism of the turban as well the many other ruined crowns in De Quincey's substantial oeuvre (Barrell 25–36, 104–25, 157–67).

De Quincey subsequently recalls in his "Autobiography" how White was again called to attend a friend of his mother, Mrs. Schreiber, who was dying from a cancer, during which period he claims to have become "intimate" with the surgeon (19: 257, 258). De Quincey evokes the powerful but shadowy impression made upon him as a child by White's personal anatomical museum which enigmatically "furnished attractions to an unusually large variety of tastes." He describes how he has forgotten, and gratefully so (and why so?), the contents of the museum, "all the earthly trophies of skill or curious research," with the exception of two notable "*humanities*" (he does not mention White's specimen of the African penis). One was the mummy of a Miss Hannah Beswick, a patient of White, who, terrified of premature burial, had requested that her body be kept above ground. She was embalmed, swathed in cloth, and made to stand upright in a wooden case in White's museum, with the veil withdrawn from her face but once a year in the presence of two witnesses. De Quincey reports seeing the English clock case in which the mummy was contained as a child but never the mummy within, on either of his two visits. The second exhibit, however, was seen. This was the skeleton of a highwayman and probable murderer, Thomas Higgins, whose story is alluded to in De Quincey's *On Murder considered as one of the Fine Arts* (1827) (6: 125–26; 19: 260–63; 466n) The skeleton had been embalmed by White with the assistance of the surgeon William Cumberland Cruickshank, William Hunter's associate (Cullingworth 18–22).[35]

De Quincey's recollections of White's attendance on his dead sister and the anatomical museum he possessed leads to several psychological enquiries about death, memory, curiosity, mystery, and violence with White's uncanny mummy troped within an Orientalist *Arabian Nights* narrative, but it does not lead to any identification with the racial theories of the man who may have opened his sister's skull, which appear to amuse and intrigue De Quincey, rather than convince him. In his essay of 1824 on "English Physiology" De Quincey attacked the contemporary state of such endeavor on Coleridgean lines for its "unphilosophic" nature and its increasing tendency to materialism. Though he does not mention White's work in this essay, his target is very much the notion or concept of gradation in nature that White espoused. Instancing the contemporary controversy surrounding William Lawrence's *Lectures on Physiology, Zoology, and the Natural History of Man* (1819), De Quincey criticizes the argument that one can determine racial intelligence from the dimensions of the skull:

> On examining certain African skulls Mr. Lawrence is disposed with many other physiologists to find the indications of inferior intellectual faculties in the bony structure as compared with that of the Caucasian skull. In this conclusion I am disposed to coincide: for there is nothing unphilosophic in supposing such a gradation amongst different races of men, any more than in supposing such a gradation of individuals of the same nation. But it is a high degree unphilosophic to suppose, that nature ever varies her workmanship for the sake of absolute degradation. (3: 182)

De Quincey argues that nature pursues differences in kind in addition to those of degree and that if "the negro intellect be in some of the higher qualities inferior to that of the European" we must posit that this is because such "inferiority exists for the purpose of obtaining some compensatory excellence in lower qualities that could not have else existed." In so distributing her "gifts" nature is pointing to "that same intermixture of all the races with each other...we have reason to suppose one of her final purposes, and which the course of human events is manifestly preparing" (182–83). De Quincey defers to Kant's *Kritik der Urteilskraft* (1790) in positing a teleology which obliges us to find purposiveness in the world.

In 1830 De Quincey indicated a wish to write an essay on Kant's "idea of *Race* in natural history, which deduces the physical varieties of man from a single aboriginal pair" (7: 88, 310n). In 1824 he had translated Kant's essay "On National Characteristics, so far as They Depend upon the Distinct Feeling of the Beautiful and Sublime" (1764). Kant's essay, discussed above, analyzed national character in accordance with its feelings for the Sublime and Beautiful, though Kant indicated that whether these differing manifestations of character were occasioned by "the colour of the times and the quality of government" or "were bound to the climate by a certain necessity" remained uncertain. The translation is mainly notable for De Quincey's objection to Kant's claims that manumitted African slaves have never contributed to the arts and sciences: "[C]ommon sense demands that we should receive evidence to the intellectual pretensions of the Blacks from the unprejudiced judges who have lived amongst them, not from those who are absurd enough to look for proofs of negro talent in the shape of books" (4: 149-50, 157n).

De Quincey's consciously held model of race, to the extent that it may have been formulated at all, probably owes more to Kant's anthropology than to other models, in that he assumes that there are kinds of biological racial difference and that there is a teleology occasioning the difference. This is similar to Coleridge's notion that all human races will be reunited at some stage in the future, though this inevitably posits a universal whiteness or Europeanness. In his essay on "Modern Greece" of 1842, however, De Quincey casts doubt on the notion of race as a permanent stock or bloodline. He concurs with those who doubt that even "one drop of genuine Grecian blood, transmitted from the countrymen of Pericles, now flows in the veins of any Greek subject." Rather than glimpsing the morphological type of a "Grecian cast of face," one sees instead an "Albanian face," whatever that may be. The Albanians are no more "the old legitimate Greeks" than "the modern English represent the Britons." The Albanians are representatives of the "Sclavonic race," thus connecting modern Greeks with the Russians, "the supreme branch of the Sclavonic race." De Quincey here clearly defines race in the modern biological sense of the race idea, using terms relating to the purity or impurity of an established bloodline. Discussing the stationary nations of Greeks, Egyptians, Persians and Afghans, De Quincey argues that, although one might expect purity, "the fact is the four nations mentioned have been so profoundly changed by deluges of foreign conquest or foreign intrusion, that at this day, perhaps, no solitary individual could be found, whose ancestral line had not been confounded with other bloods." Only the Arabs and Jews have avoided this "hybrid mixture" of bloods. For De Quincey the intensity of the reciprocal hatred between Jews and Christians has served to maintain "the intense purity of the Jewish blood through probably more than six millions of individuals" (13: 205-6). De Quincey, however, does not seem preoccupied by the idea of race per se but more intrigued by the notion of racial hatred. He does not represent peoples in the context of racial schematics, like Coleridge, but in the context of an economy of fear and loathing in which typically orientalized subjects are represented as less than human, rather than as a part of racial hierarchy or as part of a teleology of human development. De Quincey's depictions of Oriental people is discussed in chapter 6 of this book.

The "Race idea' thus was strongly present in the late eighteenth and early nineteenth centuries. Although its point of origin is contested and unclear, it became increasingly influential as the century wore on. The Race idea was not one single hypothesis but several competing theories about the origins of the differences between human beings. Though not all writers in the period engaged with it as directly as Coleridge and De Quincey did, those who were scientifically interested were aware of its impact in some shape or form.

CHAPTER 2

ROMANTIC ANATOMIES OF RACE:
THE NEW COMPARATIVE
ANATOMY AND THE CASE
OF VICTOR FRANKENSTEIN

COMPARATIVE ANATOMY AND THE
CLASSIFICATION OF HUMANITY

The new Comparative Anatomy was a Romantic science. It was also a racial science, possibly the most racial of all the newly emerging professional and scientific disciplines of the early nineteenth century. It is significant that Britain's first permanent chair of comparative anatomy was given to Robert E. Grant, one of the main proponents of the new philosophical anatomy of Etienne Geoffroy Saint-Hilare, by the new London University in 1827 (Desmond 81). The practice of comparative anatomy was a long-standing one, in one form or another, but it established itself as a fully modern science in the Romantic period (Cole). Enlightenment attempts at classification and description of the natural world in the systems of Linnaeus, Buffon, and others were enhanced by an examination of the internal structures of bodies and the form and function of their organs. One of the great tasks of comparative anatomy was to more correctly situate the place of man in the natural world. In 1698, arguably the progenitor of the comparative anatomist, Edward Tyson, famously dissected the body of a chimpanzee because he was struck with the similarity of the creature to that of human kind. Tyson was the first to suggest that the ape was structurally more closely related to mankind than any other animal. Tyson's views were supported by Samuel Thomas von Sömmering who dissected and measured the bodies of several African subjects, alleging that they were closer in formation to the ape than the European. Other surgeons and anatomists, such as Pieter Camper in Holland and John Hunter and Charles White in Britain, seemed to confirm this general thesis. More extreme were the speculations of Rousseau and Lord Monboddo, the latter of whom argued that humanity was related to the apes (Moran 125–44, Wokler 107–34, and Muthu 31–45). This view of things was contradicted by a more orthodox Christian conception of comparative anatomy developed by J.F. Blumenbach in Germany and Georges Cuvier in France that stressed the unity of humanity and its clear separation from the other orders of animals on anatomical grounds. This chapter explores the racial aspect of the Romantic science of comparative anatomy and its implications for that most famous of fictional Romantic comparative anatomists, Victor Frankenstein.

LINNAEUS AND BUFFON

In his *Orang-Outang, sive Homo Sylvestris: or, the Anatomy of a Pygmie* (1699), Edward Tyson, chief physician to Bethlehem hospital, commented on the similarity he observed between "the lowest Rank of men, and the highest kind of some Animals." Tyson found about forty-eight ways in which his "pygmie" resembled human beings, as well as about thirty-four in which it differed (Tyson v–vii; Montagu 225–307).[1] He argued for the importance of comparative anatomy in further understanding humanity's relationship with the animal kingdom. Tyson believed in the importance of gradation in nature approximating to the Aristotelian notion of the Great Chain of Being (Lovejoy). Tyson's orangutan was actually what we know as the chimpanzee and his anatomizing of the ape proved that is was not a human being. He concluded that it was something in between man and ape: the "Pygmie more resembles a Man than Apes and Monkeys do; but where it differs, there 'tis like the Ape-kind" (Cole 223). The pygmy was thus the link in the Great Chain of Being prior to humanity. Nevertheless the uncertainty about what was ape and what was human, fueled by the confused and conflicting accounts of travelers' tales, is reflected in his work. Tyson's conflation of the chimpanzee with the orangutan and pygmy also had the unfortunate effect for many years of consigning the African people known as pigmies to the status of ape on the assumption they were identical with the subject of his study.

John Ray's *Synopsis of Quadrupedal Animals and Serpents* (1693), arguably an early Enlightenment text, informed as it was by the principles of the scientific revolution, did not classify humankind with other animals. Linnaeus departed from the practice of his predecessor by including, in his *System of Nature* (1735), humanity among the order Anthropomorpha (in the class Mammalia), which also included the genus *Simia* or Apes and *Bradypus* (sloths) (Schiebinger 1994, 28–39, 40–74). For the seminal tenth edition of the *Systema naturae* of 1758, Linnaeus changed his term from Anthropomorpha to Primates and enumerated its constituent genera as *Homo, Simia, Lemur,* and *Vespertilio.* He was unclear whether or not he should "call man ape or vice versa." [2] He remained perplexed commenting that "even to this day scientists search in vain for any distinguishing mark by which apes can be separated from human" and could only find in the teeth the source of any differences for physical classification.[3] In his "Anthropomorpha" (1760) Linnaeus commented that he knew:

> Full well what great difference exists between man and beast when viewed from a moral point of view: man is the only creature with a rational and immortal soul.... If viewed, however, from the point of view of natural history and considering only the body, I can discover scarcely any mark by which man can be distinguished from the apes.... Neither in the face nor in the feet, nor in the upright gait, nor in any other aspect of his external structure does man differ from the apes.[4]

Linnaeus further divided the genus *Homo* into two species, one diurnal (with six varieties) and one nocturnal. The single nocturnal species of humanity was *Homo troglodytes* (or *Homo nocturnus*). He also speculated that there might be a third species of mankind, *Homo caudatus*, or man with a tail, but concluded that this creature, a denizen of the Antarctic, was probably just an ape (S.J. Gould 1983, 18). In his construction of *Homo troglodytes*, Linnaeus was misled or confused by numerous travelers' tales of apes behaving as humans, as well as by reports of Albino Africans. Linnaeus believed that this species of humans was related to the Atlas tribe of cave dwellers described by the Roman naturalist, Pliny (Koerner 87; Schiebinger 1994, 80–84). Similarly misinformed Linnaeus constructed a species of wise monkeys, *Simia sapiens* able to play backgammon and chess, to wage formal war, and to execute their fellow-ape criminals. Linnaeus also held that animals have souls. For him, though humanity was a Primate (of the "first rank,"), this position was shared with monkeys, lemurs, and bats. In placing one kind of ape in the genus of human and in applying human characteristics to a species of ape, Linnaeus made the boundary between ape and human somewhat confused and arbitrary. There was little understanding in the seventeenth and eighteenth centuries about the anthropoid or higher apes; chimpanzees, orangutans, gorillas (not discovered until 1847), and gibbons were conventionally lumped together under the term "orangutan" by people who had never seen any kind of ape. Naturalists worked from second-hand reports by travelers and were generally confused and uncertain as to the status of the creatures they were describing. Vague and ambiguous terminology based on European reworking of native terms such as orangutan, satyrs, pygmies, jockos, and pongos was indiscriminately circulated (Schiebinger 1994, 78–114; Meijer 33–43; Lee 66–122).

Linnaeus's species were fixed and not subject to transmutation, although toward the end of his life he accepted that they might transmute though a process of hybridity (Bowler 1983, 64–68). It was Linnaeus's conflation of ape and human in the *Systemae naturae* that led other natural historians and comparative anatomists to try and define this crucial boundary more clearly, though this inevitably involved discussing humanity in terms of its animal organization. The key question was about the extent to which human beings were special and possessed of unique attributes and the extent to which they might be related to other creatures, less special. Once humanity had become absorbed into the order of Primates then these questions became increasingly urgent. The debate, reinvigorated by Linnaeus, was to have substantial implications for late eighteenth- and early nineteenth-century views of the place of man in the natural world, and such debates would also become heavily politicized in the revolutionary decades as a materialist natural history (identified with France) clashed with a Christian or theistic natural theology.

Linnaeus was concerned with the classification of animals according to their physical resemblances and the obviousness of relationship between ape and human. His system was an artificial one that looked for certain basic identifiable physical characteristics, the sexual parts of plants, and the dentition of animals, to establish a simple and easily applicable system of classification. His critics accused his system of arbitrariness and many tried to establish a natural system of classification based on the description of a number of physical qualities and characteristics (David Knight 58–106; Sloan 1976, 356–75). Buffon, his chief opponent, was more interested in describing animals in the context of their environments and identifying species by their ability to produce fertile offspring, rather than their similarities in terms of primary characteristics. His aim was to document the variety of biological forms and behavior that were to be found within a single species such as the human. The diversity of humanity, he explained through the principle of degeneration as a result of climate and environment. The similarity of any ape to that of human kind resulted from human degeneration from an original form to that of the bestial, rather than from any close relationship between apes and humans. Such degeneration, rather than any form of evolution, was sufficient to explain any such similarity. Buffon was skeptical of Linnaeus's *Homo troglodytes* which he assumed was a confusion with the existence of Albino Africans, and understood the orangutan of the East Indies to be identical with African anthropoids known as Pongo and Jocko. Despite his theory of degeneration, Buffon was certain that the ape and the human were clearly distinct, arguing that resemblances remained at the physical level and that human intelligence and reason marked the ape from the human (Bowler 1983, 92; Schiebinger 1994, 82).

THE NEW COMPARATIVE ANATOMY: BLUMENBACH

Linnaeus and Buffon were naturalists and not anatomists. The historian of comparative anatomy F.J. Cole identifies the period between the lives of William Harvey and John Hunter as a transitional time in which the accumulated details of anatomical investigation began to be formed into a new philosophical approach to comparative anatomy. The new science of comparative anatomy was chiefly pioneered by John Hunter in Britain, J.F. Blumenbach in Germany, and Georges Cuvier in France (Blumenbach 53). Everard Home summed up the aspirations of the new comparative anatomy when he described his brother-in-law John Hunter's practice as not concerned with making "dissections of particular animals," but instead, instituting "an inquiry into the various organizations by which the functions of life are performed so that he may thereby acquire some knowledge of general principles" (Home vi). Such a comment is as true of Blumenbach and Cuvier as it was of Hunter. It is with this philosophical approach to comparative anatomy that we are chiefly concerned (Cole 177; Cross 13–14). Linnaeus had reignited the debate about the difference between human and ape but in his Primate order he had also included lemurs and bats, and he placed the Primates in the class of Mammalia, judgments that pointed to larger questions about the relationship between humanity and the animal kingdom beyond the narrower issue of the boundary between the ape and the human, contested as that was.

Blumenbach was a skillful and distinguished comparative anatomist much concerned by these questions. He claimed that Linnaeus's "great mistake" in the *Systemae naturae* was "that the attributes of apes are there mixed up with those of men....the highest work of the Supreme being" (132–33). In the 1775 edition of *De Generis Humani Varietate Nativa,* Blumenbach begins by discussing and emphasizing the "differences which separate man himself from the rest of mankind" (163). He argues that in terms of humanity's external appearance, its "erect position," "broad, flat pelvis," "two hands," and "regular and close set rows of teeth" (164) differentiate it from the animal. As Schiebinger points out, much of Blumenbach's analysis of difference also hinges on a discussion of the female sexual organs, the angled direction of the vagina, and the formation of the hymen, nymphae, and clitoris, as well as the phenomenon of menstruation (Blumenbach 168–71, 182–84; Schiebinger 1994, 88–94). Blumenbach claimed that humans may copulate whenever they wish with no distinct mating times and that males are unique in experiencing nocturnal emissions of semen: "Pliny was right in calling woman the only menstruating animal" (182). Yet the key distinction is that "Man is a bimanous animal," whereas apes are "quadrumanous;" and the "great toe" enabling him to walk erect is "given to the biped, man, alone" (171–72).

Blumenbach believed that anatomical analysis could penetrate beyond Linnaeus's fixation on external physical characteristics. It could show authoritatively those internal parts that humanity does not possess and that had been attributed to it by Galen and his followers who did not dissect human corpses, only those of animals. Blumenbach comments on the many attributes of bones that previous anatomists have found to be present or lacking in both humans and other mammals, and adds that none of the attributes appears to be conducive to a clear understanding of difference; the mass of the brain "is the largest of all" the animal world and the "position of the heart is peculiar to man" (179). Ultimately, the trait that distinguishes humans from the animal is "the use of reason" which "all with one voice declare...is the highest and best prerogative of man" (182–83). It is these "gifts of the mind and their superiority" which makes mankind "lord and master of the rest of the animals." "Reason and invention" thus allow humans to adapt to different climates and environments (183). Although Blumenbach's most important marker of difference between humans and the animals is the God-given gift of reason, he does seek to explore both external and internal differences discovered by the new comparative anatomy that will establish clearly the human's place as a unique creature. Blumenbach accepts much of

Linnaean taxonomy, combined with Buffon's notion of degeneration, but he creates a special category for humans as bimana thus separating humans from other mammals, especially the apes.

CAMPER'S FACIAL ANGLE

Both Buffon and Blumenbach espoused a theory of degeneration to explain how human and animal variety had originated. Taking the European male (or in Blumenbach's term Caucasian) as the norm, degeneration had occurred through the influence of climate, environment, and the state of society a people inhabited (civilization indicated a fairer skin). If Linnaeus's *Homo nocturnus* was a species of human, it would have achieved its apelike appearance from this process but it would still be distant from the true apes, which were a different species from the human. An older and still highly influential model for organizing the world of nature was that of the chain of being. This idea was an ancient concept that saw nature as a highly structured system designed by God in which all living things could be ranked in a hierarchy from the simplest to the most complex, with the two extremes linked by a linear chain.[5] Each species was thus assigned a place on this chain with its closest relatives above and below it. The chain represented the divine plan and was thus fixed. Everything that was created had been created at the outset, what was referred to as the principle of "Plenitude." Naturalists who adopted this model understood that this was the divine plan and that the possibility of species becoming extinct was unthinkable. Humanity was at the summit of this chain of being above the apes, and in Christian and Neoplatonic versions of the idea, above humanity were the angels and ultimately God. The concept of the chain of being was less current in the eighteenth century than earlier; however it also had a rich metaphorical life and often underlay many alternative modes of viewing the natural world.

In the 1790s the idea of gradation in nature was still an acceptable hypothesis that could be applied to human beings. In his *Philosophy of Natural History* (1790), the natural historian William Smellie applied the principle of gradation to human beings:

> How many gradations may be traced between a stupid Huron, or a Hottentot, and a profound philosopher? Here the distance is immense—but nature has occupied the whole by almost infinite shades of discrimination.

> In descending the scale of animation, the next step, it is humiliating to remark, is very short. Man, in his lowest condition, is evidently linked,

both in the form of his body and the capacity of his mind, to the large and small orang-utan. These again, by another slight gradation, are connected to apes, who, like the former, have no tails. (1: 51)

For Smellie, gradation operated in a clearly racial way. Yet it was Charles White who, in 1799, made the most systematic attempt to apply rankings to human beings within the scale. For him, gradation in human beings was an explicit rendering of biological superiority. White's ideas have been outlined in chapter 1 of this book. He argued that a "beautiful gradation...subsists amongst created beings, from the highest to the lowest. From man down to the smallest reptile" (1). White claimed that he was led to the discovery of the gradation in the human species when attending a lecture given by John Hunter "who had a number of skulls, which he placed upon a table in a regular series, first shewing the human skull, with its varieties, in the European, the Asiatic, the American, the African; then proceeding to the skull of a monkey, and so on to that of a dog; in order to demonstrate the gradation both in the skulls, and in the upper and lower jaws" (41).[6] White uses gradation to argue for a polygenist account of human origins, an account that places the species boundary above African peoples who are above the apes.

Although he claimed that John Hunter led him to this view, White found support for his beliefs in the work of the physiognomist Johann Casper Lavater and the Dutch anatomist Pieter Camper. Lavater's *Physiognomische Fragmente zur Beförderung der Menschenkenntnis und Menschenliebe* (1775–78) was translated into English between 1789 and 1798. He argued that there were fixed differences in the human skull related to sex and nationality. Lavater believed that the forehead was especially serviceable as a measurement and he invented the "frontometer," a machine to measure them (Bindman, 2002, 98). Discussing a series of four skulls (German, North American Indian, Calmuck [or Mongolian]), and African, Lavater found that "the forehead of the Calmuck is flat and low, that of the Ethiopian higher and more sharpened. And in Europeans the vault of the hind-head is more arched, and rounded in form of a globe, than in the Negro, and the African." Lavater described a European head and concluded that "the individual to whom it belonged was neither a simpleton nor a genius; he was of a character, cold reflecting and active." Lavater found the forehead of the skull of the "Nomade tartar, or Calmuck" to have "a resemblance to the monkey, not by its situation, but by its flatness." In the African he is struck by "the sensible disproportion between the forehead and the rest of the profile...the arch of the forehead considered by itself, bears not that character of stupidity which is manifest in the other parts of the head." Lavater thus believed that it was possible to read from the formation of a representative human skull national and racial characteristics, finding coldness and reflection in the European, grossness and sensuality in the Indian, and stupidity and weakness in the mind of the Mongolian and African (3: 161–62). Lavater's physiognomy was heavily influenced by Winckelmann's belief in the supremacy of Greek art, which represented the highest degree of moral and physical perfection attained by humanity (Bindman 2002, 92).

Both White and Lavater credit the Dutch anatomist and surgeon Pieter Camper with being a source for notion of gradation in human beings.[7] Actually Camper was led to his discovery of the infamous "facial angle," which became a signifier of gradation and thus the scale of human inferiority, through his interest in art. Paul Youngquist finds it no coincidence that it is at this historical moment that anatomists and physicians, such as Camper and later Charles Bell, attempted to establish themselves as experts in "artistic expression" coincidental to the burgeoning of the Enlightenment science of race. (Youngquist 57–86). Camper, an artist and sculptor, composed his work as an aid for other artists when depicting the human face in its differing varieties (Camper 1794, 50; Meijer 5; S.J. Gould 1991, 229–40). Believing that artists too often used recognizably European faces for those of other nations and races, he originated a method known as the "facial angle" to serve as a corrective and more accurate index of physical difference, though he also affirmed that the measurement had no correlation in moral or intellectual terms. The facial angle or line was constructed by measuring the angle made by lines drawn from the forehead to the upper jaw and from the lower jaw to the base of the skull, thus providing a degree of prognathism or the angle of the jaw's protuberance from the rest of the face. Camper's neoclassical notions determined that the wider the facial angle, the more beautiful the subject, thus introducing an aesthetic hierarchy into an otherwise essentially arbitrary series of measurements. Camper did not, apparently, share Winckelmann and Lavater's equation of beauty and virtue as demonstrated through a natural and universal standard, though it is clear that he had a strong preference for classical art tempered by an awareness of the relativity of beauty (50).

Camper presented his discovery of the facial angle almost as a jeu d'esprit: "it is amusing to contemplate an arrangement of these [skulls], placed in a regular succession: apes, orangs, negroes, the skull of an Hottentot, Madagascar, Celebese, Chinese, Moguller, Calmuck, and divers Europeans. It was in this manner that I arranged them upon a shelf in my cabinet" (50). He found that the two extremes of this angle were from "70 to 100 degrees, from the negro to the Grecian antique; make it under 70, and you describe an orang or an ape; lessen it still more and you have the head of a dog" (109). Camper was a monogenist who accepted Buffon's notions of human degeneration through environmental change and came to oppose Linnaeus's taxonomies. Though he admits the "striking resemblance between the race of Monkies and of Blacks" any notion that they are to be confused is mistaken: "the whole generation of apes, from the largest to the smallest, are quadrupeds, not formed to walk erect; and that from the very construction of the larynx, they are incapable of speech" (99). Camper, a distinguished comparative anatomist, had already dissected an orangutan and discovered the lack of organs of speech among other human attributes in the ape.[8] He believed that apes had a greater affinity with "the canine species" and that such clear distinctions in organic bodies marked "the boundaries which the Creator has placed between the various classes of animals" (99).

Meijer argues that Camper's treatise *Redevoering over den oor-sprung en de kleur ser zwarten* (1764) contains a clear statement of human racial equality (Meijer 101–66; Bindman 2002, 203–5). He argued that the facial angle actually operated in humans only within the comparatively narrow parameters of seventy to eighty degrees, and anything above that belonged to the realm of art and below to the order of apes. The angle of difference was thus fairly constrained for humans. Nevertheless Camper had produced a visually striking diagram that placed Europeans next to Greek gods and Africans next to apes. Though Miriam Claude Meijer claims Camper as a champion of human equality whose facial angle theory was intended to justify an empirical theory of human racial equality, his discovery would become, in the words of Londa Schiebinger, "the central visual icon of all subsequent racism: a hierarchy of skulls passing progressively from lowliest ape and Negro to loftiest Greek" (Meijer 2–3, 5; Schiebinger 1994, 149–50). Certainly, later anatomists such as Charles Bell, in 1806, would expand and develop the principles of Camper's correlation of anatomy and aesthetics to argue that the "narrow and depressed forehead" of the "Negro" results from a deficiency in the "development of the organ of the mind" and contrasts with the "large capacious forehead" of the European, "the least equivocal mark of perfection in the head" (36–37).

JOHN HUNTER AND GRADATION

Charles White indicated that his first intimation of the facial angle was gleaned from a lecture given by the most celebrated British comparative anatomist of the eighteenth century, John Hunter. White had studied with Hunter at the anatomy school of John's elder brother, William, in Covent Garden, probably in 1748, and he remained a firm friend of John throughout his life (Moore 116; Cullingworth 6). Hunter's views are notoriously difficult to reconstruct and they were famously fought over by his successors, anxious to claim his legacy. He did not publish on this subject during his lifetime and, after his death, his brother-in-law and executor Everard Home, burned his manuscripts in an effort to avoid detection as a serial plagiarist of his benefactor's works. It is therefore difficult to know exactly what Hunter believed, but there is evidence to show that Hunter may have espoused a belief in gradation in nature and humanity. White, in 1799, had described Hunter's arrangement of skulls as a demonstration of gradation in nature, though we cannot be certain whether Hunter's intent was to prove a theorem or simply display an interesting phenomenon. Evidence for Hunter's ideas can also be gathered from the manner in which he organized his massive collection of specimens at his house in 28 Leicester Square, which was open to visitors, including Pieter Camper and J. F. Blumenbach, from 1788 onward. Introducing visitors to his museum, Hunter would explain that his "design" was to "display throughout the chain of organized beings the various structures in which the function of life are carried on" (Kobler 234). As Wendy Moore comments, "[T]he collection was no haphazard assortment of curiosities... but a carefully ordered series of human and animal parts arranged expressly to investigate and illustrate fundamental principles about life on earth" (Moore 465–99; Cross 15–21; Youngquist 10–19). One contemporary commentator saw in the arrangement of the collection, "Hunter's novel and curious system of natural philosophy running progressively from the lowest scale of vegetable up to animal nature" (Moore 472). In his "Life of Hunter" prefixed to Hunter's *A Treatise on the Blood, inflammation and gunshot wounds* (1794), Home described how Hunter arranged his collection as

> an attempt to expose to view the gradation of nature, from the most simple state in which life is found to exist, up to the most perfect and most complex of the animal creation,—man himself. By the powers of his art this collector has been able so to expose and preserve in spirits, or in a dried state, the different parts of animal bodies intended for

similar uses, that the various links of the chain of perfection are readily
followed, and may be clearly understood. (note 7)

Though this description of the arrangement of Hunter's collection
does not prove that he held the notion of gradation in human beings,
it is interesting to note that "different parts" of animals intended to
perform the same function are ranged in terms of complexity, which
would argue against a simple linear chain of being. Home goes on to
describe how Hunter's subjects were arranged in four classes:

> First, Parts constructed for motion. Secondly, Parts essential to ani-
> mals respecting their internal economy. Thirdly, Parts super-added,
> for purposes connected with external objects. Fourthly, Parts for the
> propagation of the species, and maintenance or support of the young.
> In each of the classes he has procured and digested a multitude of
> particulars which are disposed of in order of gradation, beginning
> with the most simple, and advancing, by degrees, to subjects of more
> complex organization. (note 7)

Moore comments that this arrangement "demonstrated the principal
anatomical systems—digestion, bone structure, nervous systems, and
so on—through a staggering range of species" and Stephen Cross
argues that for Hunter "the concept of the anatomical series thus
functions as an *a priori* biological principle in the conceptual field,
just as it functions as an organizing principle on the shelves of the
museum" (Moore 473; Cross 17; Dobson).

Within the collection Moore describes how Hunter arranged his
series of human skulls next to those of monkeys in a progression that
began with Europeans and thence to Africans and monkeys. It is
reported that Hunter claimed "that there is a regular and continued
gradation of these from the most imperfect of the animal, to the most
perfect of the human species. The most perfect skull is the European;
the most imperfect of this species is the Negro. The European, the
Negro, and the Monkey form a regular series."[9] That Hunter also saw
this principle of gradual perfection at work in terms of human variety is indicated in the portrait painted of him in 1787 by Sir Joshua
Reynolds at the Royal College of Surgeons. The portrait, engraved by
William Sharp in 1788, shows Hunter in front of an open folio note or
sketchbook (destroyed by Home after Hunter's death) with six crania
in profile arranged apparently in descending order. These skulls were
identified by Sir Arthur Keith as running from European, Australian
aboriginal, through to chimpanzee and macaque monkey, to dog,
and finally crocodile. (207)[10] The series is very similar to that which

White had used in support of his claim for gradation in humans. The facing page of the sketchbook shows a similar progression but notably in reverse order from horse, ox, pig, dog, and monkey to human.

The evidence of the portrait is not conclusive and the similarity of the sketchbook to Camper's discussion of the facial angle might be explained by some interpolation by Reynolds of an arrangement common in the international circle of artists to which he and Camper belonged. Aris Sarafianos argues that Hunter's ordering of the skulls could only be meaningful "within the limited realm of functions to which they are specifically related," thus allying Hunter more closely with the later thinking of Cuvier. By this account Hunter is deliberately attempting to break away from the tradition of the chain of being by insisting that series are only meaningful at the local level (107–8). Camper discussed his theory in his correspondence and lectured on the subject in Paris and London. In 1777 he recalls how when lecturing to the Royal Academy of Surgery in Paris, he "drew them the facial line of a European, of a Negro, of an ape, and of an ancient statue" and describes their "pleasure and surprise" at his "discovery" (Meijer 21). It is possible that Hunter's interest in the facial angle may also have been inspired by Reynolds or George Stubbes.[11] Camper, however, seemed to think that Hunter also had a coincidental intuition of the facial angle. He visited London in 1748, 1752, and 1785, lecturing to the Royal Society on the facial angle during his last visit (Meijer 5, 21; Douglas 338–53). During this visit Camper met John Hunter and viewed his collection:

> [Hunter] has sometimes professed that he has found the facial line and had arranged several races next to each other for comparison. I quickly drew the facial line in their presence and explained my theory of quadrupeds. (Meijer 112–13)[12]

Hunter's manuscript work on gradation was destroyed by Home. We do know from Charles White that he lectured on this subject. James Ramsay, the abolitionist, also attended such a lecture by Hunter, describing it in his *An Essay on the Treatment and Conversion of African Slaves* (1784), which will be discussed in chapter 3. Ramsay argues against the notion that racial inferiority can be determined from the shape of the skull. He describes how "a gentleman justly celebrated for his accuracy in the course of his researches" had pointed to the difference in European and African skulls:

> This suggested to him the idea of drawing out a series of heads in this gradation; European, African, monkey, dog. The difference between

the first two is indeed striking; the European, by the swelling out of the hinder part of the skull, supporting itself so as to shew the face almost perpendicular to the table on which it is placed, while the African, for want of such support, recedes from the perpendicular, and shews an obvious elongation of the lower jaw. The use that he has made of the discovery, has been the classing of nations by their attributes, without taking genius into account. He rather throws it out, but only as a conjecture, that negroes might have been the originals of mankind, he having observed, that in all birds and beasts, the originals, whence the tame sorts are derived, are black, and that every variation from them approaches more or less to white. (220)

That this is John Hunter must be obvious from the inclusion of the dog among the series. Ramsay also mentions one of Hunter's more unusual beliefs; that the first humans were black or dark-skinned (Moore 474). Coincidentally, Camper also held this belief. Ramsay goes on to mention in a later footnote how he consulted "the late celebrated Dr. Hunter" as to whether, given a greater degree of civilization and better nourishment, the "tender texture of the brain" of the African embryos would be less injured and "the brain, favoured in its growth, [would] force the skull to take its natural spherical form, and...make the man more capable of improvement?" Ramsay, here is arguing that the shape and formation of the skull does indeed have an impact on the intelligence of the person. "Dr Hunter" agreed that in an anatomical sense this was "fair and conclusive." Ramsay comments:

> The same gentleman, in his course of lectures at the Royal Academy, when shewing the gradation of Skulls, a discovery which he gave to its right Author, humanely observed, that he drew no conclusion from the difference in them respecting African inferiority. Several persons, who had possessed the best opportunities of observing the capacity of Africans, had assured him, that there was no difference to be seen, but what could be traced to their depressed condition, and that there were instances, where African ability had shewn itself in spite of all the disadvantages under which it laboured. He understood, that the very doubt whether they might not be an inferior race, operated against the humane treatment of them; and God forbid, said he, that any vague conjecture of mine should be used to confirm the prejudice.—Such was the modesty of true genius. (228)

This "late celebrated Dr. Hunter," however, is not John (as all previous commentators have assumed) but his brother, William, who died in 1783 and who lectured at the Royal Academy in London from 1769 to 1772 in his capacity as professor of anatomy.[13] John died in 1793, four years after Ramsay and nine years after the publication of his *Essay*. Ramsay's note cannot therefore be taken as evidence for John's views. William's reference to the "right author" of the "discovery" of gradation most probably refers to his brother John (though it might still refer to Camper). William Hunter did not accept the notion of gradation and his skepticism concerning the significance of his brother's idea would be understandable.

According to Wendy Moore, Hunter was also a protoevolutionist regarding human beings as closely related to apes who believed that life-forms adapted or changed over time. As far back as 1779, she claims, he had "abandoned the notion of a static, unchanging ladder of creation" believing that "species were mutable and capable of developing into others" (488–89, 496–99; Rolfe 316–19, 316n). In the notes published posthumously as *Essays and Observations*, Hunter asked the question "Does not the natural gradation of animals, from one to another lead to the original species" arguing that "that everything in Nature has a connection with some other natural production or productions; and that each is composed of parts common to most others but differently arranged" (1861, 1: 9, 47) Hunter was one of the few anatomists who, like his fictional counterpart Victor Frankenstein, went so far as to make actual surgical interventions that would match the parts of different species. Hunter was fascinated with the ability of different parts of animal bodies to regenerate. While working as an army surgeon at Bell-Isle he had noticed how lizards were able to grow their tails again after the tails had been amputated. Other skin and animal tissue manifested similar properties. Experimenting further, Hunter grafted the spur from the foot of a cockerel onto the comb of a fowl, where it continued to grow. Encouraged by this success, he implanted one of the testes from a rooster into its belly and, when this also continued to grow, he repeated the experiment but this time transplanting the testes into the belly of a hen, again with success. Then he turned to humans; securing a healthy human tooth from a paid donor he implanted it into the comb of a cockerel. Several months later, when dissecting the tooth, he noted that it had grown into the cockerel's comb. Though Hunter did not repeat his success with the tooth (which had, in fact, died), the testicle in the hen's belly had developed blood vessels and was not rejected by the host body, an experiment that Moore describes as "a remarkable early organ transplant" (218–19, 577n). Hunter often performed such bizarre experiments worthy of H.G. Wells's Dr. Moreau, of whom he is a literary progenitor. He grafted a cow's horn onto the head of a donkey and developed procedures to transplant living human teeth, thus initiating a practice that would survive well into the next century, ethically dubious though it certainly was. Behind such experimentation was Hunter's fascination with the idea of life and how living tissues seemed to grow, adapt, and repair themselves according to some mysterious principle. Hunter's creation of his animal freaks, surgical chimerae, that provided evidence for the relationship between different animals and their shared vitality combined with his belief in a development from simple to complex forms of animal organization and together they show him to be Victor Frankenstein's most obvious literary model.

CUVIER AND GEOFFROY: FORM AND FUNCTION

If Hunter and Blumenbach were leaders of the new comparative anatomy in Britain and Germany, the major figure in France was Georges Cuvier, the professor of anatomy at the Museum d'histoire naturelle from 1802. Though others, such as Buffon's collaborator Louis-Jean-Marie Daubenton and Félix Vicq d'Azyr, can be associated with a new comparative anatomy, it was the conservative and orthodox Cuvier who dominated comparative anatomy and natural philosophy in post-revolutionary France. He also politically dominated the French scientific establishment. Cuvier's *Leçons d'anatomie comparée* (1800–05) can be described as the first complete work of comparative anatomy. In this Cuvier described the regularity of natural forms and processes, developing his theory of the "correlation of parts" to explain and compare the functional basis of living structures and processes (Appel 24, 40–68). Although Cuvier was to prove a staunch opponent of both gradation and transformism, the *Leçons* contained a discussion of prognathism and racial intelligence. Cuvier argued that Camper's facial angle theorem was too crude an index of measurement. Instead he developed his "cephalic index," combining the facial line with a measurement of the dimension of the forehead, describing the size of the facial area. His notion of correlation indicated that a protruding jaw was evidence for the presence of a small brain and vice versa and he applied Camper's theorem to intelligence. Though a more sophisticated form of measurement, the cephalic index had the predictable result of demonstrating the inferiority of the Ethiopian and Mongolian races (Cuvier 1802, 2: 9). Cuvier regarded the Africans as "the most degraded of human races whose form approaches that of the beast and whose intelligence is nowhere great enough to arrive at regular government" (S.J. Gould 1981, 36; Meijer 171, 175–76).

Cuvier was a staunch Christian (of Protestant Huguenot descent). He believed that it was possible to establish a rational and natural system of animal classification that demonstrated the order of divine creativity. He upheld the concept of type, a sharply defined and morphologically stable unit used to describe animal variety, a belief reconcilable with the notion of creation and fixity of species. He observed the complex correlation between the parts of the organism that he felt would be disturbed by any change in one aspect of its structure. Like Blumenbach and Hunter, Cuvier was less interested in external appearance, advocating the description and comparison of the internal structure of animals. He stressed again the correlation of the parts, the necessary structural interdependence of the creature, essential to maintain the complex balance of life. The creature's structure was determined by its "conditions of existence." Cuvier emphasized that creatures were suited to their environment and that the key to describing and classifying their structures was function. Animals could thus be classified according to their internal structures. Those characteristics that were crucial to the animal's powers of movement and its sensitivity were given the most emphasis in Cuvier's system. The nervous system, in particular, was the most significant organizing principle for his system, hence the key role played by the backbones or vertebrae (Cuvier 1834, 24), In his substantial work *Règne animal* (1817), Cuvier felt able to classify the entire animal kingdom into four types, which he designated as "embranchments": Vertebrata, Mollusca, Articulata (animaux articules), and Radiatia (Zoophytes) (14–26; Appel 40–60). In Cuvier's scheme there was no obvious hierarchy, just different kinds of organization. Each of these types represented a fundamental plan on which animal structures were based and there was no transition between the plans. In each embranchment the number and variety of species varied according to function: the needs of the animal would determine its structure. Cuvier also refused to rank animals within the vertebrate type, as different kinds of vertebrates were adapted to different environments. Cuvier's scheme thus broke down any idea of linearity. As David Knight explains, "Cuvier had given the early nineteenth century a pattern which could be visualized, and yet seemed to represent a natural system" (89).

Mankind was thus a genus of the class Mammalia of the embranchment vertebrate. Cuvier accepted Blumenbach's separation of humanity from other mammals as bimana and quadruped: "Man forms but one genus, and that genus the only one of its order" (34). Setting humans apart within the class of Mammalia, Cuvier stressed the uniqueness of their upright stance and the magnitude of the ratio between the size of the skull and the smallness of the face (the cephalic index). He emphasized that "Man is pre-eminently distinguished in the organ of his voice," which he uniquely possesses of all the mammals. Cuvier reconciled the biblical story of the three sons of Noah with the presence of three distinct races or varieties of man: "the Caucasian, or white, the Mongolian or yellow, and the *Ethiopian* or negro." He accepted Blumenbach's and Buffon's notion that humanity is originally descended from the Caucasian stock, the most perfect variety. As for the "Negro race," Cuvier argues that the "projection of the lower parts of the face, and the thick lips evidently approximate it to the monkey tribe; the hordes of which it consists have always remained in the most complete state of utter barbarism" (1834, 34–42). Although Cuvier clearly separates the order of bimana from that of quadrumana (including the genus *Simia*), he does wish to suggest a closeness between Africans and apes that cuts across his attempt to describe a fixed plan.

Cuvier's system of classification would not go unchallenged. The main challenge concealed a whole series of scientific, political, religious, and racial assumptions about humanity. Cuvier's debate was with his erstwhile friend, mentor and collaborator, the comparative anatomist and professor of zoology at the Museum d'histoire naturelle, Etienne Geoffroy Saint-Hilare, one of the truly great clashes of early nineteenth-century science. Geoffroy, unlike Cuvier, had been identified with the Jacobins and, as such, had prospered in the early years of the Revolution. In 1794 he had declared that "while our brothers in arms are going to repel with sinewy might the futile attempts of the coalition of kings and cement with their blood the foundations of our republic," he and his fellow natural philosophers were to "acquire new knowledge in order to add new luster to the glory of the nation" (Appel 22, 71). He served as naturalist on Napoleon's Institut d'Egypt and, throughout his life, maintained liberal and deistic opinions. Geoffroy developed a theory of anatomy that was variously described as higher, philosophical, or "transcendental anatomy."[14] He argued that the unity of structure linking species within types was an idealized one and that there was a single structural plan that could be traced through, first all vertebrates then, later, invertebrates as well, what he referred to as "unity of composition." Geoffroy argued that one should ignore the function of the part and concentrate on the connections between the parts. He thus, unlike Cuvier, believed that form not function was the key to determining the structure of an organism. Geoffroy began to disseminate these ideas from 1795 onward, though it was not until 1818 that his magnum opus the *Philosophie anatomique* appeared (Appel 28). Geoffroy believed that all organisms shared a basic ideal form and that their parts were transmuted to serve different functions, counter to Cuvier's claim that function determined structure. Geoffroy and his followers came to accept the unitary composition of all animals; not only were all vertebrates built to the same blueprint, but the theory allowed that insects, mollusks, and man could be reduced to common organic components. Animal life was therefore a continuous and related series, not broken into discrete divisions, as Cuvier had argued. Geoffroy and his disciples spent much of their time searching for homologies, or those parts in different animals that were essentially the same, even though they might be employed for differing functions and have different shapes. Such homologies were evidence for the existence of an ideal plan. That the same parts could perform different functions in different animals was a direct contradiction of Cuvier's functionalism.

Geoffroy, unlike Cuvier, was a transmutationist. He held that the past, present, and future were one and that the human embryo develops through the stages of the lower animals, recapitulating and transcending them. Invertebrates thus represented stages in the embryological development of higher animals. Geoffroy came to believe that a change in the environment could affect the growth of an embryo so that new or altered organs would develop, and he undertook a series of experiments on chicks to try and prove his hypothesis. He also pioneered the new science of teratology or the study of monsters. He argued that organisms, like monstrous progenies, changed through a process of sudden mutation. Geoffroy's political sympathies were as republican and materialist as Cuvier's were royalist and Christian. His emphasis on theory and philosophy ran counter to Cuvier's espousal of careful and patient observation and description.

The simmering disagreements between Cuvier and Geoffroy finally erupted into public quarrels and debates from 1820 onward when Geoffroy began to identify homologies between, rather than within, Cuvier's four and morphologically stable embranchments. As Toby Appel has shown, this debate had strong religious and political elements as the staunchly Christian Cuvier defended a classificatory system that was irreconcilable with that of the materialist Geoffroy, whose emphasis on transmutation contradicted the notion of creation and fixity of species. In revolutionary and postrevolutionary France the debate had strong political overtones and the conservative scientific establishment, dominated by Cuvier, the Napoleon of science, battled with a younger generation of politically liberal thinkers. The dispute was also carried out over patronage and power with Cuvier defending the role of positive facts and scientific authority against the dangerous potential, as he saw it, of unrestrained speculation.

Geoffroy's philosophical anatomy became associated with liberal and radical political beliefs and was regarded by many as a manifestation of French materialism and atheism. The racial implications of the philosophical anatomy were profound and pernicious. Geoffroy had argued that mutations would develop in the embryo as a result of changes to the circumstances of the organism's life. This idea was pursued by Geoffroy's chief supporter Etienne Reynaud Augustin Serres. Serres was interested in discovering the general morphological laws of animal development, what he called "transcendental anatomy." Serres argued that homologies between organisms were more apparent in embryonic than adult form. He extended an idea, known as the "theory of arrests of development" or the "recapitulation theory" of the German anatomist J.F. Meckel to his study of human embryos.[15] In 1832 he was to claim, for instance, that the human embryo passed though a series of stages recapitulating the progress from simple to complex forms of life, fishlike, reptilian, and avian. He argued that malformations were the result of arrests of development, by which the development of a higher animal was arrested and fixed in the form of a lower and transitory phase. Thus one could explain the phenomenon of monstrosity as the appearance in a higher animal of an organ from a lower form (Le Guyader 8; Appel 121–30; Meyer 379–96; S.J. Gould 1977, 45–52). Recapitulation and the theory of arrested developments would, later in the century, be given a strong racial application. It served as a general theory of biological determinism whereby it was claimed that the white European male recapitulated in its growth the lower races. Dr. John Down, for instance, argued that certain congenital "idiots" displayed the features of non-European races; hence he used the term Mongol to indicate his belief that such people had had their physical and mental development arrested, leaving them with features resembling the lower "Mongoloid" race (S.J. Gould 1981, 134–35; Jackson 166–88). The idea that characteristics of the lower races could appear in degenerate forms of the higher was an influential belief of late nineteenth-century biology and implicit in the transcendental anatomy of Geoffroy, Serres, and their disciple Robert Knox, though none of them had gone as far as an open profession of the belief (Desmond 73; Rae 25–29; Biddiss 245–50).

WILLIAM LAWRENCE: VITALISM
AND COMPARATIVE ANATOMY

Debates about the relationship between human beings and the rest of the animal world and where the boundaries should be drawn between the various types or gradations of organism were very current in the late eighteenth and early nineteenth centuries. More than this, such debates were also politically charged in the wake of the French Revolution. We have seen how the Cuvier-Geoffroy debate was conducted in the political and religious context of the postrevolutionary France. Similarly, in Britain such debates in comparative anatomy and medicine were conducted among conservatives, radicals, and reformers. Adrian Desmond has shown how pre-Darwinian ideas about evolution were much more current in the early nineteenth-century milieu than has often been accepted and that they were espoused by liberals and radicals opposed to the conservative medical and scientific establishments of the Royal Society, and the Royal Colleges of Surgeons and Physicians. In particular, Desmond indicates how the evolutionary ideas of Lamarck and the philosophical anatomy of Geoffroy found particular favor among reformers and radicals such as William Lawrence and Robert Knox. Desmond argues that "for a wide range of reformers" the "comprehensive package imported from France in the 1820s known as 'philosophical anatomy'" was especially important. Geoffroy's ideas were influential in Britain from 1820, with innumerable courses based on his science taught by comparative anatomists, such as Knox, who had studied in Paris from 1821–22. Such ideas were characteristically taught in the private and more advanced medical schools. The radicals' belief in "nature's unity of plan, serial progression, and self-developing powers" were pitted against the conservative and antidemocratics' opposition to the combination of science and philosophy (Desmond 73; Rae 25–29; Biddiss 245–50).

In 1814 the long-running debate within Enlightenment science concerning vitalism and the principle of life broke out in a very public way with the championing of French materialist science by William Lawrence. The story of the debate has often been told.[16] Lawrence was a surgeon, comparative anatomist, and theorist of human variety. In 1799 he became apprenticed to the eminent surgeon John Abernethy at St. Bartholomew's. Abernethy, the Hunterian Professor of Anatomy and Surgery had published a series of lectures in 1814 ostensibly expounding the theories of his mentor Hunter who had died in 1793. Abernethy argued that organization could not explain life, and that life had to be considered as something separate. Mind is "superadded to life as life is to structure" (Abernethy 48,52). To explain life some "subtile, mobile, invisible substance" perhaps analogous to "electricity" and which "seems to pervade everything and appears to be the life of the world" was needed. This force would appear to be analogous to the Christian doctrine of the immortal soul. In postulating a vital force, Abernethy was close to anatomists such as Blumenbach who argued for a "formative force" that organized and determined the structure of a body. Abernethy's views had strongly conservative implications, supporting the orthodox position of an immortal soul and implying that just as a superadded external principle was necessary to control the human body, such a principle was also needed to govern mankind. In 1815 Lawrence was appointed as second Hunterian professor of anatomy and surgery at the Royal College of Surgeons and took the opportunity to use his inaugural lectures in 1816 to attack Abernethy's stance. He was well-versed in French scientific theories and he "dismissed all vital principles and mystical life forces as poetic personifications worthy of the benighted savage" (Desmond 117–21). For Lawrence life was "the assemblage of all the functions a living body can perform" (1816, 140–42). Where Abernethy represents the principle of life as the cause of living phenomena, Lawrence viewed life as the working operation of the living body. The story of Lawrence's persecution by the *Quarterly Review* as a modern skeptic and the enforced withdrawal of his *Lectures* and their subsequent pirating is well known. Lawrence was obliged to take an injunction against James Smith who had pirated his work, but lost the case when the *Lectures* were declared blasphemous and outside the protection of the law, thus ensuring their widespread distribution (Ruston 68–73). Lawrence was associated with the radical and liberal wing of the medical profession that had connections with Thomas Wakley's *Lancet* group, and a proponent of the materialist French science (Desmond 117–21).

Here I am concerned not with the vitalist debate itself, but with Lawrence's ideas as a comparative anatomist and their implications for racial science. In 1807 he translated Blumenbach's *Handbuch der Vergleichenden Anatomie* (1805) as *A Short System of Comparative Anatomy* (1807). Blumenbach arranged his system by organ and that was the system adopted by Lawrence in his *An Introduction to Comparative Anatomy and Physiology* (1816). In his 1819 *Lectures on Physiology, Zoology and the Natural History of Man*, Lawrence defends himself from Abernethy's charge of being one of the "party of modern sceptics, co-operating in the diffusion of these noxious opinions with a no less terrible band of French physiologists, for the purpose of demoralizing mankind!" (4). He considers his task as to "consider man as an object of zoology—to describe him as a subject of the animal kingdom" (103, 25–36). Lawrence's comparative anatomy is, however, confusing. He borrows Cuvier's system of classification, with its postulation of a "fixed external form" for each animal, continued by generation and follows Cuvier in dividing the animal world into Departments, Classes, Orders, Genera and Species (27–28, 82–87). He criticizes Rousseau and Monboddo, who would classify humanity in the same species as that of monkeys, and attacks White for his espousal of gradation, condemning "the poor African to the degrading situation of a connecting link between the superior races of mankind and the orang-utan" (106–8). Lawrence denies that gradation should be used to "assert identity of species between ourselves and monkeys" but that if "nothing more" is meant than "the variety and organization and its progressive simplification throughout the animal kingdom, the truth is incontestable." The human species he argues "is separated by a broad and clearly defined interval from all other animals, even from those species which, from their general resemblance to us have been called anthropomorphous" (108–9). Like Cuvier and Blumenbach, Lawrence regards the humans as a separate species and in a separate order (bimana) distinguished from other animals by the "vast superiority...in the faculties of the mind" (114, 163, 204). The *Quarterly Review*, however, was less than impressed by Lawrence's apparent privileging of humanity accusing him of deeming "the perpendicularity of the inferior incisors and the prominence of the chin quite as important characteristics of man, as his powers of reason and his intellectual faculties" (D'Oyly 247).

Despite this desire to separate humanity from the ape, Lawrence frequently invokes the notion of gradation and the concept of the "great chain" (41–42):

If we contemplate living beings arranged in one line, beginning with the most perfect, and continued downwards, we find a tolerably regular gradation from complicated to simple, through the whole series. At one end is man; at the other an animated microscopic point, of which thousands are found in a single drop of fluid. Numberless gradations are placed between these; so that, though the two ends of the chain are immeasurably remote, there is a close approximation between any two links. (87)

Lawrence claims that this "simplification or degradation of the organization" is equally apparent within Cuvier's four embranchments or divisions, as well as between them (87–88). He ranks hierarchically Cuvier's embranchments to show the principle of gradation throughout the animal kingdom: "[T]ake any organ or system of organs, and the same progress from complication to simplicity will be apparent" (89–90). Similarly, Lawrence extends this notion of gradation to human races or varieties:

> The number and kind of the intellectual phenomena in different animals correspond closely to the degree of development of the brain. The mind of the Negro and Hottentot, of the Calmuck and the Carib, is inferior to that of the European; and their organization less perfect. The large cranium and high forehead of the orang-utang lift him above his brother monkeys; but the development of his cerebral hemispheres and his mental manifestations are both equally below those of the Negro. The gradation of organization and of mind passes through the monkey, dog, elephant, horse, to other quadrupeds; thence to birds, reptiles, and fishes; and so on to the lowest links of the animal chain. (94–95)

Lawrence's notion of gradation serves to reinforce his materialistic views of life. If man's "intellectual phenomena" necessitates the existence of an "immaterial principle, superadded to the brain" this must be also conceded to "those more rational animals" differing from humans only in degree (96). Generally Cuvierian in his approach, Lawrence also briefly hints at a position that is closer to Geoffroy's philosophical anatomy when he comments on

> [t]he existence of certain parts, generally in an imperfect state, or, in the anatomical phrase, as rudiments, in some animals, where the function does not exist, and where the parts therefore are not employed. It seems as if a certain model or original type adapted to the intended function, had been fixed on as a pattern for the construction of nearly allied and analogous beings; and that this model had been adhered to, even in those cases where some particular function did not exist, and where, consequently, the corresponding organ was in reality unnecessary. (42–43)

Lawrence's speculation of a "certain type or original model" though applied only to "allied or nearly analogous beings" hints at an awareness of Geoffroy's philosophical anatomy and the importance of types. There is, however, no clear statement that such parts might become transformed to serve other functions. According to Peter G. Mudford, Lawrence's book was "concerned with an attempt to illustrate the position of the human species in zoological classification, by means of comparative physiology" in which he shows himself, if anything, the disciple of Cuvier" (430–60; Wells 319–62). Mudford is right to describe Lawrence as a follower of Cuvier in comparative anatomy as well as someone who upheld Bichat's more radical physiology, and it was the latter argument, rather than the former, that landed him in trouble. Nevertheless, as Nancy Leys Stepan argues, Lawrence's rather contradictory use of the notion of gradation, possibly derived from Hunter, cuts across his more orthodox posturing. Lawrence also argued for the importance of generation and for hereditary over environmental factors as the agent of variation within the human species. Such changes, he argued, were the result of spontaneous alteration, perpetuated by isolation and breeding, analogous to the process familiarly observed in animal variation: "[T]he differences of physical organization and of moral and intellectual qualities, which characterize the several races of our species, are analogous in kind and degree to those which distinguish the breeds of domestic animals; and must, therefore, be accounted for on the same principles" (470–71, 431–32, 436, 441–36). Lawrence, however, was discussing the variation within species, and he does not countenance the possibility of the transmutation of species.

VICTOR FRANKENSTEIN AS COMPARATIVE ANATOMIST

Anne Mellor has firmly located *Frankenstein* in the context of a feminist critique of masculine science epitomized by Humphry Davy, and Marilyn Butler has equally decisively established the novel in the context of the vitalist debate between Abernethy and Lawrence (Mellor 1988, 89–114; Butler 1993, ix–li). Mellor argues that Shelley "illustrated the potential evils of scientific hubris and at the same time challenged the cultural biases inherent in any conception of science and the scientific method that rested on a gendered definition of nature as female." For her, the works of Humphry Davy, Erasmus Darwin, Luigi Galvani, his nephew Giovani Aldini, and the writings of Adam Walker were vital to Shelley's understanding of contemporary scientific endeavor and achievement (1988, 89, 96–110). The intimacy of the connection between the Shelley circle and William Lawrence has now been firmly established (Butler 1993, xi–xii; Luke 141–52; Crook and Guiton; Ruston 74–94). Percy Shelley may first have met Lawrence in 1811 and he later consulted him about his health in 1815. Their most frequent contact between 1814 and 1817 occurred during the most intense periods of the vitality debate. Shelley, as is well known, was seriously interested in Enlightenment science, especially the works of Buffon, Condorcet, LaPlace, and Cabanis (see also Holmes; Grabo; Crook and Guiton).[17] As Butler speculates, during the period leading up to the novel's composition, Lawrence, "a high-flying professional may well have guided the couple's reading in the physical sciences from the time they became partners in 1814, to the moment of the novel's emergence" in 1818. Butler has argued that *Frankenstein* parodies Abernethy's vitalist position, in effect, allying itself with Lawrence's physiological opinions (Butler, 1993 xvi–xxi, xxxi–xxxiii, xli–xlv). Additionally, the contribution to the debates on anatomy and the principle of life that were held at the Villa Diodata in the summer of 1816 during the novel's composition were informed by the knowledge and opinions of John William Polidori, Byron's troubled physician. Polidori's contribution to the scientific discussion is now regarded as of substantial importance (Macdonald 5–24, 83–98; Frayling 6–18; Rieger 461–72). He was a graduate in medicine from the University of Edinburgh and had composed his thesis on the subject of somnambulism. From 1811 to 1815, when Polidori was there, the University was not at the forefront of anatomical research or teaching, though new ideas disseminated from France were circulating in the private medical schools, such as that run by John Barclay, which were as advanced as those in London and of which Polidori, as an especially bright and inquisitive student, would have been aware (Desmond 85–86). Polidori could have provided information relative to many medical and anatomical practices, such as the business of grave-robbing, and he would certainly be aware of the vitalist debates (Macdonald 85–86). Ironically, Polidori, when he was a student, would almost certainly have known the anatomist, Robert Knox, who graduated from Edinburgh in 1814 and would later become the chief exponent of Geoffroy's transcendental anatomy in Britain. It was Polidori who apparently initiated the discussion "about principles—whether man was to be thought of merely as an instrument" in a conversation with Percy Shelley (Butler 1993, xxi).

The Creature has been discussed in terms of its otherness, representing the newly politicized masses or alternatively female alterity and marginality.[18] From the 1990s onward the novel *Frankenstein* has received attention on account of its reflection of contemporary attitudes to race and human difference, with the Creature as a signifier of Caribbean slave revolt, or the fear of the east as mediated though scientific discourse (Malchow 9–40; Lee 171–93; Mellor 2001, 1–28). The novel, however, has not been discussed in the context of the new comparative anatomy and the debate about the classification of humanity and its relationship to the rest of the natural world developed through a concern with the bodily manifestations of difference and variety. What difference then does it make when we put *Frankenstein* into the discourse of comparative anatomy and the various attempts to classify mankind and fix the boundary between animal and human?

Victor Frankenstein, like John Hunter or William Lawrence, is a student of anatomy interested in discovering the principle of life, an obsession fueled by his romantic interest in the work of the alchemists Cornelius Agrippa, Paracelsus, and Albertus Magnus.[19] Unlike Lawrence, but like Hunter, Frankenstein is also a vitalist, who believes that something must be added to bodily organization to allow life. Frankenstein is thus led to look for "the philosopher's stone and the elixir of life" (Shelley 1966, 26). From the perspective of Lawrence and the "materialist school" this is a wrong-headed thing to do; Frankenstein should be concerning himself less with first causes and more with experimentation and observation. Disappointed at the University of Ingolstadt that the kind of natural philosophy in which he had earlier immersed himself is no longer considered to be worthy of serious attention, Frankenstein is reenthused by Professor Waldman's panegyric to empirical Enlightenment science, the modern masters of which "promise very little, they know that metals cannot be transmuted, and that the elixir of life is a chimera" (32). Nevertheless, he claims, they have achieved miracles of a different order:

> They penetrate into the recesses of nature, and show how she works in her hiding places. They ascend to the Heavens; they have discovered how the blood circulates, and the nature of the air we breathe. They have acquired new and almost unlimited powers; they can command the thunders of heaven, mimic the earthquake, and even mock the invisible world with its own shadows. (32–33)

As Mellor shows, Waldman's concept of nature and of the utility of chemistry owes much to Humphry Davy's well-known introductory lecture to a course on chemistry, delivered on January 21, 1802 to the Royal Institution founded three years earlier and subsequently published as *A Discourse, Introductory to a Course of Lectures on Chemistry* (1802), which Mary Shelley probably read on October 28, 1816. She also probably read Davy's *Elements of Chemical Philosophy* (1812) in late October and early November, when she was drafting the second chapter of her novel (Mellor 1988; Crouch 35–44). Waldman's particular interest is chemistry, one of the disciplines in which the

French ideologues had specialized, for which their opponents had accused them of reducing life to mere chemical processes. From then onward Frankenstein determines to master both physiology and anatomy dealing with "the structure of the human frame and the animal endued with life." This reference to the "animal endued with life" indicates that that he is a comparative anatomist, in the mould of Hunter, Blumenbach, Cuvier, and Lawrence (35). He studies the "natural decay and corruption of the human body," becoming somehow aware of the very principle of life itself. The French physiologist Xavier Bichat had defined life as the resistance to decay and that property which when removed no longer prevents the dissolution of the bodily frame. Frankenstein concentrates on this aspect of study observing how "the corruption of death succeeded to the blooming cheek of life," examining "the minutiæ of causation" exemplified "in the change from life to death" and the processes by which the worm inherits the "wonders of the eye and brain" (35–36). It is through these studies that Frankenstein claims to discover "the cause of generation and life" and to become capable of "bestowing animation upon lifeless matter" (36). Mary Shelley is notably reticent about how Victor accomplishes his creation and he himself refuses to tell Walton the secret for fear others will try and emulate his project.

William Lawrence's criticism of Abernethy's methodological procedures would seem to be applicable to Frankenstein: "We do profess to explain *how* the living forces in one case, or attraction in the other, exert their agency. But some are not content to stop at this point; they wish to draw aside the veil from nature, to display the very essence of the vital properties, and penetrate to their first causes; to shew independently of the phenomena, what is life, and how irritability and sensibility execute these purposes" (1816, 167). Lawrence rebukes Abernethy for his desire to engage with theological issues and to search for an immaterial principle, such as the soul "amid the blood and filth of the dissecting room" (1823, 8). His language recalls that of Frankenstein in his desire to pursue "nature to her hiding places" (37) and Waldman's imaging of the rape of nature by male scientists who "penetrate into the recesses of nature, and show how she works in her hiding places" (32).

Victor Frankenstein in terms of his methodology and personality resembles comparative anatomists such as Hunter, Lawrence, Cuvier, and Geoffroy.[20] Indeed, as Tim Marshall reminds us, any British anatomist faced with the shortage of human cadavers prior to the Anatomy Act of 1832 was perforce a comparative anatomist of some kind or other, obliged to experiment and study the carcasses of animals (71). If

Abernethy is present in the novel, it may be as the less compulsive professor of natural philosophy at Ingolstadt, M. Krempe with his "gruff voice and repulsive countenance" and "brusque manners, repulsive physiognomy and manners" who rebukes Frankenstein for his study of the "nonsense" of the alchemists (31, 34). Frankenstein is reluctant to "hear that little conceited fellow deliver sentences out of a pulpit," an intimation that Krempe is given to theological orthodoxy in his lectures (32). We are not given the details of the list of books of natural philosophy which Krempe gives Victor to read, but it is tempting to speculate that Blumenbach, Cuvier, White, and Lawrence might have been among the names (He is already familiar with Buffon's work) (28).[21] Waldman, whose ideas have been identified with those of Davy and Lawrence, is a more sympathetic character who, while upholding the Enlightenment concern with experiment, observation and discovery, acknowledges the debt that "modern philosophers" owe to their alchemical forbears. Waldman tells Victor that they have "left to us an easier task, to give new names, and arrange in connected classifications, the facts which they in a great degree had been the instruments of bringing to light" (33). Waldman is described as a chemist rather than an anatomist and under his influence Victor studies that branch of natural philosophy.

Frankenstein is an enthusiastic obsessive dissector and collector of human and animal parts. In this he particularly resembles John Hunter whose almost pathological drive to acquire specimens for his collection, such as the skeleton of Charles Byrne, the Irish Giant, became notorious. He was expert in the acquirement of cadavers for dissection for his brother's anatomy school, as Wendy Moore has recently shown. He undertook numerous experiments on living animals, which to our sensibilities appear troubling (Moore 71–99, 169–73, 397–428).[22] He was famously thought to have been involved an attempt to resurrect the corpse of the Reverend William Dodd, after he had been hanged for forgery in 1777. This was an experiment concerned with the principle of life and resulted from Hunter's investigations into what precisely constituted life and which may have involved the use of electric charges from a Leyden jar. Hunter had also cofounded with William Hawes the Humane Society in 1774, the purpose of which was to sponsor the revival of unfortunates drowned in the Thames around that time. Frankenstein's desire to visit England, prior to his attempt to create a female companion for his creature, is occasioned by his hearing of "some discoveries having been made by an English philosopher, the knowledge of which was material to my success" (115, 117, 117n). Either Hunter or Erasmus

Darwin are most likely referred to here, given the time frame of the novel and their notorious interests in the principle of life, "the subject in which my interest was so terribly profound" (122). Hunter would certainly have been included among the "most distinguished natural philosophers" to whom Frankenstein has letters of introduction (121, 121n). Frankenstein is an animal experimenter and a vivisectionist. He is "peculiarly attracted" to the phenomenon of the "structure of the human frame, and, indeed, any animal endued with life" and studiously applies himself "more particularly to those branches of natural philosophy which relate to physiology" where he becomes acquainted with "the science of anatomy" (35).

Frankenstein's interest in the "principle of life" is that of a comparative anatomist rather than that of a surgeon. Once he has discovered this principle he begins to prepare "a frame for the reception of it, with all its intricacies of fibres, muscles, and veins." He wonders whether he should create "a being like myself," a human being, or "one of simpler organization" (6–7). It is not clear what this alternative being would be, but one presumes it would be an animal organization, indicating that Frankenstein's comparative approach and his belief that his discoveries are not confined to the human but also apply to the animal realm. He decides to give life to "an animal as complex and wonderful as man," but an animal nevertheless. Frankenstein's secret toils among the "unhallowed damps of the grave," his torturing "of the living animal to animate the lifeless clay," and his "workshop of filthy creation" recall the activities of anatomists such as Hunter, procuring bodies to work on and living animals to experiment with. While constructing his "human frame" Frankenstein tells how "the dissecting room and the slaughter house furnished some of my materials" (37–38). The creature that Frankenstein constructs is thus not fully human but contains parts of animals somewhere in its anatomy; its lifeless clay is animated somehow by the torturing of living animals.

In what way does the novel engage in the debates about comparative anatomy and the place of man in the natural world, a debate in which William Lawrence was a key participant, if not an original thinker? it describes humanity as a form of animal possessing a more complex organization than other animals. The creature is not fully human, but a hybrid which would argue that its author did not accept the notion of the fixity of the species of Linnaean taxonomy. We do not know which animal parts may have been used in its creation but, if such parts were derived from nonanthropoid animals, this would suggest that the Cuvierian notion that organisms are structured according to function and that any adaptation of the parts of the organism would destroy the delicate balance of its constitution and render it not viable is also rejected. This leads to the interesting speculation that the novel, if it affirms any system of comparative anatomy, is more conducive to those hypotheses which postulate gradation and the close connections between individual organs on a rising scale of complexity or perfection, much like that of Hunter. More excitingly, it is possible that through contact with surgeons such as Lawrence, Mary Shelley and her circle knew something of the new debates about Geoffroy's philosophical anatomy which, as Desmond shows, were becoming increasingly influential among the more radical practitioners of London and Edinburgh after 1815. It is tempting to speculate that Frankenstein uses animal parts to serve for his creation, functions other than they may have performed in the original creature. And that the presence of the organs of lower animals in that of a higher, more complex being is a fictional justification of the "recapitulation theory" that Geoffroy developed with his disciple Serres and which would be used in such a heavily racialized form later in the century. The novel thus implicitly supports the radical science of the French Revolution and its British sympathizers.

The Creature is Frankenstein's first attempt at constructing a living creature. His second attempt is aborted. Persuaded by a mixture of importuning and threats, Frankenstein agrees to construct a female mate for his Creature. The novel is even more reticent about the process of the female's construction. Frankenstein describes it as a "filthy process" undertaken without the "enthusiastic frenzy" of his first foray which protected him from an awareness of the "horror" of the proceedings (127). His imagination is more horrified at the possibilities arising from the creation of a female than a male. She "might be ten thousand times more malignant than her mate, and delight, for its own sake in murder and wretchedness." She might also propagate a "race of devils" who could make "the very existence of the species of man a condition precarious and full of terror" (128). Mellor has drawn our attention to Frankenstein's excessive and pathological horror of the female and female sexuality, a horror that may explain his unwillingness to hasten the date of his marriage to Elizabeth (Mellor 1998, 220–32). He is also worried that his female creation, "a thinking and reasoning animal" might have a will of her own and "refuse to comply with a compact made before her creation," an entirely reasonable position for her to adopt. There is no doubt that Frankenstein views the female he is to create as, like his first creation, not human but another species, a view his creature reflects when he declares

"everlasting war against the species" of humans (102). Frankenstein
here raises the specter of interspecies' desire and mating notoriously
discussed by racists such as Edward Long, John Kemeys, Samuel
Estwick, and, in the 1840s, Dr. Robert Knox: "She also might turn
with disgust from him to the superior beauty of man; she might quit
him, and he be again alone, exasperated by the fresh provocation of
being deserted by one of *his own species*" (my emphasis). Frankenstein
despairs that in creating a couple capable of propagating he endan-
gers the "existence of the whole human race" in some species war.
He raises the possibility that the female creature may have desires for
"the superior beauty of man," a desire which if enacted might lead
to the creation of a hybrid race between two species. Frankenstein's
frenzied and hysterical speculations are indicative of his distressed
state of mind rather than a cool extrapolation of eighteenth-century
scientific reasoning regarding human difference, but his imagination
encompasses the possibilities of not only the propagation of a different species of anthropoids but also of hybrids between the two
species, if his female should prove fertile. His response is to tear "to
pieces the thing" he is creating (128–29).

Frankenstein's aborted female creation shares in his fevered imagination many of the characteristics of stereotypical Gothic demonic
females from M.G. Lewis's Beatrice de la Cisternas (the "Bleeding
Nun") to Bram Stoker's female vampires and beyond, who populate
eighteenth- and nineteenth-century texts. Yet, in this respect, racial
and anatomical discourse shares in this process of gothicization. In
his construction of a female creature Frankenstein, surprisingly, does
not discourse about the different challenges that this will create for
him as an anatomist. The conclusion we may thus draw is that he
does not regard the female anatomy as radically different from that
of the male of his new species, though he clearly believes that there
is an essential and biologically female body and psychology he will
construct. Frankenstein's fears of a savage unbridled female desire are
at odds with what the Creature has told him about his own Lockeian
education and transformation from benevolent vessel to vengeful
agent. Discussions of race and science historically have tended to separate race and gender, and more recently scholars such as Schiebinger
have interrogated scientific writing for its assumptions relating to
gender. The assumption of male comparative anatomists working on
predominantly male human subjects was that "the racial subject was
male and that sexual differentiation was primarily about Europeans"
(Scheibinger 1994, 147).[23] Women were thus, on the whole, studied
for their deviation from a European male norm.

As the nineteenth century progressed, race and gender were used increasingly as analogies for human difference: "[L]ower races represented the 'female' type of the human species, and females the 'lower race' of gender" (Stepan 1992, 263, 261–77). Skulls used to make craniological comparisons were typically male and when a female skull was used it could as well have been a male skull, stripped of all the accoutrements of femininity. When anatomists compared women across cultures, their concerns were characteristically with their sexual traits, and the pelvis not the skull became the "universal measure of womanhood" (Schiebinger 1994, 132–33, 126–34, 148–57). Frankenstein's method of constructing the female seems more or less identical to that whereby he first created which would argue for his assumption that, in anatomical terms, the male form is prior and the female a deviation from it. His ascription of gendered feminine traits to the body he constructs derives from the projections of fear and desire European explorers and travelers visited upon females of nations they accounted as primitive or savage. His destruction of the creature is a grim parody of Georges Cuvier's notorious dissection and mutilation of the body of Saartjie Baartman in 1816 (Youngquist 53).

In the context of racial anatomy it is the Creature's physical appearance that provides the clue to its taxonomy. Shelley describes its form and features in the following words:

> His limbs were in proportion, and I had selected his features as beautiful. Beautiful! – Great God! His yellow skin scarcely covered the work of muscles and arteries beneath; his hair was of a lustrous black, and flowing; his teeth of a pearly whiteness; but these luxuriances only formed a more horrid contrast with his watery eyes that almost seemed of the same colour as the dun white sockets in which they were set, his shrivelled complexion, and straight black lips. (39–40)

Numerous critics have pointed out that the Creature, like all monsters, defies or disrupts obvious classification, whether scientific or normative. That the monster disrupts and transgresses boundaries serving as a focus of the anxieties of a predominantly white middle-class audience has become a cliché of Gothic criticism. Amongst those anxieties critics have found one relating to race as well as class and gender. H.L. Malchow, for instance, argues that the physiognomy of the Creature combined with his powerful body suggests the "standard description of the black man in both the literature of the West Indies and that of unfolding West African exploration"(18, 17–31). Mary Shelley had just about that time read the accounts of Mungo Park's African exploration as well as Bryan Edwards's *History of the West Indies* (1793). Debbie Lee argues, on the basis of the slave revolts in Barbados and Demerara occurring at the time of the novel's composition and reprinting, that "it seems logical to contend, then, that Mary Shelley drew on attitudes toward Africans and slaves in her depiction of the monster" (Lee 173, 174, 171–93). Paul Youngquist has discussed the novel in terms of its evocation of a white and proper body and Elizabeth Bohls has shown how it serves to normalize eighteenth-century notions of taste and race (Youngquist 53–55, 56–85; Bohls 23–36). Both Lee and Malchow refer to the speech of the British Foreign Secretary, George Canning, from the debate in 1824 concerning an emancipationist motion to free the children on West Indian slaves on the attainment of their majority. Canning explicitly uses *Frankenstein* to provide a cautionary tale of the dangers of granting too precipitate a freedom to those who had been enslaved: "[H]e finds too late that he has created a more than mortal power of doing mischief and himself recoils from the monster which he has made" (March 16, 1824; Baldick 60).

In an attempt to move the focus away from the black-white binary, Anne Mellor has argued that if we locate the Creature in the context of racial science, the racial variety of humanity which he most-obviously resembles is the "Mongolian" (Mellor 2001, 1–28). The Mongolian is one of the five varieties of humanity Lawrence described in his lectures of 1819, based on Blumenbach's typology. Lawrence attributes a yellow complexion to the Mongolian variety of humanity:

> *Yellow* or *olive* (gilvus or buxeus, a middle tint, between that of ripe wheat and boiled quince or dried lemon-peel) characterizes the Mongolian tribes, usually called together with the inhabitants of great part of Asia, Tartars (Tatars). (1819/1823, 249)

His description of the Mongolian peoples, as Mellor argues, bears a clear physical similarity to Shelley's representation of the Creature:

> The Mongolian Variety is characterized by olive colour, which in many cases is very light, and black eyes; black straight, strong, and thin hair, little or no beard; head of a square form, with small and low forehead; broad and flattened face, with the features running together; the glabella flat and very broad; nose small and flat; rounded cheeks projecting externally; narrow and linear aperture of the eyelids; eyes placed very obliquely; slight projection of the chin; large ears; thick lips. (480)

Though Mellor develops a more generous reading of Lawrence's racial thought than the *Lectures* warrants, downplaying his strong sense of gradation in humanity, the physical characteristics of the Creature do evoke Mongolian racial variety discussed in chapter 6 of this book, with the yellow skin and lustrous black hair, especially if we focus on the skin as the crucial signifier, which the comparative anatomists did not. Crucially the Creature, like the Mongolian and the races of the Americas, has "little or no beard." The lack of a beard or any mention of its subsequent growth serves to infantilize and feminize the Creature as well as identify him with a number of non-European races. In 1848, for instance, Charles Hamilton Smith made a clear division between "The Bearded, Intermediate, or Caucasian Type" and the "The Hyperborean, Beardless, or Mongolic Type" (Charles Hamilton Smith, 279, 385). As Schiebinger has argued, the presence of a full beard became a key marker of both masculinity and of the European or Caucasian kind of humanity.[24] The Creature's lustrous and flowing hair, however, would associate him more closely with the Caucasian or European in contrast with the woolly hair convention- ally attributed to the African. Yellowness also, like the absence of a beard, is applied to the Carib Indians. Bryan Edwards, for instance, comments on the "sickly yellow" complexion of the Eboes and their eyes that appeared to be "suffused with bile" in his *History* (2: 58,69; Malchow, 18). Similarly Peter Hulme has drawn our attention to the ways in which anthropologists and linguists attempted to make dis- tinctions between "Black and Yellow Caribs" in St. Vincent and the " 'True' Caribs" of the mainland in writings from the late eighteenth century onward (Hulme 2000, 3, 12; 2003, 182–94). The Creature's pearly white teeth also recall frequent descriptions of the dentition of the ferocious cannibal in popular writing of the period; William Frankenstein's fear is that the Creature wishes to "eat me, and tear me in pieces," although he identifies the Creature with the ogres and monsters of his childhood reading rather than the fully racial- ized cannibal (106). From the Creature's physiognomy and gigantic stature it is difficult to ascertain a clear racial typing and it would appear that he shares characteristics of the different human variet- ies commonly enunciated in the period. If Mellor's identification is valid, however, the Creature would have been placed by Lawrence, and those who accepted racial gradation, at the lowest level of human development, akin to the African.

The Creature is naturally highly intelligent and educable, capable of assimilating complex ideas from his reading and from the overheard conversations of others. From his reading of Frankenstein's journal, to the works of Volney, Milton, and Goethe, the Creature demonstrates a formidable linguistic and intellectual grasp. This, combined with his natural resourcefulness and cunning, would certainly place him high on any imaginary scale of being and at a certain remove from the disparaging remarks of Lawrence and others on those varieties of human being that they placed at the base of human development. The Creature, however, displays strong animalistic traits; he has an infantile and uncontrollable rage, which leads him to murder a child, William Frankenstein, as well as Elizabeth Lavenza, Henry Clerval, and, indirectly, Justine Moritz, all of whom have done him no personal injury beyond their familial or social relationship to his creator. The Creature's violent and vindictive nature places him more closely with contemporary views of the savage and violent tendencies and thirst for revenge of untutored savages. In Frankenstein's eyes, the Creature, like an African slave, has no legal status as a human being. The Creature taunts his creator by claiming, correctly, that he would "not call it murder, if you could precipitate me into one of those ice-rifts, and destroy my frame, the work of your own hands" (108).

The novel is tantalizingly vague about its science but it does address questions or raise issues about the place of humanity within the animal world. The Creature does not appear to conclusively represent any contemporary racial type. Rather the Creature is constructed as not human but another species. However, in the world of the novel the relationship between species is close, allied closer to transmutationist notions of the animal world as found in Erasmus Darwin, John Hunter, and the speculative tenets of the transcendental anatomy of Geoffroy. The Creature is clearly a hybrid in any case. Thus readings that wish to locate the Creature as an African slave or Mongolian Tartar essentially miss the point. The Creature is a new species, formed from the materials of others. Nevertheless in a transmutationist and evolutionary world, the difference between species, races, and varieties becomes increasingly meaningless. This does not mean that the novel cannot be read as a commentary on the ways in which different kinds of sentient beings may relate to one another. It does have a racial politics but its politics is not that of antislavery or the fear of eastern peoples. It affirms an anatomy of race in which viable humanoid or anthropoid creatures could, conceivably be created through a science of hybridity. Such creatures, at least in Frankenstein's fevered imagination, are capable of procreating with humans, though their offspring might be infertile like those of the donkey and the horse, affirming Buffon's ideas about the species. The novel does not thus argue for the fixity of the species for which Linnaeus, Cuvier, and more confusedly Lawrence maintained. The Creature represents another species of humanoid life, composed of human and animal parts and gestures in the direction of the kinds of evolutionary speculation that is found in Erasmus Darwin, and Geoffroy. Viewed thus, it may be read as a disquisition on the tragic impossibility of the peaceful interaction of species which closely resemble one another but whose members have clear and emphatic markers of difference. If taken as a commentary on issues of human difference in the period, the novel accepts that humanlike creatures who share much of the same anatomy may be scientifically of different species, rather than races or varieties. Though the novel may identify key moments when its tragic consequences for Frankenstein, his family, and his Creature could have been either averted or transformed into alternative social negotiations, its overriding depiction of the relations between its two bipedal, intellectual, and linguistically sophisticated hominoid creatures is uncannily proleptic of the coming century of race conflict and imperial warfare between creatures who would not, like Frankenstein, call it murder to kill and annihilate each other.

CHAPTER 3

"CANDID REFLECTIONS:" THE IDEA OF RACE IN THE DEBATE OVER THE SLAVE TRADE AND SLAVERY IN THE LATE EIGHTEENTH AND EARLY NINETEENTH CENTURIES

RACE AND TRANSATLANTIC SLAVERY

In describing the natural world, Enlightenment and Romantic natural philosophers may well, for the most part, have been attempting to assert a Baconian objectivity and disinterestedness in their work in trying to describe the world as they saw it. With the privilege of hindsight we can see how their works were infiltrated with assumptions and prejudices about society, race, and gender that rendered their speculations and hypotheses anything but neutral and the belief that such neutrality was possible, illusory. However, what happens when such ideas are taken out of the arena of an allegedly objective science and are, instead, put into a polemical context in which they can be used as evidence for the support of a political or economic position? What happens when the participants in a debate have a vested interest in employing (or not employing) arguments that they may or may not believe, but the presence of which may convince others or their deliberate withholding may fail to prevent others from taking up a position? Historians of transatlantic slavery have long accepted the presence and importance of racial ideas in the debate about slavery and the slave trade and they have debated the nature of the relationship between capitalist expansion and the development of racial and racist ideologies.

In 1944 Eric Williams famously made the case, in his *Capitalism and Slavery*, that slavery was essentially an economic phenomenon that arose through the imperative to secure cheap labor and that racism was one of its consequences and not its cause: "slavery produced race." The trade and the institution were abolished with the rise of cheap labor and the spread of European colonial rule in Asia and Africa.[1] Other commentators have argued that slavery, especially in the Americas, was primarily racial in origin. Oliver Cox and George Fredrickson, have stressed the importance of the prior existence of a race prejudice, which allowed one group of people to exploit the labor power of those they considered culturally or racially inferior (Cox). Fredrickson maintains that it was in the early nineteenth century that proponents of slavery established a biological notion of black inferiority to counter the arguments of abolitionists (2002). However, despite anticipations, this full-fledged racial doctrine was not developed until *after* the period in which Britain abolished its trade in slaves. Winthrop D. Jordan (1986) also maintains that racial prejudice and slavery may well have been equally both cause and effect of each other. Jordan charts the change in perception suffered by black people from the sixteenth century onward, arguing that later representations were inflected by the experience of slavery and economic oppression. Peter Fryer has argued the link more forcefully. He claims that the scientific ideology of racism arose as a justification for the slave trade, originally begun for primarily economic reasons. Scientific racism was "the weapon of a class whose wealth, way of life, and power were under mounting attack." Fryer argues that from the 1770s onward, the empire, "and the pseudo-scientific racism that served it, developed side by side" (134, 133–90). Not so narrowly focused on biological and physical characteristics, Henry Louis Gates, Jr., examining early slave narratives has claimed that Europeans used literacy and reason as a means of distinguishing sub-Saharan Africans from Europeans. He argues that Africans were seen as less than human because their civilizations were not based on literacy and the pursuit of the arts (1986; 1996, 1–20). James Walvin, in substantial agreement, comments that "it was the late eighteenth century attacks on slavery, from all angles, that conjured forth pro-slavery defensive theories. And one of the easiest pro-slavery cards to play was race." The African already had a place in the cultural demonology of Europe before the system of colonial slavery was established and this body of prejudice was buttressed by plantocratic voices assuring their audience that its suspicions of black inferiority were, indeed, proved by experience: "[H]ere lay the foundations of a debate about race which derived from the experience of the slave empire and was, in turn, used to promote and to defend that same slave system" (Walvin 72–95). Similarly, Stuart Hall, discussing the period of plantation slavery and its aftermath in the United States, argues that proslavery discourses were structured by a series of binary oppositions of which one was "the opposition between the biological or bodily characteristics of the 'black' and 'white' races, polarized into their extreme opposites—each the signifiers of an absolute difference between human 'types' or 'species'" (246, 223–90).

Such arguments tend to be situated in the realm of representation and intellectual history, rather than socioeconomic reality. In contrast, Theodore W. Allen defines race in the context of North American slavery in terms of legislation. He describes the legal and economic process by which "whiteness" was established as an unmarked and normative category in a racial economy of difference. Allen views whiteness as the self-interested creation of a racialized Western capitalism and organization of labor (1994, 1–24).[2] Whiteness is thus a legal and economic fiction and not a biological phenomenon; its hegemonic invisibility and normative status lead to the creation of a nonscientific form of racist oppression. Allen focuses not on black slavery, but the ways in which English, Irish, Scottish, and other planters were transformed into the single and all-inclusive category of "whites." For many historians and critics "blackness serves as the primary form of Otherness by which whiteness is constructed" (Hartigan 184).[3] Such readings, of course, run counter to Roxann Wheeler's conclusions that complexion was only one of several signs of difference prior to the late eighteenth century and not in itself the most crucial marker. For Anthony J. Barker, actual racialist thinking was not common in the debate about the slave trade but, crucially, more apparent in abolitionist refutations than proslavery apologias. He argues that the debate was "not marked by urgent preoccupation with the most radical theories of racial inferiority," largely because the "the debate over the slave trade never developed into a debate over the nature of the Negro," it was "the racism of slavery rather than the racism of ideology which dominated attitudes" (159). In his history of the British slaving factory, Cape Coast Castle, William St Clair also claims that "for most of the slaving era, the British were largely free of notions of racial superiority" with even the "most hardened British slavers" praising the "intelligence, commercial acumen, prodigious memories, ability to make complex arithmetical calculations, and skill in languages" of the local African peoples on the "Gold Coast" of West Africa, with whom they traded (St Clair 99–100).

This historiographical debate concerning the connections of race and slavery has been conducted between two models of race, one of intellectual history and the other of social history. Barker's distinction between the "racism of ideology" and the "racism of slavery" is an important one. For Jordan, Fryer and others, the preexisting belief that blacks were inferior, articulated through a range of beliefs, allowed racial slavery to develop. Williams and Allen, in different ways, argue that race thinking is a specific product of historical practices, the dictates of the plantation system. The nature of race as a social, historical, or intellectual construction is central to this discussion and returns us to the larger questions explored in chapter 1 about whether race should be addressed as a system of group domination (as argued by Goldberg) or as a specific ideology of oppression (as argued by Appiah) defined by a concern with biological essentialism. The focus of this chapter is deliberately narrowed in its more modest aim to consider the importance of only one of the languages of racism, that is, what has been variously described as, "classic racism," the "racism of ideology," or "scientific racism" to the abolitionist and slavery debate. It may well be that this is a discussion of the surface language or one of the idioms of racism and not the deep structure or grammar of the ideology that Goldberg attempts to delineate in his work. Similarly, I make no larger claims about the causal relationship between slavery and the race idea. In focusing, primarily, on the intellectual constructions and rationalizations of human difference, it becomes clear that the leading ideas surface long after the establishment of colonial slavery as a practice, and, that when we consider especially the contribution of German thinkers to the debate, such ideas derive substantially from states not heavily involved in the practice. In addition, such ideas are, for the most part, metropolitan in origin, rather than derived from the colonies. Nevertheless by juxtaposing an understanding of this idiom in the context of the slavery debates, we still may gain some understanding of how the deep structure of racism reveals itself. When looking at prominent works about the natural history of humanity it is surprising that many of the most notable proponents of notions of racial inferiority (outside the U.S. South) seldom explicitly supported the slave trade, or, after its abolition, the institution of slavery. It is also clear that all such discourses, including those supportive of human equality, were infiltrated by racist thinking in other ways.

SLAVERY AND THE RACE IDEA

The relationship of writing that opposed or supported the abolition of the slave trade (and the ameliorationist writing which desired the serious reform but not abolition of the institution) and the institution of slavery to the race idea is highly controversial. When discussing slave trade discourse, Roxann Wheeler helpfully draws our attention to that the puzzling and paradoxical fact "the anti-slave trade position relied more heavily on appeals to racial similarity than slavery advocates relied on appeals to racial difference." Wheeler, however, also remarks on how the increasing tendency in the eighteenth century to enumerate "minute differences among groups of people" makes "claims about the irrelevance of exterior features difficult to reconcile with the increased propensity to note them" (1999, 236, 237). Philip Curtin, remarking on the distance between colonial and metropolitan justifications of slavery, observes that "Men most connected with the slave trade, and even the West Indian planters...were less inclined to emphasize racial factors than those who stayed in England" (27). The difference between colonial and metropolitan views of African slaves is thus striking and provides evidence for the view that the race idea flourishes most *outside* the contact zone of transcultural exchange, where peoples meet, interact, collaborate, and negotiate. Though it is clear that some plantocratic voices justified slavery in terms of biological race thinking, when looking at the abolition debate, it seems that, whatever their private opinions may have been, in print racial justifications of slavery and the slave trade, in the period 1780–1815, were comparatively rare. Indeed, plantation owners and defenders of the slave system were often resistant to a fully developed polygenist account of race, which might have provided the best available contemporary scientific justification for their practice, because it contradicted the account of Creation and the dispersal of Noah's sons, as set forward in Genesis (S.J. Gould 1981; Young 118–41). Most historians of the slave trade have come to the conclusion that the primary arguments for the trade and the institution were not racial but economic, though, confusingly, race seems always to be present in one form or another.[4]

The works of Edward Long, Samuel Estwick, Christoph Meiners, and the comments of William Cobbett are certainly evidence for the manner in which theories of biological inferiority were used to justify enslavement of Africans and their enforced labor. Nevertheless, key writers against the slave trade, such as James Ramsay, Thomas Clarkson, and William Wilberforce, felt that they had to defend the

African against charges of racial inferiority, or, if they did not, were keen to make the accusation against their opponents for strategic reasons. Edward Long's polygenist ideas about race are discussed in chapter 1 of this book. He became the most notable, indeed, infamous, spokesmen for the polygenist account of separate species (Wheeler 1999, 209–33). Although not a champion of the plantocratic cause, his *History of Jamaica* (1774) argued that the African, or "Negro" constituted a separate species from that of the White kind of humanity. He claimed that the institution of slavery benefited the African by civilizing him or her as well as benefiting Britain commercially in his polemical pamphlet *Candid Reflections* (1772), produced at the time of the Somerset case and the debate about the legal status of slaves in England.[5] Long argued that African slaves were essential for the survival of the sugar colonies because their biology made them better suited to plantation labor than white Europeans, "the nature of the West India climate, and the impossibility of clearing and cultivating the soil there, by any other than Negroe labourers, as it was first the occasion of employing them, so it must ever remain, so long as the colonies exist." "Nature" and the "Divine Will" appropriated the African for work in "these climates" (3–14, 21). In addition to his support for slavery, Long was also horrified at the prospect of miscegenation between black men and white working women. In a notorious passage, he commented how

> [t]he lower classes of women in *England*, are remarkably fond of the blacks, for reasons too brutal to mention; they would connect themselves with horses and asses if the laws permitted them. By these ladies they generally have a numerous brood. Thus in the course of a few generations or more, the English blood will become so contaminated that this mixture, and from the chances, the ups and downs of life, this alloy may spread so extensively, as even to reach the middle, and then the higher orders of the people till the whole nation resembles the *Portuguese* and the *Moriscos* in complexion of skin and baseness of mind. This is a venomous and dangerous ulcer that threatens to disperse its malignancy far and wide, until *every* family catches infection from it. (48–49)

Historians have disagreed about how influential or aberrant Long's arguments actually were, and his *History* certainly contained severe attacks upon the morals and behavior of the planters, and the attacks were used by Wilberforce in his own speeches against the trade. For that reason, as Barker maintains, Long had few friends or defenders among West Indian planters (1–76).[6] It is not easy to determine the extent of Long's influence, but he did, however, have *some* among writers, the most notable of whom was John Kemeys who explicitly used his polygenist ideas to justify black servitude. Kemeys' *Free and Candid Reflections Occasioned by the Late Additional Duties on Sugar and on Rum* (1781) represented Africans as "Barbarians, amongst who, perpetual war is raging even for the horrid practice *of eating their enemies*" and as a people "but a few degrees removed from the ouran-utang." Kemeys repeats Long's slur, derived from Buffon, that female Africans may "copulate" with "those brutes" (71–72, 70–81).

Alarmed by the popularity of abolitionism, the trade's defenders appear to have tested public opinion concerning the effectiveness of appeals to African racial inferiority. This was done in a series of letters to the London *Morning Chronicle*, signed "Civis." Anthony Barker argues that these letters were primarily strategic and were meant to estimate the potential appeal of such arguments. Civis put his case with the qualification that he was intervening on the "side of the question, which has scarce found a single defender." By the conclusion of the correspondence the critics of Civis outnumbered his supporters eight to one (quoted in Barker 160; Drescher 1977, 370–71). Defenders of the trade, such as Bryan Edwards, James Tobin, and William Beckford Jr. vigorously denied that the biological racial inferiority of Africans was in any way an issue for them. Although the polygenists Meiners and Long explicitly justify the enslavement of Africans in terms of their alleged racial inferiority, by far the vast majority of the thinkers who wrote on the subject claimed that they were opposed to slavery. It is salutary to recall that Voltaire, the eighteenth-century's Enlightenment voice of Reason and humanity, and staunch opponent of the slave trade also declared himself in favor of the notion that Africans were a distinct species from the European when he declared that "bearded whites, fuzzy Negroes, the long-maned yellow races and beardless men are not descended from the same man.... Whites are superior to these Negroes, as the Negroes are to apes and apes to oysters" (1989, 423). Voltaire's polygenist ideas were conditioned by his skeptical dismissal of the scriptural account of human origins, but he was no advocate of human equality. Lord Kames also believed that Europeans and Africans were products of a different origin but, *contra* Voltaire, ascribed perceptions of their African inferiority entirely to their condition as slaves: "Abroad they are miserable slaves, having no encouragement either to think or act" (Kitson, *Theories of Race* 1999, 58–59 [24–66]). Charles White declared in his *Account* that the slave trade was "indefensible on any hypothesis, and he would rejoice at its abolition" (137). It was with some justice that George Forster responded to criticisms that his own polygenist racial views were conducive to supporting slavery with the question,

> whether the thought that Blacks are our brothers has ever anywhere even once meant that the raised whip of the slave driver was put away. Does he torment the poor long suffering creature with an execution-er's rage and a devilish delight in the full conviction that they are of his blood?[7]

A belief in monogenist theories of human origins never stopped its adherents from enslaving Africans when it was in their interests to so do. As an example of this, we have the radical journalist, William Cobbett, who fulminated in 1804 that

> [t]he state of San Domingo is as wretched and the deeds committed upon the whites as bloody, as any negro-lover could possibly wish.... The negroes are a bloody minded race: they are made and marked for servitude and subjection: it is the purpose which they were obviously intended for, and every day affords us fresh proof. (*Political Register* July 28, col. 125–26; quoted in Wood 2002, 160)

Monogenist thinking was similarly fractured when it came to dealing with slavery. Those who upheld this account of human origins could still develop a theory of racial inequality. Buffon, in the *Histoire naturelle*, argued that

> if the Negroes are deficient in genius, they are by no means so in their feelings; they are cheerful or melancholy, laborious or inactive, friendly or hostile, according to the manner in which they are treated. If prop-erly fed, and well treated, they are contented, joyous, obliging, and on their very countenance may we read the satisfaction of their soul. If hardly dealt with their spirits forsake them, they droop with sorrow, and will die of melancholy. They are alike impressed with injuries and favours. To the authors of the one they are implacable enemies; while to those who use them well they imbibe an affection which makes them deny all danger and hazard to express their zeal and attachment. (1792 4: 291–92)

Buffon accepts that Africans have less intelligence than Europeans. He presents them as creatures of feeling, subject to extremes, as irra-tional beings. He repeats the standard eighteenth-century trope of the "grateful Negro," discussed by George Boulukos: "when...they have a liking for a master, there is nothing they are not capable of doing to show him their zeal and devotion" (Boulukos 1999, 12–29; 2007). For Buffon slavery, under a kind master, is a state with which Africans, possessed of "excellent hearts" (1992 4: 292), might be content. Buffon, however, is no proponent of slavery:

> Are they not sufficiently wretched in being reduced to a state of slavery; in being obliged always to work without reaping the smallest fruits of their labour, without being abused, buffeted, and treated like brutes? Humanity revolts at those oppressions, which nothing but the thirst of gold could ever have introduced, and which would still, perhaps, produce an aggravated repetition, did not the laws prescribe limits to the brutality of the master, and to the misery of his slave. Negroes are compelled to labour; and yet of the coarsest food are they sparingly supplied. Their unfeeling masters say, they can support hunger well; that what would serve an European for one meal is to them a sufficient subsistence for three days; however little they eat or sleep, they are alike hardy, alike capable of fatigue. How can men, in whom the smallest sentiment of humanity remains, adopt such maxims, and on such shallow foundations attempt to justify excesses to which nothing could ever have given birth but the most sordid avarice? (292–93; Roger and Bonnefoi 181–82)

Buffon's position is conflicted and based on a divide between Africans ("them") and us ("men who...have some feeling of humanity"). He hints that Africans may have a different physiology, which may justify the maxim that they are more robust than humans and require less sustenance. Buffon then distances himself from such beliefs that appear to become the prejudices of others, but his opposition to slavery is not based on his rejection of such racist arguments, but on the belief that these are rationalizations of European greed and thus immoral. Buffon's theory of degeneration, as we have seen, was reversible, but only after some considerable time and, to all intents and purposes, his view of the race was one where changes occurred over large periods of time.

Kant, often credited as the originator of biological racism, actually said very little about slavery. Though, as Bernasconi comments, we have his statement that "ethics would seem to be a perfect instrument with which to combat chattel slavery," Kant's silence on such matters is deafening (2002, 150). More than this Kant tended to choose for his sources those texts that presented a less favorable view of African accomplishment. He cited from C. K. Sprengler's *Beiträge zur Völke—und Länderkunde*, a German paraphrase of James Tobin's proslavery *Cursory Remarks on Mr Ramsay's Essay on the Treatment and Conversion of African Slaves* (1787), rather than texts from the abolitionist side of the argument (Bernasconi 2002, 148). Kant referred to Africans as "born slaves" and commented that "Africans and Americans cannot govern themselves. They thus serve only for slaves" (152). It could be quite plausibly argued that Kant, though a monogenist, held beliefs or suspicions that Africans were suited for slavery and that such a situation was thus justifiable.

Blumenbach's attitude to slavery and to those who denied African equality is reasonably clear: he vehemently opposed both. The monogenist view of human origins, however, did not always guarantee Blumenbach's clarity or Buffon's ambivalence about the institution. A support for slavery, albeit humanized and reformed, could be expressed in terms of contemporary natural philosophy or as a more general faith in the universalism of Christian thought. One of the most significant statements of the monogenist position was that of the American Presbyterian minister, Samuel Stanhope Smith. His *An Essay on the Causes of the Variety of Complexion and Figure in the Human Species* (1787) attacked, in particular, Lord Kames's polygenist position that Smith saw as an assault on the validity of the scriptural account. Smith put forward the classic Buffonian environmentalist argument that physical variety among humankind was due to natural and social causes, not to the existence of separate species. Implicit in this account was a literal understanding of scripture. In 1810 Smith published a substantially enlarged and more fully informed edition of his *Essay* to vanquish Charles White and the whole panoply of polygenist thinkers from the scientific field. Again Smith stressed the importance of natural, environmental, and social factors as causes of human variety. Following Buffon, Smith argued that blackness was caused not only by such factors as extreme heat and cold, but also by the state of savagery itself, and thus the more civilized a people were, the fairer they became. This process he claimed to witness among those slaves who were domesticated on the plantations of good masters. Descendants of Africans, he claimed, were "gradually losing these peculiarities so offensive to our eye." In "Princeton and its vicinity," he opined, "I daily see persons of the African race whose limbs are as handsomely formed as those of the inferior and laboring classes, either of Europeans, or Anglo-Americans" (1965, 157, 105n). The optimally temperate climate and civilizing influence of America were thus transforming the African into a "white" person. America would thus, in time, render all its inhabitants a single people, negating the need for the institution of slavery itself. As Winthrop Jordan acutely comments, in Smith we can see how "thoroughly the assumption of racial inferiority had infiltrated the citadel of equality" (1965, xlvi). Smith was, however, not an open supporter of slavery; he elsewhere criticized the institution; nevertheless, the tenets of his *Essay*, which is strangely silent on the subject, could provide as strong an argument for using black slave labor in the Southern states as that which the later polygenist racialists, such as Samuel George Morton and Nott and Gliddon, would provide.

The British natural philosopher and surgeon, William Lawrence was a monogenist who accepted a modified version of Blumenbach's fivefold typology of human variety, which had developed through a process of degeneration determined by a form of sexual selection. He dispensed with the scriptural account of the origin of man, which he believed to be irrelevant to scientific research. Lawrence, for many modern critics a forward-looking natural philosopher whose secular thought was wrongly seen to anticipate Darwinian notions of evolution, had absolutely no doubt whatsoever about the "inferiority of organization" and the "corresponding inferiority of faculties" of the "Negro" and he strongly criticized both the abolitionist and the pro-slavery lobbies for their respective misunderstandings:

> The abolitionists have erred in denying a natural inferiority, so clearly evinced by the concurring evidences of anatomical structure and experience. But it was only an error in fact; and may be more readily excused, as it was on the side of humanity. Their opponents committed the more serious moral mistake of perverting what should constitute a claim to kindness and indulgence into justification or palliation of the revolting and antichristian practice of traffic in human flesh; a practice branded with the double curse of equal degradation to the oppressor and the oppressed. (1823, 312–13)

Lawrence here shows that the issue of race inferiority was certainly a term or argumentative ploy that was used in the debate. He, along with White, Forster and others, demonstrates how a firm belief in the racial inferiority of the African, or in his terms Ethiopian, does not necessarily lead to a defense of slavery or the slave trade. Like Charles White, Lawrence was a declared opponent of the institution of slavery but he was not an advocate of human equality so far as it stretched to encompass sub-Saharan Africa. Others, however, saw little in Lawrence's thought that was antithetical to slavery. In the long article he wrote in the *Quarterly Review*, denouncing Lawrence's theories of vitalism as atheistic, George D'Oyly made the following swipe against Lawrence's egalitarian hypocrisies:

> If at any time a slave-driver in the West Indies should feel some qualms of conscience for treating the blacks under his care as a herd of oxen, he would only have to imbibe Mr. Lawrence's idea respecting their being as inferior to himself in mental faculties as the mastiff is to the greyhound in swiftness, and his mind would at once be set at ease on the subject. (249)

D'Oyly identifies a common link in the minds of conservative Christian moralists of the *Quarterly Review,* between scientific endeavor, normally identified with French materialism, and extreme racist thinking. The suspicion was that once the biblical account of human origins is dispensed with, there is little to prevent the estrangement of different races of humanity. This supports the argument of Phillip D. Curtin that the reason polygenist thinking did not take off as strongly in Britain as it did in France was due to the rise of Evangelical religion in the early nineteenth century and the conservative reaction against the French Revolution (235–36). D'Oyly certainly represents the conflation of these views in his probing of the familiar fault line that race manifests in egalitarian thinking: where to draw the line between that community of humans who are equal and those who are excluded. For all his metropolitan radical chic, Lawrence cannot bring himself to proclaim the slave his brother or sister and equal, a linguistic formulation which Evangelicals could at least manage in theory, if not in practice.

RACE AND PLANTOCRACY

Evidence that the planters themselves did not articulate their racism in terms of polygenist scientific theory is easy to find. Seymour Drescher's view that "the merchants and planters restricted their defense of slavery largely to reasons of law, politics, and, above all, economic expediency" is an apt summary of their position (1992, 371). In fact Richard Ligon's comment in his *History of the Island of Barbados* of 1657 that among the slaves were "as honest, faithfull, and conscionable people as amongst those of Europe, or any other part of the world" is not atypical of a great deal of historical and travel writing about the West Indies (Krise 28). Edward Trelawny, governor of Jamaica, wrote in his *Essay Concerning Slavery* of 1746 how absurd would be the view of any planter concerning the inferiority of African slaves:

> One would imagine that the Planters really think the Negroes are not the same species with us, but that being of a different Mold and Nature, as well as Colour, they were made entirely for our Use, with Instincts proper for the Purpose, having as great a propensity for Subjection, as we have to command, and loving Slavery as naturally as we do Liberty. (19; quoted Boulukos 2007, 67)

Trelawny's phrase, "would imagine that the Planters really think" implies that they do not think this but are acting as if they did, largely in not realizing that resources are needed to ensure the subjection of those who love liberty as much as themselves. Fifty years later, in his *History Civil and Commercial of the West Indies* (1801), the West Indian merchant and historian Bryan Edwards gives a detailed account of the dispositions of the various African people that were transported to Jamaica as slaves. When describing the "Eboes" he observes that "the conformation of the face" resembles "that of a baboon" and that this is more visible in these slaves than any other. However, he adds that such an observation does not imply any "natural inferiority in these people" as it is "perhaps purely accidental" and can be "no more considered as a proof of degradation, than the red hair and high cheek bones of the Natives of North of Europe" (1: 73–74). Edwards, often regarded as one of the more liberal and humanitarian voices of plantocracy, defended the slave trade and slavery on the grounds that they were necessary evils, essential for the economic health of the colonies and mother country (Kitson, *Abolition Debate* 1999, 325–47).[8]

Maria Nugent, the American wife of Lord George Nugent, the governor of Jamaica from 1801 to 1805, similarly does not regard the African slaves in essentialist terms. She records in her journal her sympathies for the "poor blackies" whose "want of exertion" proceeds not from biological causes but from the institution of "slavery" itself. Although Nugent regards Toussaint, then in ascendant in neighboring St. Domingue, as "a wonderful man…intended for very good purposes," she can still express herself in contemporary racist terms; when seeing two baby boy Africans, she comments that they "were exactly like two little monkeys." Assiduous in promoting Christianity among her black servants, she believes abolitionist claims that the slaves are ill-treated to be exaggerated. Generally she sees the slaves as good-natured children, and a subject for sentimental discourse. Would the whites set a better example by behaving less licentiously, then the African would propagate and remove the necessity for the existence of the slave trade. Nugent does, however, claim that the planters consider "the Negroes as creatures formed merely to administer to their ease" and confesses difficulty in persuading "those great and superior beings, our white domestics, that the blacks are human beings, or have souls" (13, 14, 33, 43, 45, 86–87, 98). This does not seem to be a prejudice shared by the slave owners, however. The historian John Stewart, in his *Account of Jamaica* (1823), describes the variety of African slaves and their various dispositions but generally sees them as capable of civilization:

> The Negroes, though so rude and ignorant in their savage state, have a natural shrewdness and genius which is doubtless susceptible of culture and improvement. Those who have been reared among the whites are greatly superior in intellect to the native Africans brought at a mature age to the county. Many are wonderfully ingenious in making a variety of articles for their own use, or to sell. (256)

Stewart also points to the example of Toussaint L'Ouverture who "though an uneducated slave, acquitted himself as a general and a statesman" confounding those "who maintained that Negroes were incapable of intellectual improvement" (265).

The planter spokesman, James Tobin, claimed that the biological racial argument was "not of much consequence" and that it "has never been pretended that the slaves were, or are, any way inferior to their masters, except in strength, policy, or good fortune." If his antagonist, James Ramsay "feels any triumph in the idea of having confronted the opinions of Hume, Voltaire, Lord Kaims, Long &c he is welcome to enjoy it without the smallest interruption from me." Tobin here distances himself from skeptical accounts of human origins. He makes the familiar argument that the slaves were better treated than the laboring poor of Great Britain and that if freed they would do no work at all. He nevertheless repeats the racist slurs that Africans are "lazy, sensual and cruel" and "totally averse to the least civilization" as well reiterating Long's fears relating to "the dark and contaminated breed" that results from miscegenation (1785, 1). Like Edwards, Tobin justified the "odious traffic in the human species" as an evil necessary for the maintenance of the colonies. He also argued that enslaved Africans were "the only class that will stand the climate, and, at the same time labour" (1788, 11). As the pseudonymous "Philo-Xylon" brusquely put in a letter to the *Barbadoes Gazette* in 1788, "I shall not take up your Time, in an useless discussion of *white Men* and *Negroes:* They are both admitted to be of the *human Kind*; and both *species* have all the necessary Abilities, of Mind and Body suitable to their being *Cultivators* of the *Soil*, which is to feed them" (No. VIII).

The planter advocate William Beckford, Jr., (a poor relation of the enormously wealthy Beckford slave-owning dynasty) admitted that the "poor Negroes are seldom considered as human creatures" in Jamaica which provides some evidence that ideas of African racial inferiority were routinely bandied about in private discourse, but goes on to say that their situation under a "kind owner" is superior to that of the majority of British laborers. Beckford once again denies that the slaves are "of a different species" from the European and rhapsodizes that, the "sun that shines on all, enlightens them; and if genius be the consequence of heat, and the beams that fertilize the earth, irradiate the mind; the African in geniality of climate, and warmth of soul would blaze; when the inhabitants of Europe would freeze" (1788, 30, 39, 84, 86). In his picturesque *Descriptive Account of the Island of Jamaica* (1790), Beckford denied that it "was the colour of the skin…that degrades humanity" but claimed, instead, that "Providence" had thickened the slaves' skins "to enable them to bear what would otherwise be insufferable." Beckford maintains that those that claim that the Africans are "but one degree removed from vegetable existence" argue both weakly and impiously and that nevertheless, he can still claim, somewhat confusingly, that "the negroes are slaves by nature" (1790, 1: 200–201; 2: 60, 350, 383).

The planter and proslavery view then seldom relied on Long's polygenist argument or any explicitly stated theory of biological racial inferiority. It did not need to. Proslavery writers could justify just about anything they wanted to about the practice of plantation slavery by taking recourse to the view that humanity was of one species, providing one understood that Africans were of a lower social and cultural level. The proslavery writers were actually delighted to refute Long's theories with their impious Enlightenment and atheistic associations and to be heard to do this. Certainly, whatever their private opinions were, the official spokesmen of the plantocracy saw no merit in publicly arguing for slavery and the trade on the grounds of scientific racism. If proslavery writing reinforced any of the beliefs in human variety, it was that of the monogenist camp with its stress on the determining powers of environment, climate, and savagery to thicken and blacken the skin of the African that allowed him or her to stand strenuous labor in the field and the excruciating punishment of the whip if he or she slackened.

ABOLITIONIST CONCEPTIONS OF RACE
AND THE "UNIVERSAL FRECKLE"

One therefore wonders why defenses of the humanity and equality of the African slave were prominent in abolitionist writing? In 1787, for instance, the Reverend Robert Boucher Nickolls claimed that: "the stupidity of negroes is...urged by the friends of slavery as a plea for using them as brutes; for they represent the negroes as little removed above the monkey, or the oranoutang, with regard to intellects." Nickolls went on to urge the cases of both the poet Phillis Wheatley and Francis Williams to demonstrate the falsity of this claim, "I never heard of poems by a monkey, or of Latin odes by an oranoutang"(quoted Carretta 1995, xi). Mary Wollstonecraft in her review of Olaudah Equiano's *Interesting Narrative* in *The Analytical Review* (May 1788) wrote how

> [t]he life of an African, written by himself, is certainly a curiosity, as it has been a favourite philosophic whim to degrade the numerous nations, on whom the sun-beams more directly dart, below the common level of humanity, and hastily to conclude that nature, by making them inferior to the rest of the human race, designed to stamp them with a mark of slavery. (1989. 7: 100)

Wollstonecraft and Nickolls fail to identify the authors of the "philosophic whim" nor those who then employ such ideas as a justification for slavery, although the language they use suggests that David Hume and Edward Long are the probable targets of their critique. Both also point to the literary accomplishments of the black writers as an argument against racist arguments about incapacity.[9] Similarly, the fourth chapter of James Ramsay's influential *Essay on the Treatment and Conversion of African Slaves* (1784) contains a detailed and extended rebuttal of Edward Long's opinions (along with those of David Hume and John Hunter) and a statement of the full humanity of the African slave. In chapter 2 we saw how Ramsay was keen to criticize the facial angle of racial anatomy. He denies that "marks that distinguish the African" from the European such as "flat noses, prominent chins, woolly hair, black skins; to which the curious anatomist adds skulls less capacious, calves of the legs less fleshy, and elevated more towards the hams" signify inferiority. Even allowing all of these, including the "less capacious skulls," Ramsay argues that there is nothing to justify belief in African inferiority. He subscribes to the Buffonian environmental hypothesis that allows for a process of reverse degeneration: "West Indian children, educated in England improve not only in complexion, but in elegance of feature." Ramsay argues that there are recognizable "sets of national features" independent of color, and color itself gradually verges "from white to black, through every intermediate degree of tawny and copper." Thus physical features are incapable of determining mental capacity or inferiority.

> Mr. Hume, because a tall bulky man, and also a subtile philosopher, might have denied a capacity for metaphysical subtilty to all who wanted these his great bodily attributes, as well as suppose capacity and vigour of mind incompatible with a flat nose, curling hair, and a black skin. (214)

Ramsay denies that the brains and blood of Africans are black; if they are in some cases it must be due to their poor diet rather than an essentialist physiological phenomenon.

He minimizes the importance and permanence of physical characteristics, arguing that a black skin was as accidental a response to climatic change as a freckle might be in a fair skin. He argues that the freckle of a white person and the black skin of an African had their origin in similar causes: "for a freckle may be defined a partial black skin; a black skin an universal freckle" (216). Ramsay's hypothesis, ridiculous to modern readers, is part of an attempt to minimize the importance of physical characteristics in determining intelligence. He argues that it would be foolish to assess the intelligence of a person with reference to their freckles and, in the same way, nothing can be read about an African's intellect form the blackness of his or her skin. Nevertheless, Ramsay equates blackness with a blemish on a fair skin, rather than with the European skin, indicating the priority of the white in his scheme. Ramsay's "universal freckle" was taken up by Samuel Stanhope Smith, usually given credit for coining the term, when he argued that "colour may be justly considered as an universal freckle."[10] For Ramsay, such physical characteristics could not predetermine moral or intellectual capacities: "the soul is a simple substance, not to be distinguished by squat or tall, black, brown, or fair" (235). Ramsay also discusses at length the implications of the Africans' "diminutive skulls" (219). As discussed in chapter 2, Ramsay while accepting a difference in the skull formations of Africans and Europeans strongly criticized ideas concerning gradation, and assured his readers that John Hunter's notion of gradation was not meant to signify anything other than an interesting phenomenon. Ramsay feels it is necessary to combat arguments justifying slavery on the basis of racial inferiority, yet he does not accuse the planters of believing in the inferiority of Africans; rather he argues against Long, Hume, and comparative anatomists, such as John Hunter.

We have seen how James Tobin simply conceded this argument to the abolitionists, claiming that it had no bearing on the issue of the slave trade and plantation slavery, but it remained a persistent theme in much abolitionist writing that continued to argue as if this *were* one of the main planks of the plantocratic argument position. Representations of Africans generally in the eighteenth century may have showed strong elements of Eurocentricism and even xenophobia, but they do not emphasize any conception of biologically essential difference.[11] This attitude can be seen in Anthony Benezet, America's most prominent eighteenth-century opponent of the slave trade. He published his *Some Historical Account of Guinea ... with an Inquiry into the Rise and Progress of the Slave-Trade* (1771) to persuade his readers to end the trade and to swiftly emancipate the slaves. His work was hugely influential in England and France (Davis 214). Benezet represented the inhabitants of Guinea as noble savages living a happy and pastoral life until interrupted by Europeans. In fact it was probably Benezet who was instrumental in fashioning the eighteenth-century abolitionist myth of the noble Negro. Wylie Sypher finds Benezet's work important in that it "marks the point at which religious, primitivistic, humanitarian, 'philosophic,' and practical objections against slavery fuse" (69, 92–93). Benezet stated that the Africans had a developed, if not sophisticated, civilization involving agricultural cultivation, and several trades (smiths, potters, saddlers, and weavers) as well as established systems of law and justice. He paid tribute to the quality of the work of the goldsmith and silversmith and the fine cloths of the weavers. He employed a range of sources to authenticate the quality of the Africans work and their industry in trade, fishing, and agriculture. Guinea appeared a fertile and Edenic place where the inhabitants have a sense of a one true God and a future state, but they are also "superstitiously and idolatrously inclined" (32). Yet ultimately, for Benezet, the Africans' were barbarous and savage and he exhorted Europeans to use "their endeavours to make the nations of Africa acquainted with the nature of the Christian religion" (58, 82). He questioned the moral superiority of the Europeans who had behaved so cruelly and immorally to the Africans but he never accepted that the Africans had achieved parity with the Europeans. He does not mention any linguistic or artistic excellence that they possessed. He could not imagine African cultures on their own terms, but only as primitive states of European culture. Throughout he spoke for, or allowed others to speak for, the silenced African and he accepted the oppositions of enlightenment and barbarity, and the equivalence of darkness, ignorance, and savagery, the terms which drive Abdul JanMohamed's "Manichean allegory" (JanMohammed 78–106). Benezet's account of primitive, pastoral Africa would prove highly influential for Equiano, Coleridge, Southey, and many others.

Perhaps the classic iteration of the Christian Universalist view of human difference comes in Thomas Clarkson's *Essay on the Slavery and Commerce of the Human Species* (2nd edition 1788). If both Long and Benezet, despite both their differing views of race and their conflicting aims, can be seen to accept the inferiority of the black races, Thomas Clarkson, who paid generous tribute to the effects of Benezet's work, went further than most in stressing the equality of the African.[12] Underlying Clarkson's arguments against the slave trade was his Christian Universalist view of race. His *Essay* made the case for the humanity of the African race in a rigorous and compelling way. He believed that all mankind sprang from the "same original" and that the notion of separate species contradicted both scripture and science. The premise behind Clarkson's writing is that a man is not a thing and thus cannot be traded as a commodity. Clarkson's essay argues for the original equality of all men and the contractual state of government. Slavery must always be illegal unless the person consents to place himself or herself in that position. Clarkson, famously, informed his audience of the horrors of the slave trade in a way that no other writer had so far done. He also attempted to demolish the main arguments about black inferiority. His apologia for African industry and culture marks him out as someone whose writings push the parameters of Eurocentric views of Africa to their limits, problematizing the reader's assumptions about European superiority.

Clarkson argues that the Africans in their own country "exercise the same arts, as the ancestors of those very Europeans, who boast their great superiority, are described to have done in the same uncultivated state." Although he sees African societies as at an earlier state of development than those of European nations, he is keen to stress the Africans' linguistic abilities, arguing that their songs "afford us a high proof of their poetical powers, as the works of the most acknowledged poets" (118, 120). Clarkson instances the case of Phillis Wheatley who if "designed for slavery (as the argument must confess), the greater part of the inhabitants of Britain must lose their claim to freedom" (122). Furthermore Clarkson regards certain aspects of the African manufacturing arts as surpassing those then practised in Europe. African skill in ironwork goes beyond "the workmen in our towns" and African cotton cloths are "not to be exceeded by the finest artists in Europe" (124). He attacks at some length the argument that the Africans suffer the curse of Ham and Canaan by showing that the descendants of Ham were not known by their color and that this color could not be used to distinguish them. The descendants of Cush, however, were "of the colour" yet no such curse was placed upon them. Clarkson's explanation of human difference accepts the contemporary synthesis of Christian and Enlightenment reasoning. Either the deity interposed and created such variation or it springs from climatic causes. In both cases differences in color must exist for human convenience and not as a sign of differing moral capacities. Clarkson argues against the polygenist hypothesis of race by pointing to the fertility of the offspring of black and white (Long claimed, against overwhelming evidence, that such offspring were sterile in the long run). This fertility test was Buffon's key argument for the existence of one species of humanity that Clarkson formulates as "if two animals of a different species propagate, their offspring is unable to continue its own species" (132).

Clarkson's speculations about secondary characteristics are quite fascinating in their mixture of Christian essentialism and contemporary scientific awareness. He postulates that the color of "dark olive; a beautiful colour, and a just medium between black and white" was probably the complexion of Noah and that of all our ancestors. He does not see white, nor, following Camper, Hunter, or Prichard, black as the primary color of humanity; "there is great reason to presume, that the purest white is as far removed from the primitive color as the deepest black" (134). Clarkson's insistence on the relativity of our perceptions of the primacy or beauty of skin color is not exactly unprecedented: Sir Thomas Browne, Joshua Reynolds, even Camper, and others had made the same point. What is new is Clarkson's attempt to confute scientific racialists, such as Long, by giving his arguments a scientific underpinning. His speculations into the origin of color lead him to minimize the key human difference as simply resulting from the "*mucosum corpus*" which lies under the skin. The actual skin of the "blackest negroe" is of the same transparency as "that of the purest white." Not having an awareness of modern-day genetic theory, Clarkson cannot account for the gradations of color or its inheritance but he assumes "the epidermic complexion" in all its many and various gradations to result solely from climate. He borrows Ramsay's hypothesis of the "black skin" as no more than a "universal freckle" (134–38, 144–45). Clarkson is attempting to efface the sign of difference between white and black, unsettling such binary oppositions by positing a dark olive as the primary color, so removing the grounds for the workings of any Manichean allegory based on such an opposition. Although he does not explicitly state them, Clarkson must have realized the implications of his discussion in decentering Western assumptions of white as privileged and primary. Ultimately the African is positioned as a being at a more primitive level of development from that of the European and in his *Essay on the Impolicy of the African Slave Trade* (1788) Clarkson looks forward, like most of the abolitionist writers, to the African's Christianization. This substantial essay serves to confute the whole range of arguments about colonial slavery. It also includes Clarkson's own speculations about human difference, which combine a Christian essentialism with contemporary scientific awareness. Again the fact that Clarkson feels he must discuss the status of Africans in terms of biology would provide evidence for the view that, at some level, he considered that essentialist arguments required refutation.

ABOLITIONIST LITERATURE: COWPER, MORE, AND COLERIDGE

Statements of the humanity of African slaves were common in abolitionist literature. [13] Probably the most famous of these comes from William Cowper's "The Negroe's Complaint." Written in response to John Newton's request for a series of popular ballads on the trade, Cowper produced a series of poems of which "The Negroe's Complaint" is one. The poem is written from the perspective of an enslaved African who appeals in eloquent lines for a recognition of his common humanity:

> Still in thought as free as ever,
>   What are England's rights, I ask,
> Me from my delight to sever,
>   Me to torture, me to task?
> Fleecy locks and black complexion
>   Cannot forfeit Nature's claim;
> Sins may differ, but affection
>   Dwells in White and Black the same.
> ....
> Deem our nation Brutes no longer
>   'Till some reason ye shall find
> Worthier of regard and stronger
>   Than the Colour of our Kind.   (Cowper, 3: 13–14)

Cowper's brilliantly economic lyrics encapsulate the abolitionist argument, once again begging the question who exactly is deeming the slave a brute. The speaker of the poem establishes through his literary accomplishment his intelligence and appeals to the common human love of freedom established by nature. The physical, however, does intrude into the poem with the unfortunate "Fleecy locks and black complexion." That the African slave is defensive about his appearance indicates that he accepts there is a case to answer, a case established by his complexion. The assumption behind the lines is that though such features are less attractive than the European, they are not so bad as to "forfeit Nature's claim." The common comparison of the African's hair with the wool of the sheep also identifies the African with animalistic features. Cowper's ventriloquized African is an innocent victim who has absorbed the leading features of abolitionist thought about his own status and is able to question the moral superiority of the reader, though not his or her sense of racial superiority.

Abolitionist racial thought is most clearly articulated in the writings of Hannah More on the subject. Like Cowper, More first became interested in the slavery issue as a result of John Newton's example. Her *Slavery: A Poem* of 1788 encapsulates her views on the subject. More begins the poem by carefully deconstructing the term "Liberty" to exclude any beliefs that do not coincide with her Christian paternalist worldview. As Wood comments, the poem is a "testimony not only to abolition ideas on slavery, but a stern treatise on the necessary policing of the political thought of the poor" (Wood 2002, 73). More goes on to determine the status of the African slave and the wrongs of slavery, raising the issue of African inferiority:

> Perish th' illiberal thought which would debase
> The native genius of the sable race!
> Perish the proud philosophy, which sought
> To rob them of the pow'rs of equal thought!
> What! Does th'immortal principle within
> Change with the casual colour of a skin?
> Does matter govern spirit? Or is MIND
> Degraded by the form to which 'tis join'd?
> No: they have heads to think, and hearts to feel.
> And souls to act, with firm, though erring zeal;
> For they have keen affections, soft desires,
> Love strong as death, and active patriot fires:
> All the rude energy, the fervid flame

Of high-soul'd passion, and ingenuous shame:
Strong, but luxuriant virtues, boldly shoot
From the wild vigour of a savage root.[14]

More, as an Evangelical Christian, is an opponent of the "proud phi-losophy" of scientific polygenesis. Again it is not clear who exactly she has in mind here, though she seems to imply a connection between skeptical and materialist thought and the denial of the humanity of the African. What is objectionable is the denial of the "immortal principle within to" all humans as descendants of Adam and Eve. More is at her most generous to the Africans here, allowing them the power of "equal thought" and "heads to think." Complexion here is "casual" and does not signify. Nevertheless in claiming that spirit and mind are not "degraded" by the forms to which they are joined, More shows that she does not accept any notions of cultural or aesthetic relativism. Nor is she willing to concede any concept of civilization to those who "boldly shoot / From the wild vigour of a savage root." Returning to the same reasoning after a powerful evocation of the violence and sav-agery of the traders on the West African coast, More is less generous:

What strange offence, what aggravated sin?
They stand convicted—of a darker skin!
Barbarians, hold! Th'opprobrious commerce spare
Respect HIS sacred image which they bear.
Though dark and savage, ignorant and blind,
They claim the common privilege of *kind*;
Let malice strip them of each other plea,
They still are men, and men should still be free.   (105)

More, like Cowper, insistently hectors the reader with the thought that the owning of a darker skin is not a sufficient excuse for buy-ing and selling other human beings. This, of course, cuts both ways. It argues that skin color is not crucial when assessing some-one's humanity, while at the same time reinforcing the significance of complexion as something that must be discussed. A darker com-plexion might not justify the enslavement of human beings, but it might justify other forms of inequality: "Though few can rea-son, all mankind can feel" (106). Clearly for More a darker com-plexion does signify inequality. It signifies savagery and a lack of reason and civilization. As Moira Ferguson puts it, "Even though Africans are ugly, rationally inferior, and basically savage, Christian values dictate that they do feel" (1992, 8–9). The cure for these ills involves Christianity and commerce: ideas strongly advocated in the later half of poem "The Sorrows of Yamba" which More coauthored (A. Richardson 2002).

I discussed Coleridge's theories about race and his movement from Enlightenment universalism to his later anthropological racism in chapter 1 of this book. His published writings on the slave trade in the 1790s clearly owe most to the Clarksonian position, although they are much more sophisticated at the level of representation. When writing against the trade in slaves, Coleridge anticipates his later Kantian distinction of the difference between a person and a thing: as every human is born with the faculty of reason "a person can never become a Thing, nor be treated as such without wrong" (1969, 2: 125). He is willing to apply Kant's categorical imperative to the issue of slavery, unlike its originator, who was oddly silent on the issue. His lines in the version of "Religious Musings" published in 1796 make this point most tellingly, "where more hideous TRADE / Loud-laughing packs his bales of human anguish." The oxymoronic juxtaposition of the noun "bales" and the adjective "human" functions as a powerful reminder of the European's category mistake in forgetting that humanity is a single species (2:140–41; 2003, 1:180). Coleridge's "Lecture on the Slave Trade" of June 1795 clearly owes much to Clarkson. The day before the lecture he borrowed Clarkson's *An Essay on the Impolicy of the African Slave Trade* and C.B. Wadström's *An Essay on Colonization* (1794–95) from the Bristol Library (1974, 232). Benezet's *Account* and Wadström's *Essay* provided Coleridge with descriptions of the idyllic life of Africans, and Clarkson's *Essay on the Impolicy of the African Slave Trade* gave him details of the manner in which the trade was conducted. Coleridge inflects this source material in significant ways. He uses a view of African pastoral culture to criticize political economy, anticipating Marxist ideas of alienation (Morton 87–106). He provides an account of pastoral simplicity behind which stands his advocacy of a pantisocratic community of property, one of the fantasies, according to Hayden White, often visited upon the New World (White 187; Coleman 1994, 345–46). Here Coleridge sees Africa through the filter of his own concerns at that time. Nevertheless he explicitly gives to the African "an acuteness of intellect" lacking in the European mechanic and, in comparing the African with the European peasantry, he implicitly subscribes to Clarkson's Christian and Enlightenment view of race. Like Clarkson's his stress is also on the European's category mistake whereby people are turned into things: that is into "bales of human anguish."

Coleridge's "Lecture" is perhaps most interesting to us in its much discussed virtuoso deconstruction of the binary opposition of savagery and civilization:

> A part of that Food among most of you is sweetened with the Blood of the Murdered. Bless the Food which thou hast given us!—O Blasphemy!—Did God give Food mingled with Brothers blood! Will the Father of all men bless the Food of Cannibals—the food which is polluted with the blood of his own innocent Children? Surely if the inspired Philanthropist of Galilee were to revisit earth and be among the feasters as at Cana he would not change Water into Wine but haply convert the produce into the things producing, the occasioned into the things occasioning. (1974, 248)

The ingenuity of the trope is clearly designed to impress his educated audience. Here the Unitarian Coleridge attacks the Anglican practice of Sacrament but also accuses the sugar-eating European of cannibalism—which travel accounts from Columbus onward had attributed to the savage races.[15] Hayden White, in an argument based on Freud's treatment of cannibalism and incest in *Totem and Taboo*, demonstrates how European taboos of cannibalism, nakedness, community of property, lawlessness, and sexual promiscuity are common in European reports of the savage. He argues that, "this may be, in the European commentators, a projection of repressed desires onto the lives of the natives... but if it is such it is desire tainted by horror and viewed with disgust" (White 187). Coleridge's question relating to the grace, "Will the father of all men bless the Food of Cannibals," in implicating the European in acts of cannibalism, preempts White's theory of taboo and repression. Equiano does something akin to this in his *Interesting Narrative* when he remembers, upon embarking on the slave ship, how he asked his fellow slaves "if we were not to be eaten by those white men with horrible looks, red faces, and long hair" (55). Although Coleridge is preeminently concerned with defining his own Unitarian version of dissent in attacking the Sacrament and with outlining the modern-day miracles of a messiah who is no more than an "inspired Philanthropist," he does try to make his audience aware of the horrors of both the slave trade and of the processes of representation itself.[16] Ultimately in this lecture, Coleridge is trying to undermine the argument that the two radical indicators of savagery, absence of language and cannibalism, apply to the African.

As we have seen, Coleridge's views of race underwent revision and development as he attempted to synthesize contemporary "scientific" accounts of the varieties of humanity (derived from

Blumenbach), with his larger philosophical ambitions. Moreover, as he became dissatisfied with his earlier pantisocratic notions of property, he increasingly came to see Africa as a market for commercial development and the Africans as suitable subjects for conversion to Christianity. He makes such points in a review of Clarkson's *The History of the Abolition of the African Slave-Trade* in 1808 which imagines, somewhat inappropriately, the old slave forts on the coast of Africa becoming centers of civilization. He projects a glorious future if "African industry were awakened" whereby the "articles necessary for our consumption" could be manufactured by African labor and thus "come to us more cheaply." Christian conversion will also be effected by "a systematic repression of all religious proselytism" (1995, 1: 240–41). Although this advocacy of an aggressive and commercial colonial policy sounded suspicious to contemporary ears, it should be noted that Equiano advocated much the same thing at the close of his *Interesting Narrative* (1789), as did Clarkson in his *Impolicy of the African Slave Trade*. Commerce as a panacea for all cultures was seldom, if ever, questioned in abolitionist writing. However in moving from his 1795 advocacy of the pastoral, communitarian, happiness of the idyllic African society to his stress on the importance of commerce and Christianity in civilizing Africa, Coleridge was at one with the general nineteenth-century drift of opinion regarding what became known, as it was explored in the 1850s, as the "dark continent" (Brantlinger 1988, 173–98).

BLACK ABOLITIONIST THEORIES
OF RACE: CUGOANO AND EQUIANO

It would seem therefore that there was some confusion regarding how African men and women were understood in the eighteenth century. Felicity Nussbaum argues acutely that the literature of the time reflects that "the public consensus concerning the actual nature of African men had not yet jelled, and it vacillated erratically from pro-slavery racism, through benevolent amelioration bolstered by Enlightenment humanism to abolitionist sentiment."[17] Eighteenth-century Black British writers felt the need to establish their intellectual, moral and racial status by promoting arguments affirming human equality. Quobna Ottobah's Cugoano's *Thoughts and Sentiments on the Evil and Wicked Traffic of the Slavery and Commerce of the Human Species* (1787) is the first abolitionist tract to be produced by an African, one of the "Sons of Africa," a loose grouping of black

Londoners who wrote antislavery letters to the press.[18] Cugoano's radical abolitionist and emancipationist polemic draws substantially on white abolitionist writing, especially that of Wesley, Clarkson, and Ramsay. Like Clarkson, Cugoano addresses the issue of race as if it were a serious justification for the institution of slavery. He does not name those "some men" who claim that nature designed the African "'for some inferior link in the chain, fitted only to be a slave'" despite placing the statement in quotation marks as if deriving from an unacknowledged source (11–12).[19] His major opponent, however, appears to be "the Cursory Remarker," though Tobin went out of his way to deny that biological notions of African inferiority were a part of the planter case. Cugoano argues a radical Christian Universalist case of the "rational creation of man" (27). He confutes, at length, the biblical argument for slavery, the curse visited upon Ham and his descendants that "the Africans are peculiarly marked out by some signal prediction in nature and complexion for that purpose" arguing that there can be no justification for "any part of the human species" enslaving another (28). As all humans spring from the same act of creation there can be neither "different" nor "inferior species" among humanity. As the "present inhabitants of the world" all sprang from the "family of Noah" they were originally "all of one complexion," the differences in complexion and feature being derived "after they became dispersed and settled on the different parts of the globe" (29). Such variety was established by God for allowing them to endure the "respective climates of their habitations, so their colours vary to some degree" (30). Behind Cugoano's reasoning lies the environmentalist explanation for human variety though expressed in one of its most heavily Christianized forms through jeremiadic thunderings. Cugoano does not argue for the priority of blackness but accepts that variation (significantly he does not use the term degeneration) has occurred since the Deluge and that human difference derives from the various movements of Noah's descendants. The text reveals little of what Cugoano may have known of contemporary scientific thought regarding human variety beyond what he discovered in Ramsay and Clarkson.

Like Cugoano, Olaudah Equiano was keen both to raise and then confute arguments concerning the biological inferiority of Africans. In a letter to William Dickson, the former private secretary to the governor of Barbados, published in *The Diary; or Woodfall's Register* in 1789, Equiano praised Dickson's *Letters on Slavery* thanking God that "the nation at last is awakened to a sense of our sufferings." Equiano excludes from this collective, national awakening only "the

Oran Otang philosophers, who we think will find it a hard task to dissect your letters" (1995, 344). Equiano's reference here, which preempts Coleridge's similar usage, may refer to thinkers such as Long, who equated African with apes and justified slavery. In his letter of 1788 to the proslavery advocate, Gordon Turnbull, published in *The Public Advertiser*, Equiano criticizes the recipient for offering "an hypothesis that the Negro race is an inferior species of mankind." Equiano rejoins against Turnbull with Acts XVII.xxvi, "God hath made of one blood all the nations of men, for to dwell on all the face of the earth, &c" (332). To James Tobin, Equiano boldly praises the merits of interracial marriage:

> If the mind of a black man conceives the passion of love for a fair female, he is to pine, to languish, and even die, sooner than an intermarriage be allowed, merely because the complexion of the offspring should be tawney—A more foolish prejudice than this never warped a cultivated mind—for as no contamination of the virtues of the heart would result from this union, the mixture of colour could be of no consequence. God looks with equal good-will on all his creatures, whether black or white—let neither, therefore, arrogantly condemn the other. (329)

Equiano, of course, married an English woman, Susanna Cullen in 1792, but his argument for the positive benefits of such arrangements as harmonious with "Nature's own wide and extensive plan...without distinction of the colour of a skin" (330) counters the gothic apocalypticism of those, like Long, who saw in miscegenation the degeneration and destruction of the European races.[20] Equiano, like Clarkson, decenters the binary hierarchy of white and black by positing "tawney" as an intermediary complexion preferable to the whiteness of the planters, which conceals their rapes and enforced abortions against their slaves.

Equiano's advocacy of a Christian Universalist conception of race is forcefully made in his *The Interesting Narrative of the Life of Olaudah Equiano* (1789). Most criticism of the work has tended to minimize the importance of race for Equiano's conception of identity, arguing for religion or Britishness as the key issues.[21] Roxann Wheeler, understanding the importance of the increasing racialization of discourse at this time, however, more carefully delineates how through its awareness of the "general shift to a more noticeably color-conscious racial ideology, the narrative shows Equiano's attempts to keep whiteness separate from a notion of Britishness in order to keep for him, a former slave, an authoritative public identity."[22] Felicity Nussbaum relates the *Narrative* to Equiano's desire to establish a black masculine identity in competition with the many competing fictional, dramatic, poetic and other cultural representations available (2003, 189–212; 213–38). Certainly the issue of race thinking, and need to refute it, is present in the Equiano's text. He comments on how, during his childhood in Africa, complexions that are fairer than his own partake of deformity:

> [I]n regard to complexion ideas of beauty are wholly relative. I remember while in Africa to have seen three negro children, who were tawny, and another quite white, who were universally regarded by myself and the natives in general, as far as related to their complexions, as deformed. (38)

Equiano is thus a relativist in aesthetics, which he establishes as an ethnologically verifiable phenomenon. This argues against those, such as Blumenbach, who maintained hierarchies of racial beauty while denying gradations of morality or intelligence. If, however, Equiano's Igbo (Eboe) childhood is a construction or self-fashioning of the later Gustavus Vassa, as Vincent Carretta has suggested, Equiano's ethnology is opportunistic (Caretta 1996, 96–105 and 2003, 226–35). The intention is to minimize the significance, aesthetic or otherwise, of skin color.

Equiano presents his African homeland as one of pastoral simplicity in which abundance is combined with a developed political, social, religious, and artistic civilization. He comments, several times, on the similarity of its customs with those of the Jews as described in the Old Testament, "before they reached the Land of Promise, and particularly the patriarchs, while they were yet in that pastoral state which is described in Genesis." This "analogy" leads Equiano to speculate that, "the one people had sprung from the other" (43–44). Equiano cites the researches of John Gill, John Clarke, and Arthur Bedford as corroboration that his people may have been descended from the primitive Israelites. In suggesting such an explanation for the origins of the customs of his people, Equiano attempts to diminish the racial difference between Europeans and Africans at a time when the Jews were usually regarded by natural philosophers as unproblematically Caucasian, though as a wandering race without a state they provided an interesting case to test the theories of climate and environment. To explain the differences of complexion, Equiano has recourse to the Buffonian hypothesis of degeneration, filtered of its pejorative associations through the commentary of Thomas Clarkson:

> As to the difference of colour between the Eboan Africans and the modern Jews, I shall not presume to account for it. It is a subject which has engaged the pens of men of genius and learning, and is far above my strength. The most able and Reverend Mr. T. Clarkson, however, in his much-admired Essay on the Slavery and Commerce of the Human Species, has ascertained the cause, in a manner that at once solves every objection on the account. (44)

In deferring to Clarkson's explanation to account for human difference, Equiano subscribes to a theory that postulates olive not black nor white as the primary color, and both white and black complexions the results of climatic change.[23] Equiano goes on to provide familiar examples of groups of humans who have allegedly changed their skin color as they moved their location. Such instances "shew how the complexions of the same persons vary in different climates" and may serve "to remove the prejudice that some conceive against the natives of Africa on account of their colour." Rather than ascribing any perceived inferiority to complexion, Equiano suggests that this "might be more naturally ascribed to their situation...does not slavery itself depress the mind, and extinguish all its fire, and every noble sentiment?" (45) Equiano's fascination with complexion and the results of miscegenation are shown in his recollection of a "remarkable circumstance relative to African complexion," which he witnesses on his arrival in London: "A white negro woman, that I had formerly seen in London and other parts, had married a white man, by whom she had three boys, and they were every one mulattoes, and yet had fine light hair" (220). Though he does not use the circumstance to develop or support any theory of human difference, it shows his interest in the mechanisms of physical change and the potential arbitrariness of complexion. The three boys manifest the light brown skin color that results from their English and African parentage, despite the whiteness of the woman, yet her peculiar characteristic of "fine light hair" also reappears in their physical makeup. The enigma of complexion puzzles Equiano throughout the *Narrative*. Despite the rationalization of Clarkson, the boy and young man described in the *Narrative* find it difficult to come to terms with signification of skin color. When he first encounters Europeans he fears the people who have such differing complexions, the "white men with horrible looks, red faces, and long hair"

(55). When taken to England by his Master, Pascal, and left at a house in Falmouth, Equiano witnesses a mother washing the face of her daughter and making it "very rosy; but when she washed mine it did not look so." He describes how he tried to make his face of the "same colour as my little play-mate...but all in vain" and how he became "mortified at the difference in our complexions" (69). Serving aboard the *Royal George* in the Seven Years' War, in a naval community where color mattered much less than on the mainland, Equiano regards himself as "almost an Englishman" (77). So great is his acclimatization to England that he fails at first to recognize his kinship with a "black boy about my own size" on the Isle of Wight in the 1750s and momentarily turns away from his embrace. Equiano's confusion, for Carretta, represents "the double vision of someone with a dual identity," encapsulated in the sobriquet he later adopts of "the black Christian." (92)[24]

The difference between Europeans and Africans relates primarily to the stage of civilization at which they are respectively placed and not to any difference in "our common nature" (232). The difference between Africa and Europe is the same difference as that between ancient Britain and contemporary Britain, in a word, "civilization" (233–34). Equiano does not argue for the equality of African civilization in the present but foresees the process by which this could be achieved in the future through commerce and Christianity. In this, he subscribes to a model of African inferiority, but one that is social and economic not biological. As Goldberg and Wheeler have pointed out, such models also can serve to establish group domination of one people over another. Equiano does have a biological notion of human difference, but it is one that does not argue for any kind of superiority for a fair complexion. Equiano's stress on civilization as a model for human development, however, combined with his notion of the environmental and climatic causation of physical difference, could be reconciled with the Buffonian model refined and adapted by Samuel Stanhope Smith, though Equiano nowhere argues that moral and intellectual qualities are influenced by climatic change. Slavery is wrong because it is built on the "traffic in the human species" and humans should not be treated as commodities. It is a system that is maintained not by white racial superiority but by white technology (what he describes as "magic") and overwhelming and exceptionally brutal force, supervision, and coercion, "[t]ortures, murder, and every other imaginable barbarity and iniquity" (234, 104–112, 171–72). Like those of Clarkson and others, Equiano's *Narrative* also details this regime of fear and punishment in agonizing and shocking detail. Ultimately, Equiano argues for a system of free labor and free commerce in a Christianized Africa. His early involvement in the Sierra Leone scheme is well known. (220–29; Caretta 2005, 223–35)[25] But it is "the endless field of commerce" exploited by "British manufacturers and merchant adventurers" which will show that "the abolition of slavery would be a universal good" (234–35). Although the *Interesting Narrative* explicitly refutes theories of biological racism and subscribes to the environmentalist hypothesis of human difference, it does not clearly accuse the planters of upholding a biological theory of African inferiority. This is certainly implied when he claims that slavery debases humans:

> You stupefy them with stripes, and think it necessary to keep them in a state of ignorance; and yet you assert that they are incapable of learning; that their minds are such a barren soil or moor, that culture would be lost on them; and that they came from a climate, where nature (though prodigal of her bounties in a degree unknown to yourselves) has left man alone scant and unfinished, and incapable of enjoying the treasures she has poured out for him! (Equiano 111–12)

The claim that Africans may be "incapable of learning" hints at a widespread view of their biological incapacity for advancement, although this claim was compatible, as we have seen, with a monogenist and environmentalist account of physical difference. Difference is discussed in a wide variety of contexts in *The Interesting Narrative*, as English, French, Spanish, Greeks, Turks, South American Indians, Anglicans, Methodists, Catholics, Jews, Dissenters, and Muslims make up the rich tapestry of Equiano's encounters. Dominance and subservience are not defined in racial terms; Equiano comments, for instance, on his surprise at seeing "how the Greeks are, in some measure, kept under by the Turks, as the negroes are in the West-Indies by the white people" (167–68). Race is present in the *Interesting Narrative* but it is not the primary polemical concern of Equiano's critique of slavery. Nevertheless Equiano's concern with the significations of his complexion and those of others and the relationship they have to his often and understandably troubled sense of identity are prophetic of the growing racialization of discourse in the nineteenth century, when it becomes hard to imagine narratives of slavery that do not concern the race idea as their most prominent feature.

Ironically it is perhaps in the writings of the abolitionists then that the ideas of "scientific racism" are probably most apparent, albeit under pressure of refutation. While much of abolitionist writing might be considered positive on issues of race and equality, the parameters of its worldview are limited to a Christian universalism, which stressed a humanity grounded on feeling rather than on reason. As Hannah More puts it, "They still are men, and men should still be free" because "though few can reason, all mankind can feel" (M. Wood 2003, 106). While not in the category of Long's or White's extreme speculations about difference, Ramsay's hypothesis of the "universal freckle," which both Clarkson and Smith adopt is dismissive of blackness which, in the contemporary parlance of scientific racism, is usually seen as a degeneration from a primary racial color of white or "dark-olive." Thus the relationship between the slave trade, slavery, and the emergence of scientific racialist thinking is an ambiguous and contested issue in which the various combatants line up in confusing ways. Certainly scientific racialism began to emerge more strongly at this time and it did feature as a part of the debate about slavery and the slave trade, but it was not a necessary argument for the West-Indian interest at this stage. Proslavery writers could argue everything they needed to within the parameters of Christian Universalist thinking, a worldview that could encompass both vehemently racist thoughts and practices as well as ideas that we can recognize as humanitarian and progressive. Such a view of human difference might be articulated in a scriptural or scientific mode or it might share of both, as in the work of Thomas Clarkson.

Once the authority of the biblical account began to decline, other, skeptical and secular versions of the natural history of mankind were needed to justify the domination of the whites. Certainly, in Althusserian terms, it seems that the ideology of racism is possessed of a relative autonomy that allows it to change its idiom without a direct causal relationship to material conditions. Commentators on race matters, such as Memmi and Goldberg, are thus right to highlight the racist aspect of group domination and subordination, which express themselves in a variety of ways beyond the merely physical and somatic. They are also right to point out that this is a change in the grammar of racial discourse rather than a specific attempt to justify the class interests of the West Indian planters and their mercantile supporters. However we should also maintain the space for those ideas and thoughts that challenged and upset the prevailing orthodoxies of race thinking in the period as well as understanding that racialist notions of hierarchy and inferiority infiltrated the discourses of human equality and could be seen to be supportive of exclusions and oppressions based on racial constructs, even if their adherents were opposed to trade and slavery itself.

CHAPTER 4

ROMANTICISM, RACE, AND CANNIBALISM IN THE "SOUTH SEAS"

DEFINING OCEANIA

This chapter moves the focus of the debate about human difference in the Romantic period away from the anatomy theaters and far from the transatlantic concern with the slave trade to another crucial area of geographical discovery, exploration, and exploitation, the area now known as "Oceania," but usually referred to in the period and after as the "South Seas." The discovery of new varieties of human being with quite striking physical differences often located in comparatively close proximity to each other created new puzzles and problems for the philosophers of human difference. It forced Blumenbach to expand his fourfold typology to include a fifth human type, the "Malay" in the second edition of his *De Generis Humani Varietate Nativa* of 1781. It also made Europeans confront, once again, but perhaps more urgently, the strangely compelling phenomenon of human beings eating other human beings. As the nineteenth century wore on, anthropophagy or cannibalism also became a key marker of the essential differences between human beings and increasingly it became a racialized phenomenon. This chapter attempts to show how this gustatory practice in Oceania also served to distinguish between varieties, then races, of humans who inhabited the region. Enlightenment empirical observation was never neutral and the highly charged and richly symbolic discussion of Southern and

Central Pacific diet reveals much about the ideological desires and anxieties of the West.

The "South Seas" has been the subject of much intellectual exploration in the last few years of Romantic and other nineteenth-century criticism. Most of this writing has stressed how the South Seas figured as a construction of Western desires and fears. In particular, Neil Rennie, has explored the construction of the South Sea Islands as paradise and paradise lost.[1] Most recently, Jonathan Lamb has argued that rather than exporting confident colonial subjects to the Pacific, the Europeans "spread ignorance before they spread trade routes and disease" and that the "uncertainties" that assailed the Romantic self were "intensified in the Pacific" at the same time as the "Polynesian self" was being forced out of its own tribal identity (Lamb 5). Nicholas Thomas has also maintained that this colonial encounter is one marked by ambiguities and exchanges and not a simple matter of the fatal impact of the West on a victimized and tragic native people (1997, 1–20). Such new perspectives, which combine the anthropological, cultural and literary approaches, are very conducive to a sustained analysis of diet, appetite, and difference in the Southern and Central Pacific. Combined with a substantial body of postcolonial or skeptical anthropological discussions of the nature of cannibalism, they offer a fruitful and exciting way to reappraise the colonial encounter and its most notorious, enigmatic, and fearsome subject, the cannibal.[2] In this chapter, I concentrate on the division of the South Seas into racialized groupings of Polynesia, Melanesia, and later Micronesia, arguing that the figure of the cannibal becomes key to effecting a racist division between the fair and the dark-skinned inhabitants of the Pacific. Concentrating on the distinction between Tahiti and the Maori tribes as described in ethnological and travel texts of the Romantic period, I then argue that the "imaginative" literature of the period was partially complicit in ossifying an arbitrary Enlightenment classification into a politics of the body, which justified the exploitation, conversion, and terrorization of native peoples. Focusing on the function of the symbolism and meaning of diet in the process, I show how empirical observation of taste and appetite, and the symbolism inscribed in such representations, were central in this psychopolitical creation of difference.

MELANESIANS AND POLYNESIANS

In some of the most poignant and haunting lines in all of English literature, Coleridge's Ancient Mariner strikes the sustained note of what we may call the "colonial uncanny": "We were the first that ever burst / Into that silent sea" (2:105–6; 2003, 380). In 1797, when those lines were penned, the Western maritime penetration of the Central and Southern Pacific (more properly "Oceania"), was well under way. However, in the late eighteenth century vast areas of Oceania were still unexplored by the European powers, and peoples, cultures, as well as flora and fauna remained unknown to the West. The last quarter of the century witnessed the sustained and systematic European attempt to explore, chart, describe, classify, and eventually exploit the Southern and Central Pacific. The area became the location of the stereotypes of travel writing: the dusky maiden, the noble savage, and the fearsome cannibal. As Mary Louise Pratt has argued, this moment in colonial history marked a shift in the public motivation for exploration from the earlier goals of conquest, plunder, and exploitation to an agenda of scientific exploration, devoid of any explicit program for the conquest of territory or the terrorization of native peoples. Pratt argues that in this period we see the growth of a "planetary consciousness" driven by Enlightenment imperatives to classify and arrange the various peoples and products of the natural world (15–37, 39). James Cook included in his three great voyages of discovery in the Southern hemisphere natural philosophers, botanists, astronomers, and mathematicians, such as Joseph Banks, Carl Solander, George [Georg] and John [Johann] Reinhold Forster, Anders Sparrman, William Wales, William Anderson, and others. These explorers took with them the theoretical equipment of Enlightenment classifiers, including Linnaeus, Buffon, and Blumenbach, and used such systems to order and arrange this new and extraordinary world in a grand narrative of progress and civilization.

During this process, between say 1750 and 1830, years that bear a congruence with what we have come to call the "Romantic period" in English literature, something interesting happened to the cannibal. As Roxann Wheeler and Frank Lestrignant have argued the figure of the cannibal changed from being a marker of cultural difference, the object which set up the differential between savagery and civilization, or paganism and Christianity, to being a sign of racial and moral degeneracy (Lestrignant; Wheeler 2000, 49–98). In the process cannibalism became less of a social and customary activity, a matter of culture, or, as in the theories of Voltaire and Malthus, a response to protein deficiency, than a bestial and lustful business, a practice governed by the desire for human flesh (Sanbourn 21–73; Kitson 2001, 218–20). The cannibal's skin got darker and his or her hair seemed to be, in the parlance of the time, "crinkly or woolly." Cannibalism became one of the key signs of racial inferiority, as pronounced and specific a marker for a nineteenth-century readership as the physical features of skin, skull, and hair. The practice was to be understood as a somatic or physical and innate aptitude, a justification for empire and for the civilization of the dark places of the earth.

Cannibalism thus became a marker of difference in the nascent Enlightenment and Romantic science of human variety and race, and eating people was understood to be the specialty of the dark-skinned human whether in Africa or the South Pacific. In *The Philosophy of History* (1837), Hegel wrote that "the eating of human flesh is quite compatible with the African principle; to the sensuous Negro, human flesh is purely an object of the senses, like all other flesh" (183; Sanbourn 38–39). Cannibalism as sign of racial degeneration was very much the view applied by the young Charles Darwin to the natives of Tierra del Fuego in 1846 (Sanbourn 38–39). By the mid-nineteenth-century, as Nicholas Thomas has shown, the classification of the peoples of the Central and Southern Pacific into the racial groupings of Polynesia (Eastern Pacific), Melanesia (Western Pacific), and later Micronesia (North Western) had been accomplished (1989, 27–34; 1997, 133–55). Taking the central dichotomy of Melanesian and Polynesian, the Melanesians (Solomon Islands, New Hebrides, and New Caledonia) were dark-skinned and had crinkly hair, and were susceptible to cannibalism. The Polynesians (Tahiti, the Marquesas, Samoa, Tonga, and the Society Islands) were fair-skinned with flowing hair and, if they were cannibals it was long ago in the past or, alternatively, evidence of an uncharacteristic backsliding. Gary Hogg, for instance, in his popular study of cannibalism of 1958, reflected this equation between Melanesian culture and cannibalism: "It is in Melanesia that cannibalism was longest in dying...[its inhabitants] like the vastly larger island to the west of them, New Guinea, just to north of Australia, are peopled by inhabitants who clung obstinately to their ancient tradition of devouring human flesh long after the tradition had begun to fade, or had even been wholly stamped out, elsewhere" (23). The ambiguous position of the Fiji Islands (not properly known until the 1830s) in this racial divide is solved for Hogg by the substantial number of missionary accounts describing the Fijians as fierce and unregenerate cannibals. Hogg accepts that the Fijians are Melanesians because they are cannibals, and because they enjoy eating human flesh, as do other members of their racial grouping in New Guinea.

Although the practice may have occurred in Polynesia "it certainly began to die out amongst those islands long before the process began in Melanesia" (Hogg 157). Where it exists in Polynesia, it is due to Melanesian influence. Hogg presents a populist and unthinking absorption of an anthropological distinction that still persists, but that originated in the late eighteenth century. Behind this belief is the axiom propagated by some theorists of race that one approaches more closely to humanity as one's skin approaches to whiteness. Late eighteenth-century Pacific explorers were puzzled by the difference between the fairer-skinned Tahitians' and their darker-skinned neighbors. Louis de Bougainville in his voyage of 1766 to 1769, noted that "Nothing distinguishes" the Tahitians "features from those of the Europeans." If they were "less exposed to the sun at noon, they would be as white as ourselves." The darker-skinned habitants of the New Hebrides he found to be "short, ugly, ill-proportioned." He further added that he generally observed that "the black men are much more ill natured than those whose colour comes near to white" (249, 291, 320). Bougainville's distinction was not a racialized one. Yet as early as 1799, the evangelical preacher, Dr. Thomas Haweis, implied a racial dimension in his contrast of the lighter-skinned Pacific peoples with a "darker race," which occupied Australia, New Guinea, New Caledonia, the Solomons, Vanuatu, and Fiji. These people, he hypothesized, were the original inhabitants of the islands who had been conquered by the Tahitians. Haweis found "The stature of the Fijians is superior, their complexions are darker, and their hair approaches to wool." They also "retain their practice of eating the bodies of their enemies whom they have killed, which is now abhorred by all the lighter race, except the individuals of New Zealand" (lxxi, lxxxvi; N. Thomas 1997, 142–43; Rennie 159–61, 164). In his *History of the Tahitian Mission*, written in the 1830s, John Davies comments that the "mild generous and hospitable" Tahitians have "fewer horrid customs" than the New Hollanders who are "wretches...below the state of nature many degrees" (31). The missionary William Ellis could dogmatically expound with certainty, at the same time as Davies, the view that "the islands of the Pacific are inhabited by two tribes of men totally distinct, and in some respects entirely different from each other." One of these tribes is composed of "Oceanic negroes" and the other "belong to the physical character of the Malayan and aboriginal American tribes." The latter "tribe" or "race" has a "facial angle frequently as perpendicular as in the European structure" (1: 78–79). That Ellis, a missionary with a view of humanity based on familial structures, could nevertheless appeal to the facial angle in the 1830s to discriminate between the two "tribes" is a testimony to the ways in which race thinking had infiltrated other discourses of human variety. The distinction had become entrenched by the 1840s when the Rev. Michael Russell's *Polynesia*, describes the Fijians properly as belonging "to the black tribes of Melanesia and New Guinea" as with "strong indications of Negro ferocity, they combine some of the worst habits which disgrace the whole population of the Southern Pacific, especially the horrible practice of eating their enemies, now abhorred by all the fairer-skinned families of the windward clusters" (27). Later in the century, when such biological racial distinctions had become accepted in mainstream thought, Thomas Williams could claim that the Fijian is distinguished by his "cruelty" that is "relentless and bloody." The islanders suffer from an "inner depravity" marked by their cannibalism, which they practice from motives of lust and revenge, even to the extent of "the most fiendish cruelty...of cutting off parts and even limbs of the victim while still living, and cooking and eating them before his eyes" (112, 212, 205–15). The Rev. Josiah Priest, in *Slavery* (1843), tells us that the "horrid and heart-appalling practice of cannibalism has, in all ages, attached more to the African race than to any other people of the earth." The dark-skinned, denizens of the Western Pacific of Africa, he claims, "have been irrespective of civilization, actually more or less in the practice of the dreadful crime of eating human flesh, as an article of food, the same as dogs or any other carnivorous animal" (191, 199; Sanbourn 27). The Fijians, as even a cursory look over missionary accounts in the era makes clear, were alleged to be cannibals because they enjoyed eating human flesh and because they were addicted to cruelty. It is this that confirms them as Melanesian. As Geoffrey Sanbourn puts it, "Through its association with race, the fixed desire for human flesh had been made visible; through its association with addictiveness, the visible sign of cannibalism—the dark skin—was fixed" (29). The cannibal has come along way from the honorable and noble warriors of the Tupinamba Indians that Montaigne idealized in his essay "Of the Cannibales" of 1580, and the friendly, tractable man Friday, who despite his hankering after human flesh was eminently capable of being civilized to be Crusoe's servant.

The distinction between Melanesians and Polynesians was a result of Enlightenment science, an arbitrary mapping of cultures in terms of physical type, customs, and language. The term "Melanesia," as N. Thomas informs us, lumps together populations with very different backgrounds, such as Papuans and Austronesians, while ethnologists now inform us that "Polynesia" is best understood as a subgroup of Austronesian "Melanesia." These categories have been sustained though "reiteration and redefinition, rather than on the basis of self-evident human differences" (1997, 133–55). Even when the distinction between the races is not made on narrow physical traits, the Melanesians are most often considered the inferior grouping. The missionary George Brown in 1910, for instance, could argue that though descended from "one common stock," "the Melanesian is the oldest representative at the present time" and that the "brown Polynesians" "represent a later and greater admixture caused by successive immigration of Caucasian peoples" (15–17). The distinction is often repeated uncritically in accounts of the exploration of the area. In 1965, for instance, John Dunmore could comment relating to the encounters of the French explorer Louis Bougainville: "The dark Melanesians were obviously more warlike and of a less happy disposition than the 'Indians' of Tahiti" (Dunmore 1: 101). Certainly the presence of the "dark and ugly" Melanesians in close proximity to the beautiful Polynesians was an enigma that troubled theorists of human variety. As George Forster archly put it when critiquing Kant's racial theories about the peoples of the South Seas, "many a hypothesis would be improved if one could argue away the ugly Blacks from the South Seas. But they are there, and that is that" (quoted in Bindman 2002, 175).

One of the several key figures in establishing this distinction was the natural philosopher, Johann (or John) Reinhold Forster (Hoare 1976). Forster and his son, Georg (or George), sailed as naturalists on Cook's second voyage of exploration (1772–75) in search of the disputed great southern continent, *Terra Australis Incognita*. This voyage brought to their attention a vast diversity of peoples scattered over a wide area of the globe. This variety and its possible origins puzzled Cook's natural historians who attempted to find a way of explaining it in terms of the migration of Asiatic peoples. J.R. Forster's *Observations Made during a Voyage Round the World* of 1778 was the most systematic of a number of attempts to provide a mapping of the Pacific.

> We chiefly observed two great varieties of people in the South Seas; the one more fair, well-limbed, athletic, of a fine size, and a kind benevolent temper; the other blacker, the hair just beginning to become crisp, the body more slender and low, and their temper, if possible more brisk, though somewhat mistrustful. The first race inhabits O-Taheitee, and the Society Isles, the Marquesas, the Friendly Isles [Tonga], Easter-Island, and New Zealand. The second race peoples New-Caledonia, Tanna and the New Hebrides, especially Mallicollo. (153)

Forster's movement in this passage from the term "variety" to that of "race" is significant. The term "race" is synonymous, in Forster's usage, with variety, which implies arbitrary change. "Race" implies the biological and morphologically fixed type in the sciences of human classification, closer to the term "species." Forster's distinction between the two great "races" is not made simply on the basis of physical characteristics and temperaments, but on a whole series of cultural phenomena, including language, customs, and diet. He speculates that these two races are descended from different ancestors, though how this happened is a mystery. Within the "Polynesian" or Eastern Pacific group, Forster arranged the islanders he observed on a graded scale with the Tahitians at the apex down through New Zealanders, New Caledonians, New Hebrideans, with the peoples of Tanna and Malekula as the most debased. Forster, however, is not the physical or evolutionary anthropologist we might expect. He attempts to classify the peoples of the Pacific in terms of their approach toward civilization, in the manner of Enlightenment writers, such as Montesquieu, Lord Kames, John Millar, and Adam Ferguson. In so doing he distinguishes between the states of savagery and barbarism. Forster argued that humanity evolved from a childlike state of savagery to an adolescent state of barbarism. His theory of humanity was basically evolutionary rather than biologically racist, unlike his successors who were to accept the superiority of Polynesian over Melanesian culture and the innateness of their physical and moral characteristics.

COOK, FORSTER, AND THE CANNIBALS

Forster had difficulties in classifying what he called the "New Zealander," who for us are the Maori peoples. They appeared to be a recognizably Polynesian (a term not used by Forster) or Eastern Pacific people, yet, as eighteenth-century explorers discovered to their cost, they were fiercer, more warlike and less manageable than the Tahitians. Cook recorded in all the three of his voyages a people who seemed to practice cannibalism. During his second voyage two incidents, in particular, confirmed a skeptical crew of the Maori's cannibalism.[3] On November 23, 1773 at Totaranui (renamed Queen Charlotte's Sound), some of the crew of the *Resolution* who had gone to trade with the natives came across the severed head of a young man of about sixteen or so (George Forster 1777, 1: 511). The intestines, liver, and lungs of the youth were lying around, and the natives gave the party to understand that they had eaten the rest of the body (Barber 251). One of the ship's lieutenants, Richard Pickersgill, purchased the head for two iron nails and returned with it to the *Resolution*. There, as a cultural experiment, a different group of Maori, who showed a desire to eat the head, were allowed to devour a piece of flesh from it. It is reported that the flesh was devoured "most ravenously," by a man who "suck'd his fingers...in raptures" (Marra 103). Cook, who returned shortly after, recounts in his journal what happened:

> The sight of the head and the relation of the circumstances filled my mind with indignation against these Cannibals, but when I considered that any resentment I could shew would avail but little and being desireous of being an eye wittness to a fact which many people had their doubts about, I concealed my indignation and ordered a piece of the flesh to be broiled and brought on the quarter deck where one of these Canibals eat it with a seeming good relish before the whole ships Company which had such an effect on some of them as to cause them to vomit. [Oediddee, one of the Tahitians aboard the ship] was [so] struck with horror at the sight that [he] wept and scolded by turns, before this happened he was very intimate with these people but now he neither would come near them or suffer them to touch him. (1961, 293)

The racial dynamics of this encounter are interesting. The Europeans' humanity and their distinction from the savagery of the Maori are defined in this recoil from the cannibal scene. "Odiddy," (the Raiatean Islander, Hitihiti), shows a racial kinship with the European in that he reacts with horror, more violently than Cook and the rest. His distress is a feminized response (he wept and scolded) to the events that places himself apart from the Maori, but close to the European, although lacking the European's clinical reason and anthropological balance. When confronted by cannibalism the European either speculates or vomits, rejecting or distancing himself from the spectacle.

Readings of this Maori cannibal scene were various. William Wales, the astronomer and the future mathematics tutor of Coleridge and Charles Lamb, believed that this instance of cannibalism was motivated by the simple lust for flesh and, thus, implied degeneration and savagery. George Forster reported that the flesh was eaten "with the greatest avidity" (1777 1: 512), and John Elliott remembered that it was eaten "with all the avidity of a Beef Steak, to the utmost horror of the Whole Quarter deck" (Holmes 22). Elliot's discomfiting equation of the "Beef Steak" greedily consumed by the English sailor with the human flesh devoured by the cannibal focuses the reader's mind, perhaps unwittingly, on the kinds of meat acceptable for eating and the ways in which difference is created through distinctions within the carnivore set. The issue of whether Maori cannibalism was a matter of appetite or taste, custom, or necessity was thus left open. Neither Cook, nor either of the Forsters believed that the cannibalism was a matter of hunger. Through his interrogations of the Maori, Cook discovered that the youth had been an enemy of the tribe and that the incident had its origins in revenge or warfare, though Wales, for one, believed it was explicable only as bestial desire.

Sadly, the New Zealanders were not the only group to exploit the poor young man's remains. Pickersgill, who had purchased the head, presumably with a desire to sell it in Britain as a much sought-after curiosity, had it preserved in alcohol. Daniel Carl Solander, writing to Joseph Banks on the *Resolution*'s return in 1775, reports how Pickersgill "made the Ladies sick by shewing them the New Zealand head of which 2 or 3 slices were broiled and eaten on board of the Ship."[4] Solander states that his friend, the surgeon, anatomist, and collector of skulls, John Hunter, was to travel to Deptford with him the subsequent day with a view to obtaining this grisly "curiosity," presumably for his own private collection and as an object for racial study (Solander had proposed John Hunter for admission to the Royal Society in 1767). The final destination of the remains of the head of that unfortunate victim of Maori violence and British anthropological tomb robbing has not yet been traced.[5]

The meaning of cannibalism was further impressed upon Cook's crew by a more intense and urgent event, an encounter that was to indelibly color their recollections of earlier visits. On the second visit to New Zealand, Cook's *Resolution* had lost her sister ship, *Adventure*, which arrived on November 23, 1773, four days after Cook had left. On the morning of 18 December, Captain Tobias Furneaux sent a long boat in search of the ship's cutter, which had not returned from the previous evening's task. On a small beach close to Grass Cove (Wharehunga Bay), the party found some fresh meat that they assumed to be of a dog. The commanding officer, Lieutenant James Burney, then recorded how they found about twenty baskets, some "full of roasted flesh & some of fern root which serves them for bread." A severed hand was discovered with the tattooed initials of "T.H," identifying its owner as the crewmember, Thomas Hill (Burney 96–97). Proceeding further into Grass Cove the party came across further evidence of cannibalism. Burney's account of this was published in the official narrative of the voyage:

> We found no boat, but instead of her, such a shocking scene of carnage
> and barbarity as can never be mentioned or thought of but with horror;
> for the heads, hearts, and lungs of several of our people were seen lying

on the beach, and, at a little distance, the dogs gnawing their intrails.
(Cook 1777, 2: 258)

The party returned with two hands, one belonging to Hill and the
other to the master's mate John Rowe who commanded the expedition,. The party also found the severed head of Captain Furneaux's
black servant. These and other remains were wrapped up in a ham-
mock and thrown into the sea, and not preserved and transported back
to Britain as cannibal curiosities as was the case with the mutilated
Maori head. Most interested parties, including Cook, Furneaux, and
the Forsters presumed that this attack was an act of revenge, resulting from a misunderstanding between the two groups in which the
aggressive Rowe may well have been culpable. Certainly, as Anne
Salmond has shown, the similar killing and possible eating of the
French explorer Marion Du Fresne and some of his crew in 1772,
resulted from the Frenchmen's ignorance and violation of Maori *tapu*
(Salmond 1991, 359–430). On his third voyage Cook satisfied himself that the blame for this attack lay as much with the British as the
natives and that the cannibalism that followed had to be understood
in the context of revenge (1967, 815).

The desire hypothesis, however, though not the consensus view,
was still held by some. William Wales remained convinced that the
practice occurred not through scarcity or custom but "from Choice,
and the liking which they have for this kind of food" (Cook 1967,
819). Though a minority view at the time, Wales's opinion would
become the leading nineteenth-century consensus in racialized scientific discourse. Nevertheless, this encounter remains ambiguous. The
Europeans were, after all, interlopers whose observation and reporting
of the custom may have impacted on the behavior of the participants,
a third term in the cannibal occurrence and, as Barber points out,
they had already shown that they were obsessed, perplexed and fright-
ened by the possibility of cannibalism (Barber 255). The Europeans
themselves were avidly collecting partially eaten native human body
parts, such as the young man's head. Gananath Obeyesekere has also
argued that the Europeans' anthropophagic preoccupations resulted
from *their* not uncommon practice of survival cannibalism at sea
(Obeyesekere 1992, 630–50). Thus the Maori's cannibalism might
also be understood in terms of their desire to terrorize the Europeans
or to demonstrate their masculinity.

How then did George Forster, who also witnessed this scene,
account for cannibalism among the New Zealanders and how did this
custom become almost exclusively associated with the Western Pacific

Melanesians? In his account of the voyage, written with his father's journals, George Forster rejected explanations that cannibalism first developed as a response to scarcity, and argued that the origin of the practice lay in the "strong passion" for revenge. The New Zealanders, "never eat their adversaries, unless they are killed in battle; they never kill relations for the purpose of eating them; they do not even eat them if they die a natural death and they take no prisoners with a view to fatten them for their repast" (1777, 1: 514–18). J. R. Forster's treatment of the subject, in the *Observations*, is the most philosophical and ethnologically developed in the period. He argues that the New Zealanders are of the same racial grouping as the Tahitians, but occupy a lower rung on the ladder of progress. The Tahitians with their physique and their developed government have passed through the childhood state of savagery and are now progressing from the adolescent state of barbarism, as a prelude to attaining the civilization of the Europeans. In terms of diet, the Tahitians are not cannibal; their diet is typified by its reliance on the breadfruit, a freely growing staple food that does not need cultivation. (Fulford, Lee, and Kitson, 2004, 108–26). But they were also carnivores who eat hogs, with their varied diet a sign for Forster of their social complexity.

Forster argues that the Maoris, however, are defined as "bold and intrepid warriors; implacable and cruel enemies, carrying even their thirst of revenge to such a degree of inhumanity, as to feast upon their unfortunate prisoners, the wretched victims to a ferocious and uncultured disposition" (1778, 238). Thus the Maori are cannibals for reasons of revenge, not desire or lust and therefore are reclaimable (as were Montaigne's noble savages, the Tupinamba), whereas the Fijians will be declared to be cannibals because they enjoy eating human flesh and are thus racially inferior. For Forster the key sign of New Zealand savagery is their cannibalism. Human difference is created by the powerful influences of "climate, food, and peculiar customs upon the colour, size habit, and form of the body." The New Zealand diet is not so various as the Tahitian. Forster, and others, report that they "absolutely feed on fish," which is plentiful. This staple of diet "by no means contributes to the increase of numbers in a nation" necessary to the development and progress of a people from animality, savagery, barbarism and civilization. (315). Forster thus refutes the argument that Maori cannibalism is occasioned by a shortage of protein by citing the plentiful supply of fish around the islands. Cannibalism may have been a custom practised by all the South Sea islanders in the past, but which they have now outgrown, apart from in New Zealand. Indeed, Forster argued that cannibalism is one of the steps by which a "debased humanity" is prepared for a better happiness, as it demonstrates a passion and vigor that leads a people away from the indolence of animality (330–32).

Forster's Enlightenment anthropology thus hypothesized a movement to civilization from animality and savagery, whereby progress was determined by climate, mode of living, and diet. All peoples may have been cannibals in the state of savagery and barbarism. His distinction between the Western and Eastern Pacific peoples was couched in the discourse of Enlightenment Universalism, which regarded all humanity as essentially one and the same, made different by processes of degeneration occasioned by climate and environment. This distinction was, however, to ossify into a strict and clear racial dichotomy by the 1830s. Nicholas Thomas has demonstrated how this process occurred, citing, in particular, the accounts of their Pacific voyages by the French explorers Labillardière, Jules-Sébastien-César Dumont D'Urville, and the American Horatio Hale (1997, 139–51).

This nexus of diet, race, and food was seductive for a number of nineteenth-century surgeons, anatomists, and natural philosophers. William Lambe, one of Shelley's physicians, had also pondered the Tahitian diet and its implications for racial classification. Lambe, influenced by Enlightenment anthropologists like Blumenbach and Forster, could find in the Tahitian the ideal kind of physical beauty that was defined in the classical aesthetics of the Medici Venus and the Apollo Belvedere. The Tahitian physical and racial superiority derives, according to Lambe, from their having a diet mainly consisting of vegetarian food. Lambe comments how an inhabitant of Nukuhiva was measured and the measurements later compared with those of the Apollo Belvedere by Blumenbach in Göttingen:

> The latter compared the proportions with the Apollo of Belvedere, and found that those of that master piece of the finest stages of Grecian art, in which is combined every possible integer of manly beauty, corresponded exactly with our Mafau. (Quoted in Morton 1994, 166, 160–68)

Again diet and race are seen as constituent parts in a cultural mindset that brings the Polynesian closer to the European, at the cost of degrading those peoples whose features do not correspond to European neoclassical ideals.

If cannibalism was to come to be associated with Melanesian dark skins, what was to be made of the blatant cannibalism of the Polynesian New Zealanders whose fairer skins precluded them from being classed with their cannibal brethren in the Pacific and elsewhere? Forster had argued that the New Zealander was a Polynesian at an earlier stage of development. Yet to argue this was to bring the dark-skinned and, by the standards of eighteenth-century neoclassicism, ugly Melanesian closer to the European. The missionary John Davies saw them as "a far superior race to the New Hollanders" though "their rude behaviours, furious temper, and horrid customs" differentiated them from the Tahitians who were "vastly their superiors in amiable dispositions sociability and mildness and resemblance of their customs to those of civilized nations" (Davies 31). So as the nineteenth century progressed a process of elision and blaming began: where cannibalism existed, it was due to an importation from Melanesia and not a well-practiced Polynesian custom. Anthropologists of the nineteenth and early twentieth centuries thus had recourse to the "The Great New Zealand Myth" whereby Melanesian people from a "lower plane of culture" had originally settled New Zealand and that cannibalism among the Maori in that area resulted from an earlier contamination with Melanesian peoples, reinforcing the great racial and cultural distinction (Barber 267–68).

RACE CANNIBALISM AND BYRON'S
THE ISLAND (1823)

Although a substantial body of missionary and travel writing about New Zealand existed in the period, it is apparent that poets, novelists and dramatists were attracted to the more Edenic aspects of Polynesian cultures for their subjects. Literary representations of Melanesian peoples are also comparatively few, outside the travel and exploration accounts. When such representations occur, as for instance in Southey's "Botany Bay Eclogues," they are thinly drawn characters in a scarcely imagined topography that serves as a backdrop for the presentation of explicitly European issues. Imaginative writers of the period were captivated by the paradisial themes and the possibilities for excitement and romance. For Anna Seward, Tahiti is "the smiling Eden of the southern wave" (Seward 14) For Helen Maria Williams "Otaheite's isle" is the place "Where Spring...Lives in blossoms ever new" (Williams 147). Male poets, such as the young Coleridge and Byron were keen to stress the sexual freedoms of Tahiti and to figure the island as a place of retreat and escape (Fulford, Lee, and Kitson 108–26). James C. McKusick has convincingly argued for the importance of South Sea narratives as another source of the pantisocratic scheme of Coleridge and Southey, a place where there might be no personal property and no arbitrary government (McKusick 1993, 102–6 and 1998, 107–208).

Coleridge's sympathetic identification with a South Sea islander is shown in his poem "To A Young Lady" where he mourns the death of Lee Boo, the Pellew Prince, who came to England and died of small pox, as told in George Keate's literary account: "My soul amid the pensive twilight / Mourn'd with the breeze, O LEE BOO! o'er thy tomb" (2003, I: 136). In William Lisle Bowles's dramatic monologue "Abba Thule's Lament for His Son Prince Le Boo" of 1794, Abba Thulle is a vehicle for the dignified and touching expression of sensibility: "I linger on the desert rock alone / Heartless, and cry for thee, my son, my son," close in treatment to the forsaken or bereaved parents of *Lyrical Ballads*, such as the Cumbrian shepherd, Michael (Bowles 1: 51). In all these accounts the sympathetic attraction to the South Sea Islander is premised on a racial assumption that the Polynesian is close to the European. Indeed this is a kind of absorption or cannibalizing of the Polynesian by the European, effacing substantial cultural difference. No such effusion of sensibility was possible for the cannibal New Zealander or the darker-skinned Melanesian peoples (Rennie 168–80). This, at best, elision and, at worst, a demonization of the Western Pacific peoples can be argued to be complicit with the anthropological racial project then under way in Oceania.

Byron's fictionalized account of the *Bounty* Mutiny, *The Island* of 1823, provides an example of how this process was reflected in imaginative literature.[6] Heavily influenced by Byron's enthusiasm for John Martin's rendition of William Mariner's *Account of the Tonga Islands* of 1817, the poem sums up the variety of the Southern Pacific in terms of the Polynesian paradise of Toobonai (Tubuai). Byron's Enlightenment anthropological assumptions allow him, in the tradition of Montaigne, to use the native islander as a rebuke to European civilization. In so doing, he attempts to efface the difference between Polynesian and European, presenting such physical differences as having no moral significance, functioning mainly as a spur to desire and passion:

> True, they had vices—such are nature's growth—
> But only the Barbarian's—we have both:
> The sordor of civilization, mixed
> With all the savage which man's fall hath fixed.
> Who hath not seen Dissimulation reign,
> The prayers of Abel linked to deeds of Cain?
> Who such would see, may from his lattice view
> The Old World more degraded than the New.
> (Byron 1980–93, 7: ii: 67–74)

Byron thus constructs a fable of the tensions between Northern Duty and Southern Pleasure. Toobanai and its metonymic dusky maiden, the "soft savage" (1: 32), Neuha, is defined as a place of desire and freedom where mankind has no master "save his mood." It is a place of plenty stocked by "the gushing fruits that Nature gave untilled" and "promiscuous plenty" (1: 33, 35):

> Where all partake the earth without dispute,
> And bread itself is gathered as a fruit;
> Where none contests the fields, the woods, the streams:-
> The Goldless Age, where Gold disturbs no dreams,
> Inhabits or inhabited the shore,
> Till Europe taught them better than before,
> Bestowed her customs, and amended theirs
> But left her vices to their heirs.   (1: 213–20)

Neuha, the "gentle savage of the wild" (1: 123), the "infant of an infant world" (2: 127), indulges in an adolescent romance with Torquil, the Northern Scottish boy, ultimately rescuing him from the retribution of the British naval establishment by hiding him in a womblike hidden cave on an inaccessible island. Neuha is depicted as not racially distinct from the European but as a voluptuous savage whose "wild and warm yet faithful bosom knew / No joy like what it gave" (2: 146–47). Both Neuha and Torquil are offspring of island races, one northern (the Scottish Hebrides), with fair hair and blue eyes, and one southern, with brown eyes. Both are in their own way savages, as Byron breaks down the traditional binary of European civilization and native savagery. Torquil, "the blue-eyed northern child," is "scarce less wild" than Neuha (2: 163–65). The "mutual beauty" of the two lovers unites "the half savage and the whole" (2: 303–4). Fletcher Christian himself is described as "Silent, and sad, and savage" (3: 141). Similarly, the face and limbs of Ben Bunting, Byron's comic tar, are so sunburnt they might "suit alike with either race" (2: 485). It seems that for Byron difference is eroticized and priority is accorded to races on aesthetic and not moral criteria. The Polynesians are closer to us because they may be as beautiful as we ideally could be; they evince a physical perfection and beauty that serves as a reminder of a lost neoclassical ideal. Europeans are thus as savage as Polynesians, but more degraded by their hypocritical, corrupt, and greedy civilized values.

Byron minimizes cultural and physical difference in assimilating Polynesian and European peoples, but that assimilation carries the cost of widening the gap between fair-skinned, European-Polynesian peoples and the dark-skinned, Melanesian peoples who are presented only at the fringes of the poem. Byron's islanders are not cannibals. The fertility of the island "flings off famine from its fertile breast" (2: 264) preventing scarcity. Nor are its inhabitants ritual or lustful cannibals. But cannibalism does exist at the fringes of the poem as an absent presence. The poem's chief source, John Martin, blames the cannibalism that William Mariner actually witnessed on Tonga upon the Fijians (soon to be assimilated into nineteenth-century Melanesia). It was this group that imported the practice. Cannibalism was not a Tongan practice, Martin tells us, it was the "younger chiefs" who indulged, and they "have contracted the Feejee habits." Mariner, apparently, did not partake of this "kind of diet," despite his hunger and despite the fact that the human flesh when cooked "was exceedingly delicious." Martin writes how when Cook had first visited the island, cannibalism was "scarcely thought of amongst them" but "the Feejee people soon taught them this, as well as the art of war; and a famine, which happened some time afterwards, rendered the expedient for a time almost necessary" (1: 115–17). Byron uses this passage in Martin to account for the Toobuaians practice of war but significantly he fails to mention the scandalous issue of cannibalism at all, though the Fijians were by 1823, when the poem was published, famous for the practice:

> we too recall
> The memory bright with many a festival,
> Ere Fiji blew the shell of war, when foes
> For the first time were wafted in canoes.
> Alas! for them the flower of manhood bleeds;
> Alas! for them our fields are rank with weeds:
> . . . . .
> But be it so:—*they* taught us how to wield
> The club, and rain our arrows o'er the field;
> Now let them reap the harvest of their art!   (2: 33–43)

Byron's poem avoids depicting the Polynesian Tongan customs of infanticide, human sacrifice, and cannibalism, which were in his chief source. These would muddy the distinctions he is attempting to make between a corrupt and hypocritical European civilization and the paradise of desire and freedom that drew Christian and his followers to mutiny. Byron's poem glosses over the refractory material of his sources. The result is that, although the Polynesian self is assimilated into the European category on the grounds that both are beautiful and objects of desire, the Fijian or Melanesian cannibal self is alienated further from the European. The cannibalism of Tonga is abjected onto the Fijian.

Another chief commentator on Pacific peoples in the Romantic period was Byron's literary, moral, and political opponent, Robert Southey. Not unsurprisingly, Southey's view of Tahiti and its neighbors is less generous and idealized than Byron's; both writers are nevertheless complicit with a process that produces the same effect. Southey's Protestant imperial comments on Tahiti of 1809 are demonstrated in a series of reviews he wrote for the *Annual Review* and *Quarterly Review* during the first quarter of the nineteenth century. In his review of the *Transactions of the Missionary Society* for the *Quarterly Review*, Southey, ridiculed the earlier Rousseauistic views of noble savagery as mediated to the South Seas by Bougainville and others:

> The philosophists who placed happiness in the indulgence of sensual appetite, and freedom in the absence of legal and moral restraints, were loud in their praise of this "New Cythera"; and even men of healthier intellect and sounder principles, regarded these islanders as singularly favoured by Providence, because their food was produced spontaneously, and they had no other business in their life but to enjoy existence. But now they are better known, it appears indisputably that their iniquities exceed those of other people ancient or modern, civilised or savage; and that human nature has never been exhibited in such utter depravity as by the inhabitants of these terrestrial Paradises!...Crimes not to be named are habitually committed without shame; and as if to show to us what loathsomeness of pollution a depraved imagination will have recourse when palled with ordinary abominations, a society was formed both in Taheite and Eimeo, who in their meetings were to eat human ordure, as the seal and sacrament of their association!...When the Creator decreed that in the sweat of his brow man must eat bread, the punishment became a blessing; a divine ordinance necessary for the health of soul as well as body while man continues to be the imperfect being that we behold him. (Southey 1809, 45)[7]

Southey wants to banish the Polynesian as well as the Melanesian to the ranks of the unregenerate and base. He does this by discoursing upon diet. He moves from the profuse breadfruit which is now a sign of sin, removing the islanders from the Christian imperative to labor, the saving curse of Adam, to the eating of human flesh (in the conventional locution of "Crimes not to be named") to the eating of human excrement. Breadfruit is no longer the sign of Eden but of forbidden fruit and ensuing damnation. So much so that Southey

can commend "Coleridge's scheme to mend" the Tahitians "by extir-
pating the bread-fruit from their island, and making them live by
the sweat of their brows" (1849–50, 2: 243).[8] However, Southey's
lumping together of the Pacific islanders as equally depraved without
the unifying bond of Protestant Christianity in the family of Christ
is less pernicious to the European mind than Byron's Enlightenment
division of Oceania: in Southey's familial scheme all could be saved;
in Byron's only the racially beautiful achieve paradise of a kind. Thus
whether through Byron's inauthentic, imagined paradise, Southey's
Protestant imperial thundering, or Forster's Enlightenment grand
narrative of civilization, false and arbitrary patterns are imposed on
the peoples of the geopolitical area of Oceania. In the process the
cannibal was transformed from the soul of honor, to the adolescent
barbarian, to the degenerate racial other whose very existence can
only point to an unredeemable alterity, the true inhabitant of the
heart of darkness of that "silent sea."

CHAPTER 5

ROMANTIC SINOPOLITANS:
NATURAL PHILOSOPHERS,
TRAVELERS, DIPLOMATS,
AND MISSIONARIES

ORIENTALISM AND THE "FAR EAST"

The two chapters that follow are focused on the European fascination with the Celestial Empire of the Qing dynasty and its charismatic and exotic ruler, Hongli, the Qianlong Emperor. Like the other chapters in the book they take as their theme the grammar of race and the ways in which the language of race thinking entwined with other critical discourses about human difference and apply this to the exoticized Other of the Manchu Empire in the period prior to the nineteenth-century Opium Wars. To some extent I am extending Edward Said's theorization of Orientalism and its stereotyping to take in the Far East which Said mentions only fleetingly in *Orientalism* (1978), [1] but also complicating this hypothesis in the light of the many revisions of Said's ideas. Adrian Hsia has attempted to apply Said's theories of Orientalism directly to China, arguing that European thinkers constructed a notion of China in the seventeenth and eighteenth centuries, before the development of the professional academic discipline of Sinology in the West, which began after the Macartney Embassy of 1793, a key event for my study. Hsia calls this construct "Chinesia," which derives from a process, analogous to Orientalism, which he calls "Sinism" (*Chinesia* 1998, 1–22). Hsia's thesis suffers from the same problems as Said's in that it tends to homogenize, is not sufficiently sensitive to the historical moment of articulation, and is overly polemical. Like Nigel Leask, for instance, I do not see Orientalism as the "closed system" described by Said, though I do accept some equation between the material processes of colonialism and commerce (both formal and informal) and the knowledge that was produced about other cultures in the period (Leask 1992, 2) and with Srinivas Aravamudan I see representations more as figurations that may "transgress their prescribed function and reanimate cultural discourses in response to different contexts and intentions" rather than approximating to Said's rather fixed and homogenizing binaries. Chinese, Manchus, Tartars, and Mongols, like "tropicopolitans" are also "troublesome tropes" that may serve consciously or unconsciously to "interrupt the monologue of nationalist literary history," reinforcing the notions of "Orientalisms" as a plural rather than a singular category (Aravamudan 12, 1–25).

Many writers and commentators of the period were fully aware of the multiple political and religious purposes to which discussion and representation of the Qing dynasty were dragooned and were capable of unmasking and decoding the assumptions which underlay such discourse, both imaginative and descriptive. It was also quite possible for those writing about China to oppose the major trends of colonialism and racism, though inevitably such resistance is time bound within parameters. To Aravamudan's formulation of "tropicopolitans" and "Levantinization," I would like to add the term "Sinopolitan," a term antithetical to "metropolitan" or "cosmopolitan" to employ in the context of China. If the Qing Empire is defined as an "other" that serves to confirm a Western self, or in Saree Makdisi's terms a refuge from and potential alternative to modernity, antithetical to the modernizing and technological project of European imperialism, it is one which in the Romantic period, at least, is plural and conflicted (Makdisi 1–22).

In some ways the year 1793, much fetishized by historians and historicists as the year which begins the French Revolutionary Terror, assumes a different though equally crucial significance in global history. This was the year that Lord George Macartney's diplomatic mission from Britain arrived in China and attempted to establish modern diplomatic relations between the two of the most powerful empires of the eighteenth century. For the diplomatic historian, Alain Peyrefitte, "Macartney's expedition was a kind of hinge in the history of relations between the West and the Far East, simultaneously a point of culmination and departure. It brought a century of diplomatic and commercial initiatives to a close and stimulated a re-fashioning of China's image in the West" (398) Peyrefitte views the encounter between East and West as the clash of two civilizations too inflexible to accommodate each other's worldviews. In this reading, the Qing Empire is inevitably doomed by its failure to engage with the Europeans, rather in the mode of the trope of the "fatal impact" of the Oceanic colonial encounter. Nevertheless, most commentators on this subject have also noticed this paradigmatic shift in Western perspectives, as Raymond Dawson succinctly sums up:

> [T]he beginning of the nineteenth century saw a striking change in the European attitude towards China. The enthusiasm of the previous century gave way to contempt. There was no sudden general change of attitude: praise was certainly not universal before 1800, nor was contempt universal afterwards... But it was certainly about this time that the tide of China's popularity in Europe began to run out. (132)[2]

Similarly Jonathan D. Spence comments on the "abyss" that opens "between China and the visitors that made a genuine meeting of the minds problematic" (1999, 61) and David Porter notices the move from "reverential awe" to "increasingly dismissive contempt." Porter argues that what underlay Western responses to China was "an implicit model of legitimacy" in religion and language that China appeared to validate in the seventeenth and early eighteenth centuries before a classicist backlash rendered its culture increasingly unintelligible and illegitimate. China was seen in the late seventeenth and early eighteenth centuries as "a uniquely privileged site not only of genealogical but also of what one might term representational legitimacy, a place, that is, where the myriad signs and symbols that constitute culture were reliably grounded in a fixed, originary source of meaning and therefore not subject to the corrupting vicissitudes of common language and history" (9, 3–12). In economic terms it was the Imperial Court's refusal to speak the universalized and naturalized languages of Western laissez faire commerce and international diplomacy that further led to the marginalizing of China, but other factors, such as the development of the racial sciences and the advent of radical evangelizing Protestant missionaries to the Far East played their part in this wholesale European degradation of the Qing Empire as the nineteenth century progressed. This chapter seeks to outline the contribution of late eighteenth-century and Romantic thought to this process, particularly as regards the growing racialization implicit in this process.

WESTERN IMAGES OF CHINA
IN THE EIGHTEENTH CENTURY

For their view of the Qing Empire and the Far East in general, those in the Romantic period had a substantial archive describing the Celestial Empire to draw upon but very few contemporary accounts. Western images of the countries and peoples we know as China were depicted in a generally favorable light in writing from the thirteenth to the seventeenth century. The first great wave of the study of China began with the Jesuit missionaries to China. Matteo Ricci arrived in Beijing in 1601 and others followed in his wake, marking a real presence in the capital until the death of Joseph-Marie Amiot in 1793. By and large the Jesuits were concerned to minimize differences between Europeans and Chinese in an attempt to effect the conversion of the ruling elite of the Ming Empire and then, after 1644, its successor the Qing. They argued that Confucian teachings were generally in harmony with those of Catholicism and came to adopt the dress and manners of the Chinese mandarins and scholars. The Jesuit strategy was to convert the upper echelons of the Chinese court, a strategy that came close to success when the young and first Qing Emperor of China, Shunzhi, developed a very close relationship with Father Johan Adam Schall von Bell (Mungello 44–72; Spence 1990, 42–44; Brockey 126–29). Ultimately the Jesuits were unsuccessful in converting the Chinese to Christianity, but they were brilliantly successful in interpreting China to the West. In the eighteenth century the Jesuit missionaries were mainly of French origin, and they represented the Qing as a polity analogous to that of the absolutist French monarchy of the "Sun King," Louis XIV.

The voluminous writings of the Jesuit missionaries formed two especially important archives, the first is the twenty-five-volume series *Lettres édifiantes et curieuses* (1701–76) and the second the seventeen-volume *Mémoires concernant...des chinois* (1776–1814). The Jesuits were extremely impressed by the early Manchu emperors and presented Europe with an extremely flattering picture of the Celestial Empire that became the basis of the eighteenth-century appreciation of China. The most significant of their writings is Jean-Baptiste Du Halde's *The General History of China* (1735; translated into English in 1736).[3] Du Halde, who never visited China, edited volumes IX to XXVI of the *Lettres édifiantes et curieuses* and they are his main source. The *History* is the largest and most comprehensive single product of Jesuit scholarship on China that became the main source of information for writers such as Montesquieu,

Rousseau, Voltaire, Hume, and Goldsmith (Marshall and Williams 84). Anthologies of Jesuit writings about China, also appeared in collections such as Thomas Percy's *Miscellaneous Pieces Relating to the Chinese* (1762), which both Southey and Coleridge knew.

Du Halde compared China favorably to the West as "one of the most fruitful countries in the world, as well as the largest and most beautiful kingdome yet known" and its peoples "powerful, politick, well vers'd in Art, and skilful in the Sciences" (1: 2). He finds the Chinese to be "mild and peaceable in the commerce of life," though they can be "violent and vindictive" when offended (1: 130). He is impressed by the "natural charms," modesty, and demeanor of the Chinese women and is not even perturbed by what he calls the "odd Custom" of foot binding, which will later become such a contentious issue for the West. The present emperor, Qianlong, believed to be sympathetic to the missionaries, is a reforming and enlightened despot, "steady and resolute, ready to hear grievances and to redress them," holding the government entirely in his hands, and "there never was a more absolute Monarch, or more to be dreaded" (1: 502). Qianlong applies his thoughts "night and day to the reforming of Errors in his government, and to procure the happiness of his Subjects" (1: 504). He commands an "absolute Authority, and Respect which is paid to him in a kind of Adoration: his words are so many Oracles, and his commands are swiftly and readily executed as if they came directly from Heaven" (212). Du Halde's *History* does not contain any sustained physical description of the Chinese or their Manchu rulers but he does mention several characteristics. He tells us that the Chinese are "naturally effeminate" unlike their Tartar masters. They esteem education and men of letters and there is "no nation in the World more laborious and temperate than this" (1: 123), although in their "private Interest" they are "naturally revengeful" and "honesty is not their favourite virtue" (132). They are also ingenious workmen, architects, and artificers. In general he tells us, "The Chinese…are mild, tractable, and humane; there is a great deal of Affability in their Aire and Manner, and nothing harsh, rough or passionate" (1: 128). Du Halde comments that the complexion of the peasants in Southern China is "olive brown," but in the cooler provinces "they are naturally as white as the *Europeans,* and, generally, their Physiognomy has nothing disagreeable" (1: 138). In contrast to later descriptions, Du Halde says little about the physical features of the Chinese in any detail, although he devotes many pages to their dress, fashion and garments, and customs. Ultimately he tends, in the spirit of the Jesuit program, to idealize and Europeanize the empire, effacing signs of difference where they would become too awkward. This is an eminently, literate, civilized, and well-governed empire.

The Jesuit version of China was very attractive to a number of thinkers, ironically the anticlerical Voltaire and the philosophes found in the Jesuit version of the Qing Empire a shining example of an enlightened despotism devoted to the public weal, governed by civil servants who obtained their posts through competitive examination and by merit, not through the hereditary principle, and with no established religion. It was a polity governed on the principles of Confucian rationalism and not Christian dogma. Leibniz was heavily impressed and advocated cultural exchanges with the West. Voltaire, in his early works, denied that the empire was a despotism at all and praised its lack of religion and priestly quarrels. It was a government in which men ruled themselves and mankind was ruled by reason, with no church or religion. In his *Philosophical Dictionary* (1764) Voltaire discoursed on European desire for Chinese products and technology, which he contrasted with the West's desire to convert the people. The Chinese constitution is the "best in the world, the only one based entirely on paternal authority...the only one that has established prizes for virtue." Four thousand years ago, when Europeans could not read, the "the Chinese knew all the indispensably useful things of which we boast today. Their religion is admirable, no superstition, no absurd legends, none of those dogmas that insult reason and nature" (1972, 114–15). The physiocrat Quesnay took China as his model when describing the most economically productive agricultural system. Adam Smith too praised China for its agricultural system, though he was severely critical of its refusal to engage with foreign trade (Spence 1999, 81–100).

JESUITS, DIPLOMATS AND TRAVELERS

Throughout the eighteenth century, China benefited from what I have denominated an Enlightened Cosmopolitan Universalism. The nation was seen to be rich in wealth, agricultural produce, and had a developed and sophisticated culture, the products of which were much prized by the West. There were, of course, actual encounters between Europeans and the Chinese Empire. During the seventeenth and eighteenth centuries several embassies journeyed to Beijing, mainly Russian, Portuguese, and Dutch. Accounts of these embassies were translated and published in Britain or in various collections of voyages. One of the most influential of these accounts was written by the Scottish doctor, John Bell who served with the Russian Court and was a member of the Izmailov Embassy sent by Peter the Great to the elderly Emperor Kangxi (1662–1772) in 1719–20. Bell's account was written nearly forty years after this and published in 1763. His narrative is also written in the mode of Enlightenment cosmopolitanism and marks what Jonathan Spence calls "a decisive shift away from the once-dominant tradition of writing about China from a Catholic standpoint" (1999, 45–51). In Bell's *Journal* there is much less stress on the religious beliefs of the Chinese and their compatibility or otherwise with Catholic doctrine, which had obsessed the Jesuit missionaries in Beijing. Bell is more interested in the manners and customs of the empire and the tone of his account is empirical, objective, humane, and skeptical. His descriptions of what he witnesses are detailed, precise, and overwhelmingly positive. Bell finds that the "characteristic of the court of Pekin is order and decency, rather than grandeur and magnificence" (125). The soldiers do "not behave with roughness to the people, as in some places of the east" but treat them with "great mildness and humanity" (127). The Emperor Kangxi is a philosopher-king, "a great lover of the arts" who discourses affably and eloquently "on various subjects in the style of a philosopher" (138) and on the "vanity and uncertainty of all human affairs" (145). Bell tells us that "his countenance is open, his disposition generous, and he gives great application to business" and that "his reign has been long and prosperous" (179). Kangxi is a broadly tolerant ruler allowing the "free exercise" of religion and the support of missionaries. Above all he is cheerful and surprisingly familiar, capable of sharing jokes with Bell and the ambassador. The Chinese are a "sober and industrious" people despite the wealth of their country. In his general remarks on the Chinese, Bell praises the arts of this

> civilised and hospitable people; complaisant to strangers, and to one another; very regular in their manners and behaviour, and respectful to their superiors; but, above all, their regard for their parents, and decent treatment of their women of all ranks, ought to be imitated, and deserve great praise. These good qualities are a natural consequence of the sobriety, and the uniformity of life, to which they are long accustomed. (182)

Bell briefly discusses the issue of the "shocking and unnatural practice" of infanticide but claims that only the poor adopt it, and that there are "publick hospitals" for those abandoned infants the authorities find. The issue of female foot binding is glossed over quickly;

Bell comments that the confinement of Chinese ladies of distinction is made less disagreeable by "the smallness of their feet," which "renders them unable to walk to any considerable distance" (184). Bell clearly shares in the Sinophilia of eighteenth-century Enlightenment thought. He is himself, a cosmopolitan, a citizen of the world far more traveled than most and in his account cosmopolitanism as a way of life finds little that is uncomfortable in China.

By the 1790s, however, views on China were beginning to polarize and Du Halde's Jesuit appreciation and Bell's Enlightenment toleration were beginning to look increasingly outmoded. The anonymous English translator of the Jesuit, Jean-Baptiste Grosier's *General Description of China* (1788) comments on the rather paradoxical situation:

> But though it might have been expected that, from so great a variety of authors who have written concerning China, sufficient lights would have been acquired, to enable the Europeans to form a just notion of the manners, character, and disposition of the Chinese; yet the learned seem to differ widely in their ideas respecting them. By some they have been extolled as the wisest and most enlightened of mankind; while others, perhaps equally, if more remote from the truth, have exhibited them in the most contemptible point of view, and represented them as despicable people, deceitful, ignorant, and superstitious, and destitute of every principle of humanity and justice. (1: iv)

Grosier's *History* represents the last gasp of the Jesuit idealization of China and the classic statement of that influential and, by no means abandoned, view for the Romantic period. Viewing itself as a supplement to Du Halde's *History*, rather than a new appreciation, Grosier's *History* sets out as "the champion of an injured people" (1: v). The Chinese, Grosier argues, "are a mild and affable people; polite even to excess." The nation must be considered as "an ancient monument, respectable by its duration; admirable in some of its parts, defective in others; the immutable stability of which has, however, been attested by a duration of some four thousand years," held together by "that progressive submission, which rises gradually from the bosom of a family, even to the throne" (2: 372). For Grosier, "No potentate on earth possesses so unlimited power as the sovereign of this numerous nation" which he employs to provide for the safety and happiness of his subjects (2:1): "The Chinese consider their monarchy as a large family, of which the emperor, whom ought to govern with parental affection, is the head" (2: 4). China is a model patriarchal government, espousing the ideals of "filial piety"

(2: 23), admirably administrated by the Qianlong Emperor and his loyal mandarins and honored and esteemed literati. Infanticide, while occurring, is "much less frequent than has been reported in Europe" and derives almost entirely from the pressures of population and then "only in certain cantons...where the people blinded by idolatry, are the dupes of prejudice, fanaticism and superstition" (2: 125–26). Similarly the practice of female foot binding is minimized as merely one "of those whimsical customs from which no nation is exempt" (2: 299).

David Porter has argued that the prestige of the Chinese in the seventeenth and eighteenth centuries depended on the notion that their culture was more authentic than that of the rest, because it was ancient and continuous. In particular, it was argued, most famously by John Wilkins, John Webb, and Leibnitz, that the Chinese language was an ideographic language conveying meaning without reference to sound and potentially universal if one held the key to decipher it (Porter 15–71; De Francis 131–60; Mungello 174–244). Grosier's *Description* is a late example of this assessment of Chinese culture in the lead up to the French Revolution. He accepts the Jesuit view that the first Chinese are in some ways closer to the original dispensation of knowledge than Europeans, that they were the "immediate descendants of Noah" and possessed of the Patriarch's "whole treasure of antediluvian knowledge," which is enshrined in their religion and customs. As an ancient polity, they are closer to "the more distinct and sensible...traces" of "the true worship" rather than more distant from it. The Chinese thus have preserved a notion of the "Supreme Being, the creator and preserver of all things" (2: 162). They also have a conception of "the Most Holy Trinity" (2: 176). Grosier's admiration for the ancient and Confucian beliefs of the Chinese is countered by his contempt for the more recent religious innovations of Taoism and Buddhism and the activities of its priests and monks, the Bonzes. As Porter has argued, the Jesuits had a clear interest in denigrating other, rival beliefs in the empire, though they assimilated ancient Chinese with Catholic beliefs, which were seen as authentically Christian. Their language "is not only one of the most ancient in the universe" but possibly "the only language of the early ages which is still living and spoken" (2: 376).

Grosier's summary of the Jesuit assessment of China, and John Bell's more secularized Enlightenment admiration probably summed up the consensus view of China prevalent in this period. There were certainly opponents of this view. Earlier in the century, Defoe's *Farther*

Adventures of Robinson Crusoe (1719) had painted an unflattering portrait of the Chinese:

> What are their Buildings to the Palaces and Royal Buildings of Europe? What their trade to the universal commerce of *England, Holland, France* and *Spain*? What are their Cities to ours for Wealth, Strength, Gaiety of Apparel, rich Furniture, and an infinite Variety? What are their Ports, supplied with a few Jonks and Barks, to our Navigation, our Merchant Fleets, our large and powerful Navys? One *English*, or *Dutch*, or *French* Man of War of 80 Guns, would fight and destroy all the Shipping of China. (152)

What Defoe found most irritating about the Chinese was their contempt for all the nations in the world except their own. In Defoe we begin to hear the voice of the Protestant, dissenting capitalist espousing the alleged superiority of his nation's products and who was aware of the military potential of his expansionist nation, which would come to dominate in the early nineteenth century. Although hardly sharing the same background as that of Defoe, Commodore George Anson who visited China in 1743 during his remarkable and profitable circumnavigation of the world, shared Defoe's sense of the superiority of his nation to that of the Chinese. The entry of Anson's battered flagship HMS *Centurion* into Canton's harbor with the captured Spanish prize galleon was bound to upset the Chinese authorities even before Anson determined that as a man-of-war, his ship should pay no duties. Anson's narrative of 1748, written up from his journals and papers, by Richard Walter and Benjamin Robbins, turns a representational corner in Jonathan Spence's view (Spence 1999, 51–56) by portraying the Chinese as speaking a form of pidgin English and presenting them as crafty, greedy, treacherous, and cowardly people, whose reputation for ingenuity, civilization and learning has been vastly exaggerated by Jesuit missionaries for reasons of their own (Anson 351, 355, 359). Anson's naval mind regards Chinese military defenses and armaments with derision and contempt. He identifies "the effeminate genius of the nation" that allowed itself to be conquered by "an handful of *Tartars*" (326, 369). Anson allows the Chinese to be "very ingenious and industrious" but affirms their inferiority to the "mechanic dexterity of the Europeans" and sees their main talent to be that of imitation "and they accordingly labour under the poverty of genius, which constantly attends all servile imitators" (366–67). Further Anson blames much of the absurdity of their culture on their language, the "rude and inartificial method of representing words by arbitrary marks," which leads to "infinite obscurity and confusion" rendering their written works simply "unintelligible" (367–68).

Anson's remarks were no doubt occasioned in part by his extreme ignorance coupled with the frustrations of his awkward diplomatic position; nevertheless in his discussion and representation of Chinese manners and peoples we can see an anticipation of the later, more bellicose readings of the Celestial Empire. Anson's account of his voyage was extremely popular and was read by Lord Macartney, Montesquieu, and Herder. Possibly Anson's reflections influenced Montesquieu's judgment of China in *L'esprit des lois* as an Oriental despotism resulting from a hot climate. Its people were weak and cowardly, necessitating a government based on fear (126–28, 278–81, 313–43, 318–21). The geographer and natural philosopher Cornelius de Pauw refuted the claims of Chinese civilization, which he regarded as Jesuit idolization of authority. De Pauw was advocate of Buffon's theories of degeneration, which he most enthusiastically applied to the detriment of North American Indians and white settlers as well as to the Chinese. Stressing the Chinese practices of slavery, infanticide, torture, and female foot binding, De Pauw characterized the Qing Empire as the worst Asiatic despotism on earth: "The two chief springs of the government are the whip and the cudgel" (2: 292). The Chinese were not the inheritors of Mosaic wisdom, as the Jesuits and others might have it, but a "people of Scythian or Tartar origin, because it requires no extraordinary penetration to perceive, that they possess at this day a remarkable resemblance to the ancient Scythians" (1: xix). In De Pauw we see the race idea emerging into the mainstream comment about China to the denigration of its people. The Chinese were, according to De Pauw, entirely deficient in science, needed the Jesuits to correct their calendars, and had no talent in architecture, art, or literature. Their language made the transmission of thought and ideas impossible and was a barrier to learning and development: "The pride of the Chinese proceeds from their ignorance and their servitude: for other nations of Asia, not more free, are no less puffed up with ideas of their own consequence" (2: 318). Such views as those of De Pauw, were reinforced by Constantin Volney's radical Enlightenment description of the Chinese Empire in the early years of the Revolution as "an insolent despotism...held in awe by strokes of the bamboo, enslaved by the immutability of their code, and by the irremediable vice of their language." For Volney they were "an abortive civilization and a race of automata" glorified by a Jesuit love for hierarchy (119, 341).

CHINA AND THE RACE IDEA

In Defoe, Anson, and others we see the growth of an expansionist Protestant and colonial view of the world, but one that is not racialized in a biological sense. Rather it relates more obviously to the processes that Linda Colley, Roxann Wheeler, Kathleen Wilson, and others have outlined whereby Britishness was defined in terms of a Protestant anti-Catholicism stressing manliness, straightforwardness, plain dealing and honesty in transactions between peoples and nations. Debunking the Jesuit apotheosis of China was something which Protestant commentators were keen to accomplish and to do this, the Qing Empire also had to be degraded along the way. This was, however, not a debate about race, but about politics and religion. Nevertheless we can see how this way of regarding other cultures became increasingly racialized as the eighteenth century progressed. In terms of the grammar of race, the Chinese and other Eastern peoples became increasingly estranged and homogenized. For Linnaeus in the tenth edition of *Systema naturae* (1758), Asian peoples were summed up under the variety "asiaticus" and described as "yellow," "melancholic," and "inflexible" (Eze, *Race and Enlightenment* (1997, 13–14). In chapter 1, I showed how Linnaeus associates physical with moral attributes; the yellow skin of the Asiatic thus denotes melancholia and inflexibility. If not the very earliest reference to the Chinese as "yellow" it is certainly one of the most influential. To describe the Chinese as yellow is, of course, an extraordinary thing to do. Thomas Pirès, the first Portuguese ambassador to the Ming court commented that "[t]he people of China are white, as white as we are" (quoted in Hsia, *Chinesia* 1998, 14). Matthew Ricci commented that the "Chinese people are almost white, though some of them in the southern provinces are quite dark because of their proximity to the torrid zone" (77). François Bernier in 1684 grouped the Chinese with numerous other peoples as a "species of mankind" describing them as "truly white" but having "broad shoulders, a flat face, a small squab nose, little pig's eyes long and deep set, and three hairs of beard" (2–3). This alleged and problematic yellowness attributed to the Chinese, as well as some Caribbean Indians, in racialized discourse would become one of the most notorious nineteenth- and twentieth-century racial markers of difference between European and Asiatic.

Voltaire, despite his Sinophilia, argued following Peyrére's *Prae-Adamitae* (1655), that humanity was composed of separate species, rather than varieties including "the long-maned yellow races and beardless men" (Voltaire 1989, 423). Buffon classified all Asian people under the heading "Tartar." For him the action of the climate renders the Tartars "tawny," the Chinese, who are of the "Tartar" variety of humanity, are "fairer than the Tartars, though they resemble them in every feature," because they are more civilized and living in towns and cities, are less exposed to the darkening effects of the "sun and air" (Eze, *Race and Enlightenment* 1997, 26). His scheme was popularized by Oliver Goldsmith's *History of the Earth and Animated Nature* (1774), which is typical of the growing tendency to discuss human variety in terms of skin color. "[T]he chief differences in men," Goldsmith writes, "are rather taken from the tincture of his skin than the variety of his figure" (212). Following Buffon, Goldsmith groups the Chinese, Japanese, and Tartar peoples together in a homogenizing and racializing process. He associates the Chinese with the Japanese even though their "manners and customs differ...the Chinese have broad faces, small eyes, flat noses, and scarce any beard; that they are broad and square shouldered and rather less in stature than Europeans." Like the Tartars they have "olive coloured" complexions. Both peoples owe their civilization to "the mildness of the climate in which they reside" (223). Cornelius de Pauw, similarly, identified the Chinese and Tartar peoples with the Scythians as described by Herodotus.

With the creation of an authentically racialist discourse of biological essentialism, "yellowness" becomes firmly associated with the Chinese. In Kant's view, the Chinese, rather than being one of the four primary races, are a mixed race occurring with the crossing of the "Hun race (Mongol or Kalmuck)" and the "Hindu or Hindustani race." Kant, in his essay "On the Different Human Races" ascribes the color "olive-yellow" to the "Asian Indians" but not to the Chinese (11). It is Blumenbach, the most influential of all eighteenth-century writers on the natural variety of mankind, who fixes this association more than most. Like Goldsmith, Blumenbach grouped the Chinese and Japanese peoples with the Tartar people under the heading Mongolian. He describes the physical characteristics of this group as "Colour yellow; hair black, stiff, straight and scanty; head almost square; face broad, at the same time flat and depressed...nose small, apish; cheeks usually globular, prominent outwardly; the opening of the eyelids narrow; linear; chin slightly prominent" (201). Blumenbach argued that white is the primary skin color and the next gradation is "the yellow, olive-tinge, a sort of colour half-way between the grains of wheat and cooked oranges, or the dry desiccated rind of lemons," which is "usual in the Mongolian nations" (143). Blumenbach, by and large, avoids attributing moral characteristics to his principal varieties, although he is keen to claim an aesthetic hierarchy for the white races. His followers would not be so reticent.

Even those theorists of human development, such as Sir William Jones, who avoided physical anthropology, also took part in this racial degradation of the Chinese. Jones argues that rather than being of Tartar or Mongolian stock, the Chinese derived their origin and their culture and civilization from the Indo-Aryan primary race of men:

> All the circumstances, which have been mentioned under the two heads of *literature* and *religion*, seem collectively to prove (as far as such a question admits proof) that the *Chinese* and *Hindus* were originally the same people, but having been separated near four thousand years, have retained few strong features of their ancient consanguinity, especially as the *Hindus* have preserved their old language and ritual, while the *Chinese* very soon lost both, and the *Hindus* have constantly intermarried among themselves, while the *Chinese*, by a mixture of *Tartarian* blood from the time of their first establishment, have at length formed a race distinct in appearance both from *Indians* and *Tartars*. ("On China" 1807, 108)[4]

According to Jones, the Chinese are descendants of the Hindus who have lost their ancient culture and beliefs. Their language is composed of "merely the symbols of ideas," their religion is "imported from *India* in an age comparatively modern," and their philosophy is "yet in so rude a state, as hardly to deserve the appellation." The Chinese have "no *ancient monuments*, from which their origin can be traced even by plausible conjecture": in short they have accomplished "nothing, which any set of men, in a country so highly favoured by nature, might not have discovered and improved" (101). Jones is keen to contradict the argument of the French Orientalist, Joseph De Guignes that the Chinese are descendants of the Egyptians. His denigration of Chinese civilization in favor of Hindu is a variation of the process that Martin Bernal has identified as part of the eighteenth-century privileging of the Hellenic and Aryan origins of Western civilization at the expense of other cultures, in this case Chinese.

With the increasing tendency to classify human variety, human beings were divided into fixed and distinctive groupings. There was thus a tendency to attribute certain aesthetic and moral qualities to particular types and a hierarchy of physical and moral types was created with the European at the top, the original, primary, most beautiful type and the Chinese as somewhere between the European and the Kalmuck. Mongolian or Tartar, in Blumenbach's terms was as far away from the primary European race as the Negro. Cuvier, anxious to retain a lineage for humanity that corresponded with the Christian story of Noah's three sons, divided humanity into three great races, the Caucasian, the Negro, and the Mongolian. The Mongolian is known "by his high cheek bones, flat visage, narrow and oblique eyes, straight black hair, scanty beard and olive complexion." Cuvier allows that "[g]reat empires have been established by this race in China and Japan" but "its civilization has always remained stationary" (1834, 40). William Lawrence similarly emphasized somatic aspects of Asian peoples, especially their complexion. Finding more evocative ways of calibrating the yellowness of the Mongolians and Tartar complexion, Lawrence described it as "Yellow or olive...a middle tint, between that of ripe wheat and boiled quince or dried lemon peel" (1823, 249) and claimed that although the race was "susceptible to civilization," as demonstrated by the empires of China and Japan, and "of great advancement in the useful and elegant arts of life," the "fact of their having continued nearly stationary for so many centuries, marks an inferiority of nature, and a limited capacity, in comparison to that of the white races" (415). In Lawrence, once again, we taste the bitter flavors of a nascent biological racism. White, not black nor yellow is synonymous with civilization, liberty, democracy, and progress: "[In] the white races we meet, in full perfection, with true bravery, love of liberty, and other passions and virtues of great soul," and it is the "white nations alone have enjoyed free governments...institutions recognizing the equality of all in political rights." For Lawrence the "superiority of the whites is universally felt and readily acknowledged by the other races" (414–15, 420). Less vehement than Lawrence, James Cowles Prichard also grouped the Chinese with the Koreans and Japanese as part of the Mongolian group, describing the countenance of the group as varying from "a tawny white, to a swarthy, or dusky yellow or copper colour" (1973, 545).

Certainly as the nineteenth century wore on, the Asiatic got yellowier, crueler, his or her nervous system less susceptible to pain, less trustworthy, and less European. By 1850, in the writings of the Edinburgh anatomist, Robert Knox, human difference is explicitly defined in terms of white Anglo-Saxon superiority and the Chinese thoroughly discredited: "China appears to have been completely stationary; she neither invented nor discovered; their arts must have belonged to some other race...their religion is a puzzle; their morals of the lowest; of science they can have none, nor is it clear they comprehend the meaning of the term" (188). Knox predicts that "Samartian or Saxon, the Celestial Empire must one day become, and its sister of Japan must one day become . . . it will belong to the Anglo-Saxon population of Australia" (186). It is a small distance from his work to that of Arthur de Gobineau who, in his *Essay on the Inequality of Human Races* (1853–55) argued that there were three original and pure races: white, black, and yellow. The crossing of the blood could only lead to the loss of racial purity and the races are unequal in their capacities, with the White race having superiority (146).

The main current of scientific writing about race prior to Darwin tends to homogenize and fix race as a permanent type. In 1851, the American natural historian Charles Hamilton Smith identified as one of the permanent races, the "Beardless Hyperborean" or "Mongolic type," which included the Chinese as "olivaceous in color, the skin varying from a kind of sallow lemon peel, through various shades of greater depth" (285). This process is exemplified by Josiah Nott and George Gliddon's materialist and polygenist account of race. In their schema the Chinese are included under the "Mongolian" "Type" with the "Malay, Polynesian and the American" (80–81). This process of racialization and the fixing of the Asian's complexion as yellow and his or her physical and moral traits was contemporary with the decline in Chinese power and China's domination by the European powers. Certainly from the 1820s or so onward, it became increasingly common for naturalists to write not just about the white and black races, but also the yellow and red races as well with color becoming one of the indelible markers of a permanent racial type. With Gobineau we are, of course, close to the final demonization of the Asiatic peoples in the guise of the notorious "Yellow Peril," the term coined by Kaiser Wilhelm II of Germany in his fear of Eastern power and invasion, and popularized in romances such as M.P. Shiel's *The Yellow Danger* (1900) and Sax Rohmer's *The Insidious Dr Fu Manchu* (1913), featuring their charismatic and atavistically cruel protagonists, Dr. Yen How and Dr. Fu Manchu.

CHINA, RACE, AND THE MACARTNEY EMBASSY

In the eighteenth-century, China was the most admired and powerful of the empires of Southeast Asia. She was ruled from 1644 to 1912 by the Qing dynasty of Manchu emperors. Her successes in the eighteenth century were spectacular.[5] By the end of the nineteenth century, however, China was derided abroad as pathetic and her government seen as woefully inadequate to the needs of its time.

Under the Manchu Taiwan, Central Asia, Mongolia, and Tibet were annexed to China to form a single polity governed by a long-standing *Pax Manjurica*. Hongli, the Qianlong Emperor, reigned from 1736 to 1795, and was an extremely capable and assiduous ruler who by the end of his reign had enjoyed sixty years of military and imperial success. He added approximately 6,000 square miles to the empire. He was also an extravagant and autocratic ruler, a great builder, and patron of the arts. By the late eighteenth century, the Qing Empire was, in the words of James L. Hevia, "the largest, wealthiest, and most populous contiguous entity in the world" (1995, 31). It was one of the largest and most powerful land-based empires of the early modern period, ruling central Eurasia along with the Romanov, Ottoman, and Mogul Empires, a formidable military and cultural presence. Nevertheless there were tensions and problems within the empire, as F.W. Mote comments, "For the Manchu Qing imperial dynasty and for the Chinese people, this reign can be seen as both the culmination of dynastic greatness and as the fore runner of an era of deep troubles" (912).

Rather than being at the margins of the world economy it was, according to André Gunder Frank, with India, the core of a single "global world economy with a worldwide division of labor and multilateral trade from 1500 onward" to around 1800 (52). In Frank's analysis it was the European desire for Asian products that created an expanding world trade whose net balance was very much in Asia's favor and that, rather than being a static or stagnant polity, the Chinese Empire was as economically dynamic as those of the European states, at least until around the end of the eighteenth century.[6] For almost a century the merchants of the British East India Company had regularly traded with the Chinese at the port of Canton, the only part of the empire where trade with Europeans was permitted. All dealings were through a body of Chinese merchants known as the "the Co-hong." The British desired many Chinese products—silk, porcelain, laquerware, and other luxury items—but most of all and most avidly, the newly fashionable beverage of tea, the consumption of which grew exponentially in the eighteenth and early nineteenth centuries. Total imports of tea grew from 50 tons in 1700 to around 15,000 tons by 1800.[7] The Chinese did not desire Western commodities in return, so their tea and silk exports had to be paid in silver bullion, necessitating a cash crisis in the British East India Company, which held a monopoly of trade with the Chinese.[8] The Qing Empire was not, as the British would often proclaim, hostile to trade or ignorant of developments in the wider world, but it considered "unrestricted foreign contact...a potential threat to national security" (Waley-Cohen 181).

After an earlier attempt was aborted in 1788, the British government sent an embassy of diplomats under Lord Macartney in 1792 to establish diplomatic relations with China. Their formal aim was to arrange the setting up of embassies in both nations' capitals as well as to facilitate trade between Britain and China, by a variety of measures privileging British merchants over their European competitors, and involving the removal of trading handicaps at Canton. The embassy was conducted on the principles of European notions of international diplomacy and of the free trade between nations, both ideas that its originators assumed to be universal. As much a voyage of discovery as a diplomatic mission, the embassy included, at Macartney's insistence, an artist and botanist, rather like those of Cook's three voyages to the Pacific. The government was advised by Sir Joseph Banks who was interested in the potential for growing tea in India as an alternative to importing it from China. Indeed, part of the expedition's brief was to engage in industrial espionage and filch Chinese expertise, skills and products, such as tea and the mulberry worm, for transplanting elsewhere in the British colonies. The expedition was also ideologically underpinned by the Enlightenment comparativist outlook found in the accounts of Cook, Banks, and J. R. Forster about the South Seas, as Macartney somewhat airily put it, "The composition of mankind, in all countries, is a mixture of the same materials, though blended in different proportions" (Macartney 227).

The Chinese response to this embassy has been much debated in Sino-British and American historiography. The established view of British historians and Sinologists has been, by and large, that the Chinese officially regarded the embassy as a foreign tribute by barbarians to the only civilized nation on earth. The empire's Confucian orthodoxy argued that the emperor's conduct would attract the attention and admiration of the barbarians who would come to pay homage. Again British historiography has stressed, perhaps fetishized, the significance of the rite of the koutou (kowtow), the ritual prostration of foreign tribute bearers from vassal nations before the emperor. This ceremony involved three genuflections, accompanied by three acts of prostration, the forehead touching the ground nine times in all. In 1793 at the emperor's summer palace at Rehe or Jehol (Chengde) on the boundary between the North China Plain and the Mongolian Steppe, Lord Macartney formally paid his sovereign's respects to Hongli. The accounts of the embassy provide the now familiar narrative of how Macartney found

the ceremony of the koutou impossible.[9] Instead, after a lengthy
and complicated process of negotiations he and the Chinese agreed
on a formal public compromise according to which he fell on one
knee and bowed (a series of bows) as he would before his sovereign George III.[10] In his notorious Edict or letter to George III of
September 1793, Qianlong rejected the British demands in their
entirety and expressed disdain for the gifts accorded him:

> Nevertheless we have never valued ingenious articles, nor do we have
> the slightest need of your country's manufactures. Therefore O King,
> as regards your request to send someone to remain at the capital, while
> it is not in harmony with the regulations of the Celestial Empire we
> also feel very much that it is of no advantage to your country.
> (Macartney 340)[11]

Qianlong's much-debated letter came to be seen as a clear statement
of China's isolationism and its much vaunted and false sense of cultural isolationism.

Two recent and influential accounts, however, have interpreted the
cross-cultural clash between the embassy and the Qing court as demonstrating the limitations of an Enlightenment cosmopolitan worldview when faced with a polity that refused to accept the assumptions
of universality on which it was based. James L. Hevia has argued that
the British government understood diplomacy and commerce as two
specific mechanisms or languages for communication across national
boundaries, a position he identifies with Habermas's postulation of
the "public sphere," arising from an eighteenth-century bourgeois
civil society that constituted a universal voice of rationality. The Qing
court annoyed and perplexed Britain in the latter half of the eighteenth century, because it "stubbornly resisted European penetration
and the public sphere definition of 'reason,' while continuing to function outside an Eurocentrically imagined world" (Hevia 1995, 42).
More than this, China became the other against which the bourgeois
British masculine identity was defined. Of this ideology, George
Viscount Macartney and Vice Ambassador Sir George Staunton were
exemplary representatives. Macartney was a seasoned diplomat who
had served in the West Indies, India, and Russia. For Hevia, this was
less of an encounter between modern pragmatic Europeans and ossi-
fied Orientals, encased in carapaces of inflexible ritual, but a complex
and fluid series of negotiations between two expansive, multiethnic
imperial formations, in which the Qing imperial court mobilized its
complicated guest rituals in a pragmatic and flexible way and in which

both sides were "aware that what was at stake were competing and ultimately incompatible views of the meaning of sovereignty and the ways in which power relations were constructed" (28). The embassy rather than being a "failure" and lost opportunity could be seen as a successful resistance by the Qing of aggressive British imperialism.

David Porter similarly comments on how the "ideal of free circulation" of trade and capital functioned for the British "as the implicit standard of cultural legitimacy" with its claims to universality and nature. China's "steadfast refusal to conform to this natural role and to accommodate western notions of free circulation" gave rise "to the commercialist denigrations of Chinese cultural institutions over the course of the eighteenth century" (202). In addition, the Macartney Embassy sought to persuade the Chinese of the superiority of Western science and technology; among the expedition was Dr. James Dinwiddie, an astronomer and physicist and amongst the tribute for the Chinese emperor were clocks, a planetarium, telescope, air balloon, and diving bell.

An immense volume of writing was generated by and about the embassy. Macartney's valet published an account in 1795 before the official version by the diplomat and botanist, George Staunton and edited by Joseph Banks appeared in 1797. John Barrow published his own, generally hostile, account of the Qing court in 1804, as well as extracts from Macartney's memoranda and journals in his life of Macartney of 1807. It is from this latter account that Fanny Price reads in Jane Austen's *Mansfield Park* when Edmund abruptly tells her that she is to act in the amateur dramatics: "[T]here was no reading, no China, no composure for Fanny" (Austen 144).[12] Parts of Macartney's journal first appeared in John Barrow's *Some Account of the Public Life and a Selection of the Unpublished Writings of the Earl of Macartney* (1807), which Fanny is reading, although the journals themselves remained unpublished until 1962.

The official account of the embassy was authored by Staunton who had access to Macartney's private journal. Like Bell's *Account*, it attempts to avoid the direct expression of opinion preferring to observe and describe Chinese customs. In Staunton's account, China emerges as a civilized but despotic nation in which the common Chinese are restrained by "the heavy hand of power" but otherwise of "a cheerful and confident disposition" (2: 14). This despotism is summed up in the ceremony of the koutou about which Staunton believes it "is difficult to imagine an exterior mark of more profound humility and submission, or which implies a more intimate consciousness of the omnipotence of that being towards whom it is made" (2: 129). The agricultural system of the country is much praised and the people are supported: "No small portion of the people seemed, it is true, to be in a state approaching indigence; but none driven to the necessity, or inured to the habit, of craving assistance from a stranger" (2: 89). Their arts and sciences are inferior to those of the West, the one exception being that of landscape gardening: "A Chinese gardener is the painter of nature; consulting which he contrives, without rule or science, to unite simplicity and beauty" (2: 172).

Generally, Staunton regards the people from the emperor down as superstitious and credulous. Unlike Bell, the embassy is quite disappointed by Beijing:

> They were indeed aware, that so slight a glimpse [of Pekin] did but little qualify them to form a judgment of it; but what they had seen, except in relation to the imperial palace, did not come up to the idea they previously had formed of the capital of China; and they imagined that a Chinese, could he be impartial, would feel a greater gratification in the sight of the ships, the bridges, the squares, several of the public buildings, and the display of wealth in the capital of Great Britain. (2: 125)

Here Staunton appeals to a Eurocentric notion of rationality that would naturally evince the superiority of the British values and achievements. Staunton also highlights, as earlier writing did not, the issues of the "cruel sacrifice" of infanticide and the mutilations of female foot binding. He accepts the Jesuit calculation that about two thousand children are exposed each year, their only chance of survival being rescue by the missionaries. It is, however, the treatment of women that is highlighted in Staunton's and also Barrow's accounts, especially the scandal of foot binding. As Nicholas Thomas has argued, Enlightenment anthropologists regarded the way a society treats females to be crucial to an estimation of the degree of civilization it possessed (Thomas 1997, 71–92). In the case of China, Staunton points out how

> [w]omen, especially in the lower walks of life, are bred with little other principle than that of implicit obedience to their fathers or their husbands. To them they are taught to refer the good or bad qualities of their actions, without any idea of virtue in the abstract. (2: 512)

Chinese women are kept in ignorance and deprived of education and allowed by their husbands to degenerate into coarse peasantry. It is for the scandal of foot binding that Staunton reserves his most critical comment:

> In forming conjectures upon the origin of so singular a fashion among the Chinese ladies, it is not very easy to conceive why this mode should have been suddenly or forcibly introduced amongst them by the other sex. Had men been really bent upon confining constantly to their homes the females of the families, they might have effected it without cruelly depriving them of the physical power of motion. No such custom is known in Turkey or Hindostan, where women are kept in greater habits of retirement than in China. Opinion, indeed, more than power, governs the general actions of the human race; and so preposterous a practice could be maintained only by the example and persuasion of those who, in their own persons, had submitted to it. Men may have silently approved, and indirectly encouraged it, as those of India are supposed to do that much more barbarous custom of widows burning themselves after the death of their husbands. But it is not violence, or the apprehension of corporal suffering, but the horror and disgrace in consequence of omitting, and the idea of glory arising from doing, what is considered to be an act of duty, at the expence of life, which leads to such a sacrifice. (1: 424)

In connecting foot binding with the Hindu rite of the sati, Staunton makes an equation between two practices that have featured in postcolonial criticism, most notably in the work of Gayatri Chakravorty Spivak (271–313). Rather than white men saving brown women from brown men, in Spivak's terms, we have white men saving yellow women from yellow men. Spivak's point that the voice of the subaltern women is lost applies in both cases. Staunton uses the occasion to make a critical reflection on the practice of British women deforming themselves to acquire slender waists as a comparison with Chinese practices. Though such a turn of thought would seem to suggest an Enlightened cosmopolitan and relativist outlook, the formulaic criticism of British absurdities, familiar from Montaigne, establishes Britain as the superior society let down by its similarity to China. Interestingly, Staunton goes further than most commentators in blaming the women for their acceptance and internalization of the practice that the men only "silently" approve and "indirectly" encourage.

The issue of foot binding is also taken up in Macartney's *Journal*. He shows himself to be more genuinely relativist in his assessment of the practice that he sees as analogous to circumcision and no worse that the practice of producing castrati for the Italian opera: "It is not a great many years ago that in England thread-paper waists, steel stays and tight lacing were in high fashion, and the ladies' shapes were so tapered down from the bosom to the hips that there was some danger of breaking off in the middle upon any exertion" (Macartney 229). Macartney's *Journal* presents the Chinese as "a strong hardy race, patient, industrious, and much given to traffic and all the arts of gain...and by no means that sedate, tranquil people they have been represented" (226). Though admiring of the Qianlong Emperor, ultimately Macartney sounds a note of disappointment and disillusionment after his formal presentation to the emperor, employing a theatrical and nostalgic metaphor to encapsulate the Son of Heaven:

> Thus, then, have I seen "King Solomon in all his glory." I use the this expression, as the scene recalled perfectly to my memory a puppet show of that name which I recollect to have seen in my childhood, and which made so strong an impression on my mind that I then thought it a true representation of the highest pitch of human felicity and greatness. (124)

Spokesman for trade, commerce, and enlightened diplomatic relations, Macartney wishes to engage the Chinese government with tolerance, respect, and mutual understanding, convinced that familiarity with English manners will win the Chinese over to a superior estimation of his countrymen; however, he is clear that should this fail, his nation is capable of taking the Qing Empire to pieces. He speculates that "a few frigates" could quickly destroy the Chinese coastal navigation and the Bengal border could be used to ferment unrest in Tibet, encouraging unrest in the other vassals of China (210–11). In an oft-quoted phrase, Macartney summed up the embassy's view of the Qing:

> The Empire of China is an old, crazy, First rate man-of-war, which a fortunate succession of able and vigilant officers has contrived to keep afloat for these one hundred and fifty years past, and to overawe their neighbours merely by her bulk and appearance, but whenever an insufficient man happens to have command upon her deck, adieu to the discipline and safety of the ship. (213)

In both the *Authentic Account* and Macartney's *Journal* we see the increasing conflict between an Enlightenment Universalist discourse of ethnological relativism and an emergent British nationalism. Set against the alleged effeminacy, stagnation, and inflexibility of the Chinese, admired by the ungodly remnant of scheming Jesuits, a British subject is constructed as masculine, white, rational, and Protestant.

This othering of China, in Staunton and Macartney, is not racialized as yet. The race idea, however, is present in one of the most influential accounts of the embassy, John Barrow's *Travels in China* (1804). Barrow's *Travels* contains some of the most belligerent writing toward the Chinese produced by the embassy. It combines a narrative of the embassy with a sustained ethnological discussion of Chinese character and morals, their manners, society, literature and their fine arts, science, civil institutions, and agriculture. Barrow presents "the sentiments of an Englishman...acquainted with manners, custom and character of the Chinese nation." He claims to show the people "in their proper colours...as they really are" divesting the "tinsel and the tawdry" with which the Jesuit missionaries have invested them, assessing the true point "which China may be considered to hold in the scale of civilized nations" (3). Barrow tells how his initial high opinion of the Chinese civilization could not be sustained in practically all aspects of their culture. "Everything" he comments "wore an air of poverty and meanness" (70). The Chinese have "remained stationary," and though they were civilized two thousand years before Europe, since then "they have made little progress in any thing, and been retrograde in many things." Compared with Europe in the present, Barrow epigrammatically describes them as "only great in trifles, and trifling in everything that is great" (355). He comments on the lack of cleanliness of the Chinese and their infestation with lice and vermin.

In Barrow we glimpse the impact of the nineteenth-century infiltration of travel writing with the race idea. He has several very positive descriptions of Chinese people, especially the two mandarins who accompanied the embassy as guides, but he does speculate somewhat surprisingly on the racial origins of the Chinese. He describes the complexion of the Chinese and Tartar as "that tint between a fair and a dark complexion" (184), although some of the Manchu Tartars he perceives as of "extremely fair and of florid complexion" (185). After his stint at the Chinese embassy, Barrow traveled to South Africa in 1802, as Macartney's assistant. He there claimed to notice a resemblance between the Chinese and the Hottentot or Khoikhoi peoples:

[T]heir physical characters agree in almost every point. The form of their persons in the remarkable smallness of the joints and the extremities, their voice and manner of speaking, their temper, their colour and features, and particularly that singular shaped eye rounded in the corner next the nose like the end of an ellipsis, probably of Tartar or Scythian origin. (48–49)

Although Barrow indicates that dark complexions may result from degeneration toward savagery, as Buffon and de Pauw had argued, he later comments that such differences have less to do with "climate, but rather to some original formation of the different species" (427). Here Barrow hints at a polygenist notion of race encompassing the formation of different species of humankind. He describes how a Hottentot traveling with him was so like a Chinese servant that he inadvertently called him by that servant's name (48–49). Barrow does not speculate on a possible shared origin for the Chinese and Hottentot, but, in pointing out an alleged physical similarity between what are regarded as "the most polished and the most barbarous, the wisest and the most ignorant of mankind," he inevitably degrades the Chinese to the European estimation of the Hottentot African. He tells us that the "aptitude of a Hottentot in acquiring and combining ideas is not less than of a Chinese, and their powers of imitation are equally great," but the difference is simply that the Chinese are brought up among "the arts and conveniences of life," whereas the Hottentot lives "among a miserable race of beings in constant want even of the common necessaries of life" (48–50). It is possible that the Hottentots have actually derived in some way from the diaspora of the Asiatic stock, which includes the Malays, characterized by their "cruel and sanguinary disposition" (51). Barrow's discussion of the Chinese is thus more heavily racialized than either Staunton's or Macartney's and is more representative of the nineteenth-century estimation of the Celestial Empire.

Barrow's discussion of the "ceremonious and effeminate" Chinese returns the focus to those areas of increasing British obsession, infanticide and foot binding. He comments on the "unnatural and inhuman" custom of foot binding females with the "constant pain and suffering it entails. Again Barrow relates this to the mentalities of savage tribes who are seldom without "the unnatural custom of maiming or lopping off some part of the human body" (73–74). He also points out that Europeans themselves have similar absurd customs of their own, such as their powdered and greased hair that occasioned much mirth among the Chinese; nevertheless the Chinese are not elevated by such comparisons in the manner of Montaigne's noble savages, but denigrated by comparison with the savage. Barrow returns us to the Enlightenment and stadial view that "the condition of the female part of society in any nation will furnish a tolerable just criterion of the degree of civilization to which that nation has arrived" (138). In savage societies the labor and drudgery fall on the female. He comments how the Chinese "have imposed on their women a greater degree of humility and restraint than the Greeks of old, or the Europeans of the dark ages" (139–140). Women are physically deprived of the proper use of their limbs "in order to keep them the more confined."

Barrow writes about the sale of young women as brides and prostitutes. Once again he associates China with savagery and barbarism rather than with the polished nations, but it is in his discussion of female infanticide, which he makes his most pungent and gothic points. It is this "horrid practice," which establishes securely "the insensible and incompassionate character of the Chinese" (167). Following the accounts contained in De Pauw, Barrow claims that in Peking persons with carts are employed to pick up the bodies of infants discarded in the course of the night. Such bodies are carried to "a common pit…into which all those that may be living, as well as those that are dead, are said to be thrown promiscuously." He adds that "dogs and swine are let loose in all the narrow streets of the capital" so that his readers can "conceive what will necessarily happen to the exposed infants" (169). Barrow estimates that possibly about twenty thousand such infants are exposed in China each year, with nine thousand being exposed within the capital itself. In addition to crimes against women, the Chinese are also confirmed sodomites, indulging in "this detestable and unnatural act…. with so little sense of shame, or feelings of delicacy" (150). Barrow's discussion of infanticide, to which he was not an eyewitness, has struck many as being fanciful and highly exaggerated, but it was as influential as it was contested. Like cannibalism, infanticide was one of those markers of savagery that travelers, explorers and anthropologists found to their dismay or excitement in Polynesia, Africa, and China. It was also, of course, a practice that was not uncommon in Paris and London. It was also something that he did not himself witness, nor did any of the embassy staff.

Although Barrow credits the Chinese whom the embassy dealt with as showing general good humor, the picture he paints of China as a whole is not positive, equating the Chinese with nations more properly designated savage in European eyes. Barrow's ethnology combines a cultural anthropology derived from Ferguson and Kames with a physical and racial anthropology, deriving from Enlightenment classificatory systems of natural history. Here we see both strands in the grammar of race thinking with the biological beginning to emerge as a significant if not yet dominant ideology. In comparing the official account with Barrow's more idiosyncratic observations, one may be unfairly privileging the latter's opinions of China that may not be representative.[13] In the wealth of writing deriving from the embassy, there are multiple and conflicting views.

The embassy's painter William Alexander, for instance, presented a less sinister view than that of Barrow of female foot binding in his unpublished journal:

> Tho' it does not appear from this specimen that the women are so closely confined, as was expected from the statements hitherto published of this country. For the lower class of females stumped along with their small bandaged feet as publickly as they would in any country town in England, where they would also on such occasion be shy of strangers & keep them in the background. The women of better sort kept behind their walls, so that their hands only are seen which are generally ornamented with artificial flowers, bodkins &c. (f20r)

Alexander finds the Chinese to be almost exclusively good humored and pleasant and is more sensitive to issues of class than race. His main observation relates to the sheer size and scale of the Chinese population: "Our Junk was sometimes so crouded with visitors that we could scarcely stir, the swarms of boats around us, the concourse of people seen on shore, was inconceivable. Of all the wonders we have seen in this interesting country, the immense population is the greatest" (f33r). Unlike Barrow he is highly impressed by Beijing and its emperor: "We now bade adieu to this wondrous metropolis, with the boast of having resided in the largest and rarest city if the world, & having seen the Sovereign of so large a portion of the civilized earth, such reflections could not be easily resisted" (f26v). In the various accounts of the Macartney Embassy we can witness the stresses which the "other" of China under the Qing increasingly placed upon a Universalist and cosmopolitan discourse and the beginnings of its replacement with an ideology of nationalism, and later, of biological racism, which would lead to the justification of the imperial violence of the Opium Wars, as the Chinese were gradually and violently forced to speak the universal and natural languages of commerce and diplomacy as the nineteenth century progressed.

Attitudes had certainly hardened on both sides when the British dispatched a further embassy to China under Lord Amherst. Again the issue of the koutou assumed a crucial significance with Amherst's final refusal and the Jiaqing Emperor insisting that the ritual must be performed. The official account of the embassy authored by Sir Henry Ellis, makes familiar points about China as a nation "satisfied with the hereditary mediocrity of ages, resisting the introduction of foreign, but superior knowledge." China "vast in its extent, produce, and population, wants energy and variety; the chill of uniformity pervades and deadens." (40) Ellis's account of China stresses the sameness and want of variety of the Chinese people and their landscape, which never rise above the merely picturesque:

> Those who landed with an impression that the Chinese were to be classed with the civilized nations of Europe have no doubt seen reason to correct their opinion; those, on the contrary, who in their estimate ranged them with the other nations of Asia, will have seen little to surprise in the conduct of either the Government, or of individuals. The leading characteristic feature here is the influence of established usage....The despotism of the Sovereign is subordinate to the despotism of manner; the highest degree of civilization that has ever prevailed is nearer nature than the artificial system, certainly far removed from so exalted a standard, that daily regulates the habits of this people; and the only positive conclusion at which I have yet arrived is that the Chinese are a most uninteresting nation....Their minds would seem to be here treated like the feet of the women, cramped by the bandages of habit an education, till it acquires and unnatural littleness. (197–98)

Though not in itself a racialized account of the Chinese, Ellis's narrative views China as old, decrepit, and simply boring. The Chinese are prisoners of ritual and ceremony and preoccupied with the "mere business of representation" (307) rather than the objective worlds of commerce and diplomacy: "It has been said that there is nothing new under the sun, certainly there is nothing new in China: on the contrary, every thing is old" (310).

MISSIONARIES

Another important strand fueling the change in attitude of the West to China was the promotion by Britain and the United States of missionary activity in the area. With the dissolution of the Jesuit order in 1773, Protestant missionaries with a very different ethos and agenda increasingly set the tone for nineteenth-century views of China.[14] The first missionary to arrive in China was the twenty-nine-year old Scot, Robert Morrison in 1807. Morrison passed as a U.S. citizen and attempted to learn Chinese despite its being forbidden to be taught to foreigners on pain of death. He began translating the New Testament into Mandarin in 1813. Encouraged by this very limited success, the London Missionary Society (LMS) sent another Scot, the former shepherd boy, William Milne to assist him to distribute the Bible. Forbidden access to the mainland, Milne retreated to Malacca in Malaya to found a Chinese school there. Progress was slow and by 1840, fewer than a hundred conversions to Christianity had occurred (Lovett 2: 399–554; Hiney 27–30).

The Protestant missionaries were less worldly and scholarly than their Jesuit predecessors; they espoused a religion that stressed spiritual rebirth with an often violent rejection of past sinfulness. Rather than effacing signs of difference between the West and East, as the Jesuits attempted, the Protestant missionaries exaggerated them. Most of their writings prior to 1850 or so stress their own sufferings and setbacks, rather than any enlightened attempt to fathom the alterity of Chinese culture. They were, as Raymond Dawson describes them, "narrow-minded, conservative, and unimaginative" (134, 132–54). Prohibited from journeying to the interior, they made a negligible mark on Chinese society, but their writings, reviewed at home by the likes of John Barrow and Robert Southey, made a huge impact an conditioned European responses to the Far East for many years to come. The Protestant missionaries worked with a familial model of humanity as descended from the first parents, but stressed the divisions of civilization (which they understood as Christian) and savagery, virtue, and sinfulness. No human being was deprived of God's mercy and grace, but many would remain resistant to it.

Morrison served as an interpreter for the failed Amherst Embassy of 1816. His view of China as recorded in his *Memoir of the Principal Occurrences during and Embassy* was of a reprobate and sinful nation:

> China does not enjoy *liberty*. Her government is a military despotism. Her virtues and her vices are those of slaves. Always artful, suspicious, intriguing, the Chinese are complaisant and servile, or insolent and domineering, according to circumstances. They affect great care to prevent irregular intercourse of the sexes; and yet are well known to be very debauched. Indecent representations were found everywhere exposed the same as at Canton. The strong arm of power intimidates them, and they acquire a habit of departing from the truth. (68)

Equally representative was the view of Morrison's assistant, William Milne. In his *A Retrospect of the First Ten Years of the Protestant Mission in China* (1820), he repeats all the stereotypes of China as a "stationary state," with the Chinese possessing "a cowardly imbecility" and "a slow calculating prudence." He presents the excesses of the "deluded imagination of an Asiatic" in a similar manner to de Quincey's Oriental Gothic sublime of terror. The adherents of the God, "Fuh," imagine "horned demons, with swords, spears, hatchets, and hooks—wretched mortals, alternately shivering with indescribable cold, and burnt to coals with devouring fire" (36). Their vast population, their antiquity, and their defects in scientific improvement confirm the "depravity of the human heart" that sinful mankind demonstrates everywhere. Milne focuses on the alleged practice of infanticide and the immorality of the concubines and "yea, even sodomites—catamites!" He uses the scriptural language of damnation to dismiss and degrade the culture of the Celestial Empire:

> For they are "sitting in darkness, and dwelling in the land of the shadow of death"— "Have changed the glory of an incorruptible God, into images made like to corruptible man, and to birds, and four-footed beasts, and creeping things"...serve "idols of gold, and silver, and wood," abound in "witchcraft, hatred, emulation, wrath, strife &c"... "under the power of Satan"... "doing things in secret which it is a shame even to mention... "Living in the wicked one"—"without hope—without God in the World." Such is the state of China. (40)

Transmitted to a nation of armchair explorers through the pages of the periodical press, the Protestant missionary view of China was widely disseminated. Later missionary activity after the breaking open of China following from the Opium Wars was much more positive and empathetic in its approach to Chinese peoples, chiefly with the establishment of the mission schools focusing on the poorest and the introduction of Western medicine. They showed concern for the poor and for the condition of women. Missionaries such as Alicia (Mrs. Archibald) Little began, in 1895, an anti–foot binding campaign that resulted in the eventual end of the practice. There is no doubting the improvements to material welfare that post-1850 missionary activity brought to China; nevertheless such activity remained very much a part of the movement to westernize China for good or for ill (Spence 1990, 202–8).

This chapter has explored the changing status of the Qing Empire in the late eighteenth and early nineteenth centuries. It has attempted to outline the main texts and elucidate the key trends in the European degradation of China. The contribution of the race idea was certainly present in the writings of natural philosophers who increasingly homogenized and racialized the Chinese. Other trends such as economic competition in an increasingly globalized economy contributed to this process. The contribution of the Protestant missionaries in China, as in the South Seas and Africa was also crucial. All these discourses, the scientific, literary, political, economic, diplomatic, and religious were heavily intertwined with each other. It was, however, the race idea that began to emerge as the most characteristic and dominant paradigm through which to view China and her peoples. In chapter 6, I take this argument further by discussing the European racial construction of the Tartar and the Chinese as a racist binary.

CHAPTER 6

TARTARS, MONGULS,
MANCHUS, AND CHINESE

TARTARS, MONGULS
MANCHUS, AND CHINESE

In chapter 5, I discussed the changing discourse of China and the extent to which this was affected, or even caused by racial thinking. The focus of that chapter was on historical, diplomatic, travel and missionary writing rather than literary texts. The emphasis in this chapter is more firmly placed on literary texts. There is not a great deal of what one might think of as purely imaginative writing about China in the Romantic period, compared with that written about other areas of the globe and compared with later periods, although there are many cultural references to China, often as a part of political or aesthetic critique. For Ros Ballaster, writing about late seventeenth- and eighteenth-century representations of China, the elements of Chinese culture that gained especial currency in England were "political and moral absolutism, belief in theories of transmigration, and willful linguistic obscurity." She also argues that for the "cult of China…the charge of inauthenticity, or fictionality, was central to the robustness and elasticity of its dissemination." Thus, like the Rococo fripperies of Chinese wallpapers and other effusions of chinoiserie, fictions of China and the Chinese are self-consciously ironized and dependent for their impact on the tacit understanding that they have no referent in an actual polity. They become, in Ballaster's elegant formulation, "that enigmatic scribal sign which is understood by western commentators as either a vestige of a pure antediluvian language or an illegible erratic mark governed by no grammatical logic" (206, 204, 223, 218, 196).

The fictional Chinese, at this time, lack the specificities of the West Indian slave trade or of Polynesian and Melanesian cannibals. Often the ascription of Chinese ethnicity in the eighteenth century is simply assimilated into an undifferentiated form of Orientalist stereotyping. This is the case, for instance, in the "Grub Street" English translation of Antoine Galland's *Mille et une nuits* (1706–21). The hero of one of its most famous tales, Aladdin, son of Mustapha, lives in "the capital of one of the largest and richest provinces of the kingdom of China." The province is ruled by a Sultan with whose daughter, Badroulbadour, Aladdin falls in love; she is "the most lovely beautiful brown woman in the world: her eyes were large, lively, and sparkling; her looks sweet and modest; her nose was of a just proportion; her mouth small; her lips of vermilion red and agreeable symmetry; in a word all the features of her face were regular and beautiful" (Mack 1). Similarly with the Chinese elements of Galland's imitators, François Pétis de la Croix's *The Thousand and One Days: Persian Tales* (1714–15) and Thomas-Simon Gueullette's *Mogul Tales* (1736) and *Tartarian Tales* (1759), China and Tartary serve as a conventional Orientalist backdrop not distinguished from the Baghdad of Haroun Al Raschid. This chapter addresses how representation of the Chinese became increasingly racialized as the eighteenth century progressed.

One aspect of the orientalizing imagination of the West that becomes increasingly notable in the eighteenth century is the recurrent stereotyping of the Chinese and the Tartar, a pattern that is apparent from the early modern period, if not before, and which begins to disappear in the Romantic period in favor of a more fully homogenizing racial discourse. Like the constructions of the peaceful and friendly Arawak and the savage, cannibalistic Carib Indians of Columbus's New World, as discussed by Peter Hulme, this distinction is slippery and loose, and partakes of the imaginary: a projection of European concerns (1986, 1–25). The first use of the term in English, according to the OED (*Oxford English Dictionary*), was by Chaucer in 1386 in the *Squire's Tale*: 'This noble kyng this tartare, Cambynskan" (1: 41: 169). Generally, the word is used to describe a northern, warlike, nomadic, fierce, and superstitious people, while the Chinese are southern, civilized, feminized, and literate. Conventionally, the term "Tartar" refers to the northeastern and northwestern peoples of Central Eurasia who were not Chinese, rather than to a specific ethnic or linguistic grouping. According to Pamela Kyle Crossley, "Tartar" was originally a linguistic not an ethnic category, the name of a Turkic-speaking medieval people of Central Eurasia. This people became a significant element in early Mongol federations of the twelfth century, and the name became commonly applied to the Mongol peoples as a whole (1979, 1–4). Because the Turkic peoples, who settled in the Crimea and near parts of the Caucasus, were in fact called "Tatars," the corruption Tartar remained familiar in Europe (Izhboldin). The term was later applied to Temur or Tamerlaine and his followers, and, by the seventeenth century, it was also bestowed on the newly powerful Manchus. The practice of calling both Manchus and Mongols by the term Tartar persisted until the end of the Qing Empire in 1912. As Crossley puts it, " 'Tartar' then was evidently a European and American common-place for a free-spirited, horse-riding Eurasian people who harassed and in select instances conquered sedentary cultures of sober repute" (1979, 3).

Justin Marozzi describes how "Tartar" was first applied to the Turkicized Mongols of Genghis Khan's hordes, despite the fact that Genghis had virtually eliminated the original Tatar tribe, the bitter enemies of his tribe. Subsequently Europeans used the term "indiscriminately for all nomadic peoples and, because they regarded these rough barbarians with fear and loathing, spelt it Tartar, from Tartarus, the darkest hell of Greek mythology. Today the words Mongol and Tartar are often used interchangeably" (8n). John Man similarly argues that when Batu Khan's Mongols erupted into Hungary and Germany in 1241, Europeans "seized on the name of one group of Mongol subjects, the Tatars, and called all Mongols Tartars—people from Tartarus, the hellish nether regions of antiq-uity" (309). This modern usage appears to have first been made by the English monk Matthew Paris in his *Chronica Majora* (1686), which repeats the French King Louis IX's pun that made popular the identification of Tartary and the classical underworld (Saunders 124). For the Chinese the "Tartars" were generally the nomadic peoples of the northwest frontier who harassed their empire throughout history, while for Europeans the Tartars became associated with the Mongol peoples as a whole at a time of serious invasion fears. With the final conquest of the Mongolian Zunghar (Dzunghar) Empire in 1760 by the Qing, Central Eurasia became a borderland of indeterminate peoples and religions, "In the early modern period, Central Eurasia was indeed the crossroads of the Eurasian continent. Every major reli-gion reached it" (Perdue 9). The Tartars were no more religiously unified in European minds than they were ethnically; those who fol-lowed Genghis Khan into Central Asia, Persia, and Iraq assimilated to the religion of their conquered territories and had become Muslim by the end of the thirteenth century, whereas those who remained on the Mongolian plateau, such as the Manchus, remained Lamaist Buddhists.

The Manchus, who famously conquered the Ming Empire in 1644 and established a polity that would last till 1912, were a very distinct people from both the original Tatars and the Monguls, although their histories were often conflated. They were, by the seventeenth century, no longer nomadic horsemen like the Monguls, but a stable farming, hunting, and fishing people. Prior to the early 1600s, these peoples were known as the "Jurchen," but they adopted the name Manchu in 1616 in a deliberate attempt to construct a coherent and separate identity that would supersede the tribal identities of the Jurchen and other northeastern tribes associated with them (Guy 151–64; Mote 784–90; Perdue 547).[1] Both Western and Chinese historians have viewed the Manchus as foreign conquerors not fully interested in China's fortunes as a nation once the country began to falter after 1800 (Perdue 5). Paradoxically, they have also been regarded as not having an identity of their own prior to conquering China, being regarded as another example of the phenomenon of China's ability to conquer or absorb its conquerors. Rather than being a people with an ethnic identity, the Manchu were a political order. There was no clear Manchu cultural identity. For R. Kent Guy, "the Manchus were a group of people, largely but not exclusively Jurchen, who organized themselves around the mission of ruling China between the seventeenth and the twentieth centuries" (162).

The tendency to discriminate between Tartars and Chinese and to homogenize a vast array of people and cultures under the term "Tartar" is thus an old one. It is present in Marco Polo's observation that "all the *Cathayan* hated the government of the Great Khan, because he set over them Tartar rulers, mostly Saracens, and they could not endure it, since it made them feel they were no more than slaves" (133). Samuel Purchas, in *Purchas His Pilgrimage* (1613) contrasted the manners of the Tartars with those of the Ming China. Purchas discriminates between a civilized Chinese and a nomadic and warlike Tartar people; he sees the Cathayans and the Tartars as contrasting pairs of peoples, conflating the Mongolian with the Manchu, a people bent on world domination. The Tartars "are excellent Archers. Vanquished, they aske no favour; and vanquishing, they show no compassion. They all persist as one man in their purpose of subduing the world." Purchas reports the stories that the Tartars are occasional cannibals who "eate sometimes for necessitie, mans [*sic*] flesh, sometimes to delight themselves, and sometimes to terrify others." The

Chinese by contrast are an eminently civilized people who "in their offices of urbanite and courtesie...goe beyond all others, have many books thereof, and reckon it one of those five virtues which they call Cardinall" (1826, 411, 419, 444). This division can also be found in the many Jesuit sources that dominated eighteenth-century sinology. Athanasius Kircher's great compilation of Jesuit sources, *China Illustrata* (1667) emphasizes the importance of the Chinese and Tartar division. Similarly the Jesuit Jean-Baptiste Du Halde's influential *The General History of China* (1735 translated in 1736), notices the binary racial opposition between Tartars and Chinese. The Qing Empire of the Manchu is a kingdom in which "perfect Tranquility" is maintained between "an almost infinite Number of *Chinese* and *Tartars*" (1: 2). Du Halde's *History*, does not contain any sustained physical description of the Chinese or their Tartar masters, but it does discriminate between an "effeminate" Chinese and "warlike" Tartar.

The term was even more problematic in the late eighteenth and early nineteenth centuries. In his *Histoire naturelle,* Buffon divided humanity into six varieties distinguishing between the Tartar and the South Asian in increasingly racial terms.

> These circumstances are sufficient to render the Tartars more swarthy than the Europeans who want nothing to make life easy and comfortable. Why are the Chinese fairer than the Tartars, though they resemble them in every feature? Because they are more polished; because they live in towns, and practice every art to guard themselves against the injuries of the weather; while the Tartars are perpetually exposed to the action of the sun and air. (Eze, *Race and Enlightenment* 1997, 26)

For Buffon a dark or swarthy skin was a degeneration caused by the extremes of heat and cold but also by a lack of civilization (1792, 4: 348–49). Buffon identified the "Kalmuck" or Mongolian as the quintessential Tartar and as one who had degenerated just about as far as was possible from the European norm. The status of the Kalmuck, or Tartar, or Mongolian in racial discourse has been largely ignored by the Anglo-American academy because of its justifiable concern with transatlantic slavery and the racial issues of African Americans. Yet the Mongolian peoples were usually denigrated as much as sub-Saharan Africans. In the aesthetic hierarchy that infiltrated racial discourse in the eighteenth century, the Mongolian was usually ranked near the foot. Pieter Camper also uses the Kalmuck as the racial type closest to the Negro. In his influential formulation of the facial angle, Camper arranged a series of skulls from the ape through to human

beings, African, Mongolian, and then European heads. To typify the
Mongol, Camper chose a "Calmuck" skull. The Kalmuck was thus
the midway between the African and European (Kitson, *Theories of
Race* 1999, 99–117). Buffon made this clear in his description:

> The ugliest of them are the Calmucks, in whose appearance there
> seems to be something frightful.... The Calmucks, who are situated in
> the neighborhood of the Caspian Sea, between the Muscovites and the
> great Tartars, are, according to Tavernier, robust, but the most ugly
> and the most deformed of all human beings. Their faces are so flat and
> so broad that their eyes, which are uncommonly small, are from five to
> six inches asunder; and their noses so flat that two holes are barely
> perceivable instead of nostrils.... The Chinese are totally different in
> their dispositions, manners, and customs. The Tartars are naturally
> fierce, warlike, and addicted to the chace, inured to fatigue, fond of
> independence, and to a degree of brutality uncivilized. Altogether
> opposite are the manners of the Chinese; they are effeminate, pacific,
> indolent, superstitious, slavish and full of ceremony and compliment.
> In their features and form however there is so striking a resemblance,
> as to leave a doubt whether they did not spring from the same race.
> (1792, 4: 201, 202–3, 206)

Thus the Kalmucks came to be known as the ugliest of the human race.
In chapter 5, I have argued how in the Romantic period and later the
Chinese came to be increasingly described as possessing a yellowness
of complexion and how they were, in general, included with other
southeastern Asian people under the heading of Mongolian. Kant, in
his "On the Different Human Races" described one of his four main
races as the "Hun race (Mongol or Kalmuck)." He identified the
Huns with the Mongols, presumably because of their Eastern and
nomadic origins. Of the present "Huns" the Kalmucks appear to be
the purest, and after them the Torghuts and the Zingari Zhunghar.
What differentiates the Torghuts and Zingari from the Kalmuck is
their increasing adulteration with "Tatar" blood. Kant included the
"Turkish-Tatars" along with the Persians in the category of his primary race, the white race. For Kant the mixing of "the Tatar and
Hunnish blood in the Kara-Kalpaks, the Nagas, and others, has produced half races" neither white nor Hun (11–13). Kant's Tatars are
then European, though their affiliation to the white race is based on
a linguistic factor, their speaking a Turkic language and in mixing
with the Hun race they produce hybrid races. Kant eschews the word
"Tartar," and it is not clear if his Tatars are meant to be Tartars or

whether this may be a word misapplied to his Hunnish Kalmucks. Certainly Kant's nomination of the Kalmuck people as the purest examples of the Hun race, alienated from the white and other two races is an interesting and influential identification.

J.F. Blumenbach, in 1775, preferred the term "Mongolian" to describe all the inhabitants of Asia (excluding the Malays). Blumenbach influentially described the Mongolian as "Colour yellow; hair black, stiff straight and scanty; head almost square; face broad, at the same time flat and depressed...nose, small apish...the opening of the eyelids narrow linear." Yet, confusingly, he argued that the use of the term "Tartar" to stand in for the Mongolian nations was an error that gave rise to "wonderful mistakes in the study of the varieties of mankind" (265). Blumenbach, with a greater degree of ethnological precision, claimed that Buffon transferred to the genuine Tartars, who were European or Caucasian, the racial characteristics of the Mongols, mistakenly described as Tartars by ancient authors (270). Blumenbach traces this error to the *Chronica Majora* (published in 1686) of Matthew Paris in which the followers of Genghis Khan are described as Tartars (Saunders 124). Confusingly then, for Blumenbach, Tartars are not Mongols, but a borderline group located in the liminal space between the Caucasians and Mongols. In the *De Varietate*, he writes that the "Tartars shade away through the Kirghis and the neighbouring races into the Mongols," which suggests the opposite of a complete contrast, merely a series of shadings (270). The phenomena of the increasing Europeanization of the Tartar and its estrangement from the Mongolian Kalmuck and the subsequent homogenizing of both racial types, is a strong characteristic in the discourse of nineteenth-century physical anthropology. The key points to observe, however, are the increasing use of the Kalmuck as a metonymic racial expression which comes to stand for the pure racial type of Mongolian in both Kant's and Blumenbach's anthropology, as well as the growing uncertainly about what constituted a Tartar in the period and what writers actually meant by the term when they used it. The word is increasingly used as a kind of racial antinomy, or a term that denotes two contradictory states at the same time.

The word "Tartar" then is an expression that often signifies what a person is not, rather than anything more cohesive beyond the vaguely linguistic. A Tartar is thus not a Russian, Chinese, or Ottoman (the three great land empires of Eurasia in the period). He or she is sometimes not a Mongolian and not a European though the term is also used to signify both. It is a word not used by the Asian peoples themselves and is one which groups together many peoples (in particular the Mongol and Manchu) with different languages, and at different levels of social arrangements.

CONQUERED CHINA AND HER ORPHANS

The eighteenth-century discourse of China was constructed around an opposition between Tartars and Chinese, a distinction that breaks down in the nineteenth century in favor of a more mono-lithic racial grouping of far Eastern peoples. As I have demonstrated the terms of this binary distinction were constructed by Western imaginations from a confusing array of peoples and their histories. Although predating the Qing conquest of China in 1644, this distinction was deployed as a means of understanding the politics and history of China at a metadiscursive level, a discourse that revealed as much about the European imagination as about the Far East. This binary opposition was not in its inception a racialized discourse but it would come to service a racialized view of Oriental peoples in due course. The conquest of the Ming Empire by the Manchu was something Europeans knew and wrote about. They invariably saw the conflict in terms of Tartar against Chinese. The weakness of the Ming imperial formation in the north of China in the late sixteenth century had allowed bandits to invade both the north and southwest. One of these bandit leaders, Li Zicheng, marched into Peking in 1644 unopposed, and the Ming Emperor, Chongzhen, forsaken by his officials and generals, hanged himself on April 25 in the Pavilion of Imperial Longevity, overlooking the Forbidden City. The general of the major Ming army, Wu Sangui, faced with the threat posed by the bandits as well as the invading Manchu armies, decided to make an accommodation with the latter against Li Zicheng. Prince Regent Dorgon, the uncle of the future Shunzhi Emperor, defeated Li and took Peking, where he declared that the Mandate of Heaven had fallen to the Manchu Qing dynasty to rule China. It took the Manchu several more decades to complete their military conquest of China. Once established, the Qing had tremendous military success, destroying the Mongolian Zunghar Empire by 1760 and annexing Taiwan, Mongolia, Tibet, and much of Central Asia. By the mid-eighteenth century, in the words of Peter C. Perdue, "The Qing and Russians faced each other along an extended border. They had become two of the largest empires in world history" (1). Positioned in between these two world empires was the world of the Tartars.

The Ming had encouraged European missionaries but the Qing was generally less hospitable and suspicious. The subject is treated by Du Halde and other histories of China but the two main sources for the event that of the Austrian Jesuit missionary who was eyewitness to the events, Martinus Martini, *Bellum Tartaricum, or the conquest of the most renowned Empire of China, by the invasion of the Tartars* (translated in 1654) and Palafox's *The History of the Conquest of China by the Tartars* (London 1676). Martini described the Mongols as Western and the Manchu as Eastern Tartars encouraging the conflation of the two peoples in the European consciousness. Martini also claimed that the softness and effeminacy of the Chinese had the effect of enervating "the ancient vigour and Warlike Spirits of the Tartars" with their "pleasures and delices" (256). Palafox also repeatedly emphasizes the distinction. What disturbs the Chinese most of all is the Tartar Edict requiring them "to cloth themselves after the Tartarean fashion, and to cut off their hair, which the *Chineses* love most passionately, and take great care to spruce and perfume it. And generally that which they esteem the most gentle and handsome, is to have their hair, like women's, hang down to their very feet." That this is necessary, Palafox adds, is because it "not very easie to distinguish them by their faces there being so great a resemblance in the features of these two nations" (90–92). Palafox describes the Chinese as "soft and effeminate, beyond all the Inhabitants of *Asia*; and that which did produce this Effeminacy in them, and was a great cause of the ruine and destruction of their Empire, and ever will be to all other States" (343). The destruction of the empire arose from these causes combined with the Chinese distaste for military pursuits. Whereas the Tartars possess none of the effeminacy or sensuality of the Chinese,

[t]hey are very frank and open, and observe the performance of their word and promise very punctually in time of Peace, when they are out of fear of an Enemy. Their greatest vice is their Cruelty in War, where they are very sanguinary. And it is reported, that they have been transported to that excess, as to eat the Flesh of their Enemies, which is a most barbarous Inhumanity; but of this, there is no certain proof, neither does it appear that the whole Nation is guilty of that Vice; perhaps this was only the rage of some few of the most barbarous, and some of the very Dregs of the people. They cannot live out of Arms and War; they affect and desire nothing so much as to be always in the field, and have enemies to fight with, which is their joy and pleasure of their Life. They never think themselves so graceful and handsome as when they appear with their faces full of seams and scars; whereas other Nations are so careful to keep their

Faces smooth and beautiful, their complexions clear and fair, their Hair, or rather their periwigs curled, powdered, to the shame not only of the nation, but nature too who made them Men and not Women, whom they do so much imitate, and like whom they strive to appear. The Tartars are far from this effeminacy, and are so transported with a violent passion for Arms and Souldiery, that all the beautiful Provinces of China have been turned into forges, in which the Tartars employ an infinite number of Work-men in making incessantly all sorts of Arms. (518–19)

The topos of the conquest of China became a subject for drama throughout the seventeenth and eighteenth centuries, perpetuating what would become a familiar binary of the sensual effeminate Southern Chinese and their antithesis the hardy masculine Northern Tartars who, in time, would themselves be softened and feminized by their conquerors. For eighteenth- and nineteenth-century audiences such a representation dovetailed with warnings about the potential enfeeblement and feminization of Britain by the import and consumption of luxury items, typified by Anna Letitia Barbauld's apocalyptic satire *Eighteen-Hundred and Eleven* (1812).[2] In 1673–74, in what is regarded as the first piece of British imaginative writing on a Chinese subject, Elkanah Settle's *The Conquest of China by the Tartars* (published 1676) was performed in Duke's Theatre.[3] Settle's play repeats the distinction of the martial Tartars and the soft effeminate Chinese, whose best warrior is the unlikely Princess Amavanga. The tragedy depicts northern Tartars and southern Chinese in conflict. The "Indulgent Suns kind Ray / Does only on the Southern World look gay," whereas in the North, the Rebel earth

> takes forces of its own:
> And has it self from his weak power secur'd,
> With Mounts of Snow and Rocks of Ice immur'd
> Yet those strong Bars have not your Arms with-stood
> The gods that froze your Climate, warm'd your Blood. (1)

The plot is complicated but Settle dramatizes the conflict between the Tartars and the Chinese in the context of the conflict between love and duty against the betrayal and usurpation of the Ming "King" of China by the villainous Chinese general, Lycungus, a fictionalized version of the rebel Li Zicheng, who emerges as the key destructive force in the drama. It is his crime of usurpation that then serves to justify the Tartar invasion of Zunteus (a conflation of several

Manchu leaders, though chiefly Hung Taiji). The Tartar invasion and usurpation is thus legitimized by the fallen Chinese king:

> *King.* Is not deposing of a King alone
> Enough without the Wading in his Blood?
> Men may Renounce Religion, and a God;
> But so few Impious to that Fury swell,
> To Raze those Temples, where they scorn to Kneel.
> *2 Prin.* And to appear more Insolent and High,
> He calls his Bloody Treason Charity.
> To ease you of your Life after your Power,
> And Cut the Stalk, now he ha's Cropt the Flower.
> At such unknown outrageous Blasphemy
> I'm all Astonishment.   (59)

Settle dramatizes the suicide of the last Ming Emperor who hangs himself and commands his wives to stab themselves before writing his epitaph in his own blood. The emperor's daughter begs him to stab her to avoid being raped at the hands of Li Zicheng's rebels. Against this dramatic extinction of a dynasty, the rebel Lycungus discourses on the problems of the effeminacy of the Ming court which occasioned its end:

> China's Crown has 'til my Reign been worn
> By Lazy Kings, with Female Spirits born;
> Guarded by Eunuch's bred in Palaces,
> Nutur'd in Lusts, the Progeny of Peace:
> But now's the time, Fate grants the High Command
> Of this Great Empire to a martial Hand.   (62)

The drama ends with the killing of the usurper Lycungus and establishment of the Qing Empire, but this new polity is one where the warlike Tartar spirit will be civilized by the softness of Chinese civilization, through the marriage of the Tartar conqueror, Zungteus to his Chinese love, Amavanga. The civilizing force is thus a feminine one.

> *Zung.* Nor shall our Loves be Fortunate alone:
> Be yours blest too, yours is the *Tartar* Crown.
> *To Quit* Your Milder Presence will auspicious be,
> And Civilize my Rougher *Tartary.*
>   And whil'st the *Chinans* pay Allegeance here:
> I'le Teach their softer Natures Arms and War.   (67)

Here Settle somewhat unconvincingly accommodates the downfall of the Ming to Restoration discourses of legitimacy and honor. Nevertheless his popular version of this historical event served to perpetuate stereotypical views of Tartary as an antithesis to Chinese civilization combined with the notion that the feminized civilization would, in the end, assimilate and redeem the savagery of the Tartar.

The Tartar and Chinese conflict was grafted onto one of the most famous examples of Chinese literature known to eighteenth-century Europe, the play called *The Little Orphan of the House of Zhao: A Chinese Tragedy*. This play, a minor operetta of the Yuan dynasty written around 1330 by Ji Junxiang, was translated (and abridged) and adapted several times. It was first translated into French by Father Joseph-Henri-Marie de Prémare and included in Du Halde's *Description de l'empire de la Chine* published in Paris in 1735. It was available in two English translations as well as in Thomas Percy's collection *Miscellaneous Pieces Relating to the Chinese* of 1762 (which Southey among others read) (Shouyi 359–83; Ballaster 208–18). The play espouses Confucian ideals of dynastic and familial piety and loyalty and tells the story of the saving of the life of the orphan and male heir of the House of Zhao after a villainous military leader has destroyed it. To preserve the life of the child a physician allows the substitution of his own child for the orphan who is subsequently murdered by the tyrant. Twenty years later the orphan is informed of his origins by the physician and he revenges himself on the general by telling the emperor of his crimes. The play was highly thought of, praised as equal to classical tragedy by Richard Hurd, and adapted many times by European dramatists.

In Britain the play was adapted by William Hatchet in 1741 as an anti-Walpole polemic, though probably not performed (Ballaster 10–12). Voltaire next used the story, altering it significantly along the way in his *L'Orpheline la Chine* (1755). Voltaire classicized the piece imposing the three unities and changing its historical setting to that of the Mongolian invasion of China by Genghis Khan and his followers: "Je me suis arête a la grandee époque de Gengis-kan, et j'ai voulu peindre les moeurs des tartars et des Chinois" ("I settled on the great period of Genghis-Khan, and wanted to portray the customs of the Tartars and the Chinese" [quoted in Shouyi 370; my translation]). In actual fact Genghis Khan only conquered the Jin dynasty of Manchuria and not the Song dynasty of southern China before his death. In Voltaire's play the orphan becomes the heir to the throne of China who is exchanged for the son of a mandarin, Zamti. Zamti's wife, Idame, is someone Gengis-Kan has previously fallen in love with. Voltaire's Kan is an idealized monarchical figure, a paternal despot based on Emperor Kangxi. The play was translated in 1756 and acted on the British stage. Again the contrast between the Tartar conqueror, this time a Mongul, and the conquered civilization is clearly made:

> This Gengis-Kan,
> That leads this swarm from forth the Northern hive,
> This tyrant, born to be the bane of China,
> Here formerly abode, unknown and scorn'd.
> Now all-incens'd, implacable he comes,
> To glut his anger, and revenge his wrongs.
> His savage nation's form'd by other laws
> Than our sort of people: fields, and tents, and cars
> Their wonted dwelling, even the wide extent
> Of this vast city would appear confinement.
> No sense have they of our fair arts and laws,
> But mean with barb'rous rage to overturn
> These walls, so long the wonder of the world.   (10)

The Tartars are northern and driven by passion and revenge. They are savages who are compared with bees swarming from their hive, driven by dark and atavistic instincts rather than reason. They are defined as nomadic, opposed to the settlement and are figured in negatives by what they are not: "[F]orm'd by other laws / Than our sort of people." The soft and civilized Chinese are represented once more by a female presence, the Kan's love Idame. Once again it is the role of the Chinese to soften and civilize the rough Tartars and assimilate them into the mores of the empire. At the close of the play, the educated and reformed Kan now looks with "steady reason's eye" at the civilization of the Chinese:

> Though conqueror, my captives I revere,
> And praise their virtues, while I give them chains,
> I see their labours have adorn'd the world;
> I see them an industrious noble, people;
> Their kings on wisdom's basis built their power,
> To all the neighbour nations giving laws,
> And reigning without conquest or the sword.
> Heav'n has allotted us rude force alone;
> Battles our arts, and all our labours death.
> Ah! What avails so much success in war?
> Or what the glories of a world enslav'd?

We made the car of conquest red with blood:
Yet there's a greater fame, a nobler glory.
I'm jealous of their virtue, blush to see
The conquer'd soar above the conqueror.   (32)

Voltaire's play, of course, serves as his rebuttal to Rousseau's privileging of the Tartar as noble savage. Rousseau had argued that the Chinese had become corrupted and enfeebled by their sophisticated living and hence their conquest by the noble savagery of the Tartars. For Voltaire the eventual triumph of civilized values, as typified by the Chinese Empire was assured (Ballaster 213).

Three years later, on April 21, 1759, the dramatist Arthur Murphy performed his adaptation of Voltaire's tragedy at Drury Lane Theatre, with David Garrick in the role of the mandarin Zamti. Murphy's version was substantially different from Voltaire's in numerous respects. He abandoned the romance between Gengis and Idame writing scathingly in the play's Preface of Voltaire's wish that "the *role pour l'amoreux* must have its place, and the rough conqueror of a whole people must instantly become *Le Chevalier* GengisKan, as errant a lover as ever sighed in the Thuilleries of Paris" (vii–viii). Murphy's play concludes with the expulsion of the Tartars "as it was not upon the first inroad, but in process of time and experience, that they learned to incorporate themselves with the conquered, by adopting their laws and customs" (xi). Murphy's Prologue also distances him from Voltaire's neoclassical preferences: "Enough of Greece and Rome. The exhausted store / Of either nation now can charm no more," claiming that China will provide "fresh virtues to the source of light" and will "bring / Confucious' moral to Britannia's ears." If Zamti's willingness to have his son killed to save the heir to the throne shows "a patriot" too "zealous in a monarch's cause," the fault must be located in "China's tenets" "for Britain knows no Right Divine in Kings" (1). Murphy's play repeats the central dichotomy between Tartar barbarianism and Chinese civilization. Zamti tells how:

> *Zamti*. China is no more!—
> The eastern world is lost—this mighty empire
> Falls with the universe beneath the stroke
> Of savage force—falls from it's tow'ring hopes;
> For ever, fall'n.
>   Far hence, Mandane,
> Those happy days, alas! are fled, when peace
> Here nurs'd the blooming olives, and shed round
> Her fost'ring influence. In vain the plan,

Of sacred laws, by hoary elders taught,
Laws founded on the base of public weal,
Gave lessons to the world. In vain Confucius
Unlock'd his radiant stores of moral truth;
In vain bright science, and each tender muse,
Beam'd ev'ry elegance on polish'd life—
Barbarian pow'r prevails. Whate'er our sages taught,
Or genius could inspire, must fade away,
And each fair virtue wither at the blast
Of northern domination. (23)

Murphy's Timurkan is "a tyrant train'd to lust and murder, A lawless ravager from savage wilds, / Where cheerful day ne'er dawns" as opposed to "this inventive race" of Chinese whose "rich arts" have humanized the world. At the end of the play he is unceremoniously dispatched by the adult orphan and Chinese values are restored as the theme of the Tartar conqueror conquered by Chinese civilization is dropped. Murphy's play was very popular at the time of the Seven Years' War because it was seen as promoting the values of patriotism and liberty. The play was occasionally presented at Drury Lane during the subsequent decade and was revived in 1797, interestingly about the time of the composition of Coleridge's "Kubla Khan." From these plays we see that the binary opposition of Tartar and Chinese is effected and maintained despite the fact that different historical figures and peoples are subsumed, at times somewhat bewilderingly so, under the generic name Tartar, including the Mongol Yuan dynasty of Genghis Khan (Timurkhan) and the Manchu Qing dynasty of China's conquerors of 1644. Not having the ethnological knowledge and methodology to understand the complex historical and ethnic makeup of the region, the binary opposition of Tartar and Chinese became a convenient fiction with which to understand the politics of the region.

THE TARTAR-CHINESE ANTITHESIS IN GOLDSMITH, BELL, AND THE MACARTNEY EMBASSY ACCOUNTS

Oliver Goldsmith reviewed Murphy's *Orphan* in the *Critical Review* of May 1759. Surprisingly, given the nature of his next literary project, he did not express a high level of admiration for Chinese literature commenting that "of all nations who ever felt the influence of the inspiring goddess, perhaps the Chinese are to be placed in the lowest class; their productions are the most phlegmatic that can be imagined." Drawing on the humoral understanding of peoples, Goldsmith describes them as "phlegmatic," a characteristic that Linnaeus had ascribed to Africans. To the extent that Murphy deviated from the Chinese original, he made his plot more European and his work "more perfect" (*Works* 1:170–72). At the time of writing the review Goldsmith was beginning work on the 119 Chinese letters which he published weekly in the *Public Ledger*, and later collected in novel form as *The Citizen of the World* in 1762. Goldsmith's novel represents a fairly classic statement of the Enlightened cosmopolitan Universalist view of humanity.

The novel satirizes British and European culture and attitudes in a series of letters from the perspective of Lien Chi Altangi, a Chinese visitor to England. First published as a series of *Letters from a Chinese Philosopher* in the *Public Ledger* from 1760 onward, Goldsmith's novel is a version of the satirical Oriental tale employing an intelligent and refined Oriental observer commenting in a series of letters on the fashions and foibles of France as pioneered by Montesquieu in his *Lettres Persanes* (1723) and later exploited by Voltaire. With it, according to Conant, "the genre of pseudo-letters reached its highest point of development in England." [4] Goldsmith's *Citizen* was also a very popular text, unlike much Jesuit writing aimed at a religious and political elite. Lien Chi is a voice for Goldsmith to act out the role of the Enlightened cosmopolitan, as well as to satirize the notion of the Man of Reason as Swift in Book IV of *Gulliver's Travels*. As Seamus Deane puts it, "Lien Chi Altangi has many qualities which recommend him to our attention, but being credibly Chinese is not one of them" (Deane 33–50). Lien Chi declares the superiority of China over Europe, the latter being an ancient extended empire, established by laws which nature and reason seem to have originated. For Goldsmith human differences are created by the progression through stages of society and both Chinese and Europeans are civilized peoples: "The truth is, the Chinese and we are pretty much alike. Different degrees of refinement, and not of distance, mark the distinctions among mankind. Savages of the most opposite climates have all one character of improvidence and rapacity; and tutored nations, however separate, make use of the very same methods to procure refined enjoyment." Both Britain and China are "polite nations" (13–14).

For Lien Chi, standards of beauty are relative: "[W]hen I reflect on the small footed perfections of an Eastern beauty, how is it possible I should have eyes for a woman whose feet are ten inches long" (24–25). Goldsmith again effaces signs of physical difference as he complains that the English think he is not actually Chinese because he is "formed more like a man than a monster." This attitude is summed up by the fashionable lady of distinction who collects Chinoiserie and seeks to exoticize Altangi:

> Bless me! Can this be the gentleman that was born so far from home? What an unusual share of *somethingness* in his whole appearance. Lord, how I am charmed with the outlandish cut of his face; how bewitching the exotic breadth of his forehead. I would give the whole world to see him in his own country dress. (63–64)

As Porter points out, in the minds of Lien Chi's audience the idea of "China" remains "a luxuriously empty slate for their own exotic fantasies and musings." For Porter the English Sinophiles' "insistence on the vacuity of their object of admiration" is a part of the general flattening of cultural values that he sees as the hallmark of Chinoiserie in the late eighteenth century and a part of a general reaction against the more serious admiration of China earlier in the century (138, 141). The Lady's notion of the Chinese as possessing a "*somethingness*," though exoticizing the East, is devoid of the quite definite physical specificities that will mark later racialized discourse. Nevertheless Goldsmith satirizes European misconceptions of an already ironized Chinoiserie, rather than an antipathy toward a misunderstood referent, the real China which exists as an absent presence in Goldsmith's imagination. Lien Chi considers himself in "the light of a Cosmopolite," (426) and a man of reason and Goldsmith's novel, despite its many levels of self-conscious irony, demonstrates the Enlightened Universalist and cosmopolitan ethic that validates Lien Chi as an honest, if sometimes dull, philosopher. The text notably ends with the marriage of Lien Chi's son Hingpo to the niece of his English friend, an interracial marriage that arouses no anxieties.

The markers for the Chinese Altangi (and thus Goldsmith) of savagery and barbarism are the Tartar peoples. Describing his travels, Altangi reports of those countries "where the brown Tartar wanders for a precarious subsistence, with an heart that never felt pity, himself more hideous than the wilderness he makes" (47). For Altangi, however, both states of Tartar barbarism and Chinese civilization have their attractions:

> Do you sigh for the severe frugality of the wandering Tartar, or regret being born amidst the luxury and dissimulation of the polite? Rather tell me, has not every kind of life vices peculiarly its own? Is it not a

truth, that refined countries have more vices, but those not so terrible, barbarous nations few, and they of the most hideous complexion? (50–51)

Altangi generally sides with the advantages of civilization despite the dangers of luxury. The "brown savage of Thibet" may have few vices but those he has

> are of the most hideous nature, rapine and cruelty are scarce crimes in his eyes, neither pity not tenderness, which ennoble every virtue, has any place in his heart: he hates his enemies and kills those he subdues. On the other hand, the polite Chinese and civilized European seem to love their enemies.

Once again this distinction feeds into the eighteenth-century discourse on luxury and the dangers of too much refinement: "Luxury is the child of society" but it does bring more benefits than problems. (52)

The Manchu conquest of China is raised in letter 42 of the novel by Altangi's correspondent from Peking, Fum Hoam. Fum Hoam recounts the story of the Ming Emperor's defeat, the killing of his daughter, his suicide, and the final message to his people written in his own blood "Forsaken by my subjects, abandoned by my friends, use my body as you will, but spare my people." Fum Hoam repeats the standard wisdom of the conqueror conquered and, again fails to discriminate between the wandering nomadic Mongols and the Manchu:

> An empire which has thus continued invariably the same for such a long succession of ages, which though at last conquered by the Tartars, still preserves its ancient laws and learning; and may more properly be said to annex the dominions of Tartary to its Empire, than to admit a foreign conqueror; an empire a large as Europe governed by one law, acknowledging subjection to one prince, and experiencing but one revolution of any continuance in the space of four thousand years: that is something so peculiarly great, that I am naturally led to despise all other nations on the comparison. Here we see no religious persecution, no enmity between mankind for difference in opinions. The disciples of Lao Kium, the idolatrous sectaries of Fohi, and the philosophical children of Confucius, only strive to show by their actions the truth of their doctrines. (178–79)

Goldsmith's Enlightened Universalist and cosmopolitan ethic demonstrates the progress from savagery and barbarism to politeness and refinement, from that of the "unlettered Tartar" to the "polite

Chinese." His model of difference is that of the Enlightenment stadial theory, rather than of biological racism. Ultimately, differences between China and Europe are fewer than imagined as both these nations have achieved a state of civilization. The other for both Altangi and his European audience remains the barbaric Tartar who may be civilized by contact with the polite empire. In Goldsmith's account it is not the Chinese who are "othered," but the Tartar, a third term in the encounter between West and East, whether he is described as Kalmuck, Mongul, or Manchu.

John Bell also encountered Tartars on his travels and he outlined a distinction between free, nomadic, Tartars neither Christian nor Muslim, and the civilized Han Chinese, this distinction he then imposes on the denizens of the Qing. He journeyed overland from St. Petersburg to Peking traversing Siberia and what was known as "Independent Tartary" inhabited by the Kalmucks. Bell again uses this term in a loose way to describe the Central Eurasian peoples of differing cultures and religions. His Tartars are nomadic, living in tents and "removing from place to place, as called by necessity or inclination" and according to him leading "the most ancient and pleasant manner of life" (89). Bell subsumes a wide variety of peoples under the term. He comments that the "Kalmucks are not such savage people as they are generally represented" and that it is perfectly safe to travel among them. The Tzulimms "are poor, miserable and ignorant heathens," and the Tongusans are "tall, able-bodied, brave and very honest," with faces "not so flat as those of the Kalmucks." They are "unacquainted with literature, and worship the sun and the moon" (62). The Yakutzy are hunters and fishers with "flattish faces, little black eyes, and long black hair, plaited and hanging down their backs" (73). They are "humane and tractable" excepting their unfortunate custom of abandoning their terminally sick people to die. Generally, Bell finds them tractable to a conversion to Christianity.

Within Peking Bell frequently comments on the divisions between Manchu, who he identifies as Tartar, and the Han Chinese: "When a Chinese and Tartar are angry at one another, the Tartar in reproach, calls the Chinese louse-eater; and the latter, in return, calls the other fish-skin coat; because the Mantzur Tartars who live near the river Amoor subsist by fishing, and, in summer, wear coats made of the skins of fishes" (156). Bell tells us that when the Manchu Emperor Kangxi was young he insisted on his sons accompanying him on a hunting trip to Tartary to prevent their falling into "idleness and effeminacy among the Chinese" (169). Bell describes the Manchus as a small nation of the relative size of Wales to the rest of Great Britain

(177). This comparison indicates that he sees no essential difference between Tartar and Chinese beyond the kinds of cultural differences that exist between nationalities in the United Kingdom. The rebellion of Li Zicheng, the suicide of the Emperor and his court, and the invitation to the Manchus to invade are all retold.

The Macartney Embassy accounts also noted the fissure between Manchu and Chinese. In Staunton's *Account* the word "Tartar" is used to encompass the "Tartar hordes" of "Gengis-Kan's power" as well as the Manchu. Staunton notes the Emperor Qianlong's predilection for Tartars and the "secret but strong antipathy still subsisting between those two nations" (2: 65). Here again we have the conflation between Monguls and Manchus as well as the construction of the Manchu and Chinese as two different nations. Staunton writes how

> [a] military life is much more the bent of a Tartar than of a Chinese. The hardy education, the rough manner, the active spirit, the wandering disposition, the loose principles, the irregular conduct of the former, fit him better for the profession, practice, and pursuits of war than the calm, regulated, domestic, philosophical, and moral habits of the latter. Warriors seem more often the offspring of Tartary, as literati are of China. The latter are more chiefly conversant in the sciences of morals, and of the policy of government, which are often united in the contemplation, and in the works, of their lawgivers and philosophers. (2: 582)

Qianlong received the embassy at his summer palace in his "yurt" or tent. Staunton explains that the reason for this is because the Tartars though conforming to many of the practices of the Chinese "retained still a predilection for its own ancient manners...the moveable dwelling of a tent was more than a permanent palace of stone and timber, the favorite residence of a Tartar sovereign." The Qing court thus very much retained a sense of its origins and manners. Staunton recounts how the education of Tartar princes is directed to military pursuits:

> They hold the Emperor in the greatest veneration, as considering him descended from Kublai Khan, the conqueror of China in the thirteenth century. His descendants being in the fourteenth century expelled from the throne of that empire, fled into the country of the Man-choos in Eastern Tartary; and from their intermarriages with the natives, sprung the Bog-doi Khans, who, in the last age, entered China, and formed the present dynasty: a dynasty hitherto most fortunate. (2: 267)

Qianlong certainly identified himself with Kublai Khan whose cult he attempted to revive to glorify his own reign. The embassy's conflation of Mongol and Manchus as Western and Eastern Tartar was common in the period though very misleading. Staunton, like the other writers considered in this section, represents an Enlightened cosmopolitan view of difference but one where Chinese civilization meets its antithesis in Tartar barbarism, a barbarism that persists in some aspects of the sinofied Manchu despotism. Responses to Tartars, however, remained ambivalent, exuding nostalgia for a nomadic lifestyle and an admiration for a masculinity and vitality that could be stultified by an over-oppressive stress of formality and ritual.

ROMANTIC TARTARY: JONES AND COLERIDGE

For the late eighteenth century then, Tartary was a liminal space somewhere between the three great Eurasian land empires of the Romanovs, the Qing, and the Ottomans. Despite a number of revealing travel accounts, it remained for most, a place of Orientalist fantasy for the projection of desires and fears. In Antoine Galland's translations of the *Arabian Nights*, Schahriar, the Sassanid King of Persia, grants his brother, Schahzenan the "kingdom of Great Tartary" with its capital of "Samarcande" which is the backdrop for several of the Tales (Mack 1). Thomas-Simon Guellette published his imitations of Galland, *Chinese Tales* and *Tartarian Tales* in 1725 and 1759 respectively. They do not define Tartary, or for that matter, China with much distinction from the generalized Orient as a place of magic and fantasy (Conant 31–6; Ballaster 229–30). The evocation of the former Mongolian capital of "Samarcand" from which the "spiced dainties" of John Keats's "Eve of St. Agnes" are transferred by "argosy" to "cedared Lebanon" (Keats 471) is still very much a part of this fantasy, though one that was aware of the mercantile business of the spice trade and the caravan routes across Asia. Often Tartars are used for satirical purposes to comment on the domestic or European political scene as in Leigh Hunt's satirical *Account of the remarkable rise and downfall of the late Great Kan of Tartary* (1817), where the Great Khan is a cipher for Napoleon, or in the many satires based on the Emperor Qianlong by Peter Pindar, William Mason, and James Gillray that use Tartar despotism as a way of commenting on the political and sexual despotisms of George III and the Prince Regent. Numerous Tartars populate Byron's Eastern tales as well as the Ottoman parts of *Childe Harold* and *Don Juan;* usually such figures are identified by their skills in horsemanship or their "Tartar bonnets." Matthew Lewis's "grand romantic melodrama in two acts," *Timour the Tartar* (1811) conventionally equates the nation of Tartars with fierceness and equestrian skill, capitalizing on the innovation of displaying live horses on stage at Covent Garden Theatre. The most famous Tartar in Romantic period literature, however, is undoubtedly Coleridge's "Kubla Khan," variously identified as a displacement of current political figures, including George III, Napoleon, and the Emperor Qianlong himself.

The preeminent Orientalist of the Romantic period, Sir William Jones wrote extensively on both China and Tartary. Jones's "Fifth Anniversary Discourse" delivered on February 21, 1788 was titled "On the Tartars." Jones defines Tartary "on its most extensive scale" encompassing the lands between Russia, China, India, and the Ottoman Empire (72) Jones is hesitant about exactly how the region is to be demarcated, eschewing the geographically precise for an orientalizing of its sublime landscape. Tartary is a "sublime edifice":

> [T]he beams and pillars of which are many ranges of lofty hills, and the dome, one prodigious mountain, to which the *Chinese* give the epithet of *Celestial*, with a considerable number of broad rivers flowing down its sides: if the mansion be so amazingly sublime, the land around it is proportionably extended, but more wonderfully diversified; for some parts of it are incrusted with ice, others parched with inflamed air, and covered with a kind of lava; here we meet with immense tracts of sandy deserts, and forests almost impenetrable; there with gardens, groves and meadows, perfumed with musk, watered by numerous rivulets, and abounding in fruits and flowers; and, from east to west, lie many considerable provinces, which appear as valleys in comparison of the hills towering above them, but in truth are the flat summits of the highest mountains in the world, or at least the highest in Asia. (72–73)

In presenting this expansive view of Tartary, Jones is clear about the limitations of his knowledge, being largely ignorant of the "*Tartarian* dialects" (71). He identifies Tartary with classical Scythia, though he is clear that the inhabitants of the region have never used either of those terms to distinguish themselves. Despite his awareness that he is using the term "Tartar," "equally improper in the pronunciation and the application" (75), he continues as if the term does have significant and unambiguous meaning. Jones claims there is a recognizable and morphologically stable "Tartar face," a configuration "in their eyes and countenance," that encourages him to see "a common family unity among the different peoples of the region." (78).

Jones's essay has as its primary concern the refutation of the theory of the French writer, Jean-Sylvain Bailly, who, in a series of letters to Voltaire, had argued that Tartary was the "cradle of our species" (75, 77), the original home of the arts and letters from whence civilization had spread to the rest of the world. Jones argues that arts and sciences flourished among the Tartars, not from the beginning of time, but only from the time of Kublai Khan who ordered letters to be invented for his nation "by a *Tibetian*, whom he rewarded with the dignity of chief *Lama*."[5] Jones argues that as Tibetan Buddhism plays a key role in this civilizing mission, Tartary is indebted to India for its learning and not the other way around. The "general character" of the Tartar "nation" was that they "were professed hunters or fishers, dwelling on that account in forests or near great rivers, under huts or rude tents…they were dextrous archers, excellent horsemen, bold combatants…drinking the milk of mares, and eating the flesh of colts" with little taste for "poetry and the improvement of their language" (101).

In his "Seventh Anniversary Discourse" of 1790 on China, Jones was keen to refute the notion that the Chinese and the Tartars are derived from the same ancestors: "That the *Chinese* were anciently of *Tartarian* stock, is a proposition, which I cannot otherwise disprove for the present, than by insisting on the total dissimilarity of the two races in manners and arts, particularly in the fine arts of imagination, which the Tartars, by their own account, never cultivated" (98). Jones estranges the Chinese from the Tartar, and the latter he views as a definable "race":

[T]he *Chinese* and *Hindus* were originally the same people, but having been separated near four thousand years, have retained few strong features of their ancient consanguinity, especially as the *Hindus* have preserved their old language and ritual, while the *Chinese* very soon lost both, and the *Hindus* have constantly intermarried among themselves, while the *Chinese*, by a mixture of *Tartarian* blood from the time of their first establishment, have at length formed a race distinct in appearance both from *Indians* and *Tartars*. (108)

The Chinese, Japanese, and Hindus derive from a "common stem" that originated in Persia. Jones's discussion of racial difference conforms to the model that I have outlined above in its tendency to homogenize a group of culturally and socially different peoples, under the heading "Tartar" while at the same time effecting an estrangement between Chinese and Tartar, which persists despite the "mixing" of the bloods and the physical similarities that Jones perceives to exist in both. Jones thus constructs the Tartars as a kind of indeterminate, intermediate people who are not Chinese, not European, and not Hindu, and Tartary as a sublime, Oriental landscape of extremes, combining elements of civilization (derived from India and imposed by Kublai Khan) with a terrifying combination of beauty and sublimity, immensity, and particular pleasures.

We have seen how the opposition between Chinese and Tartar has informed much of the way that the West has viewed the Far East over a substantial period of history. Not only is it seen in histories, travel accounts, drama, fiction, and so on but it also informs much of the other imaginative writing about China prior to the twentieth century. When writing about China the savage other is often created against which the Qing Empire is defined for Western eyes. Samuel Taylor Coleridge's "Kubla Khan" composed sometime between 1797 and 1799 and published in 1816 is probably the most famous piece of imaginative writing about a "Tartar" in the British tradition. The poem has been discussed as a poem of pure imagination, a poem about genius, an Orientalist poem, a poem about Napoleon Bonaparte and so on.[6] If one wishes to situate the poem in the discourse of China and Tartary, a significantly different reading of the poem emerges. Coleridge says almost as little about China as he does about the poem. In the *Biographia Literaria* of 1817, Coleridge perpetuates the standard wisdom about "the immense empire of China improgressive for thirty centuries" (1983, 2: 137). His views about China at the time of the Macartney Embassy, however, are not known, and the extent to which he may have followed the published accounts of its progress is uncertain.

Nevertheless the poem can be read as work about transhistorical European exploration and the gradual discovery of China, in the same way that *The Rime of the Ancient Mariner* may be concerned with transatlantic slavery. The West's knowledge of the "Tartar" Kublai Khan's thirteenth-century empire, ostensibly one of the subjects of the poem, comes primarily from Marco Polo. Polo's *Description of the World* (or the *Travels*) is a work written by a merchant with a pecuniary eye involved in a mercantile adventure. Polo's discovery of the empire of the Great Khan and its fabulous riches is said to have inspired Columbus's westward expedition to discover an alternative route to Cathay. Here I would like to place the poem, more firmly in the ambiguous and shifting discourse of China and Tartary.

Kublai Khan, as Marco Polo and Samuel Purchas, and many others have made clear, was a "Tartar" Emperor, the grandson of Genghis Khan and heir to his throne. The Great Khan was an outsider, an alien ruler in China. When Marco Polo visited Xanadu (Shang-tu or Chengde) and witnessed the imperial palace and gardens, Kublai was eighty-five years old, and near the end of his reign and life, troubled by "voices prophesying war" (2003, 1: 30, 509–14); John Livingston Lowes, back in 1927, discussed at length Coleridge's indebtedness to Samuel Purchas's historical survey *Purchas His Pilgrimage* (1613) that contained a synthesis of just about all the accounts of China and the area called Tartary then already known. In the Crewe manuscript of the poem, Coleridge claims to have composed "Kubla Khan" in the "fall of the year" of 1797, the same year as Staunton's account of the embassy was published and the year in which Murphy's *Orphan of China* was given one of its many revivals (quite possibly capital-izing on the interest in the embassy).[7] Later in 1816 (coincidentally the date of the Amherst Embassy to China), Coleridge added the famous "Preface," to the poem, informing his readers that it was no more than a "fragment" of a larger work of about three hundred lines and now published on Lord Byron's request as "a psychological curiosity" (1: 511).

In 1998 Nigel Leask crucially resituated the poem in "the intel-lectual climate of the late 1790s," accusing Coleridge of suppress-ing the obvious contemporary sources of the poem in the Macartney Embassy accounts in favor of older exotic views of Cathay, and thus deliberately aestheticizing "Kubla Khan" and rendering it to be "a free imaginative communion with the exotic and often marvellous accounts of Polo and Purchas, rather than an engagement with the decade in which it was written" (1998, 1: 1–21). Given the conflation of Mongul, Manchu, and Tartar in the period and the historiograph-ical interest in the act of the conquest of China by the Tartars, Leask's distinction between older aesthetic accounts and contemporary more objective accounts breaks down when we realize that it is not clear that such diachronic distinctions were clearly understood in the period and that there was a synchronic discourse of China available. Coleridge's knowledge of China in the 1790s must surely have been influenced by reports and accounts of the Macartney Embassy as well as by earlier writings about Kublai which are repeated in the later dis-cussions. Certainly the Emperor Qianlong who had ruled China, the world's most populous empire, for about sixty years, an elderly ruler who would die in 1798, is conflated with Kublai in the same way that earlier writers recall in the Manchu conquest of China of 1644 that of the Mongul conquest by Genghis Khan and his grandson. Qianlong, like Kublai, is an alien ruler, a "Tartar." When the poem was written he was eighty-nine close to the age of Kublai in Polo's *Travels*, an ageing emperor at the end of his reign. Kublai hears "ancestral voices prophesying war" (1: 30), and the final years of the Philosopher-Emperor Qianlong's reign were taken up with the suppression of a growing number of anti-Manchu rebellions; the Jinchuan Wars, and after 1796, the White Lotus Rebellion of millenarian Buddhists. In the "ancestral voices" it is tempting to hear the tones of the mighty Genghis, accorded by his God Tenger, the Mongul destiny to conquer and rule the world as well as the Chinese notion that the "Mandate of Heaven" would be withdrawn from the Yuan dynasty.

For most commentators the poem constructs an antithesis between nature and culture, savagery and civilization, art and chaos. In many ways the poem enacts the discourse of China and Tartary that I have outlined. We have a Tartar emperor whose lineage descends from the ruthless and savage Genghis Khan but who has now been, at least partially, assimilated into a civilized Chinese order as indicated by Purchas and others: "In Xanadu did Kubla Khan / A stately pleasure-dome decree" (1: 1–2). The symbol of civilization here is the landscape gardens, the "twice five miles of fertile ground" that with "walls and towers were girdled round" (2: 5–6). The gardens are

> ...bright with sinuous rills
> Where blossomed many an incense-bearing tree.   (2: 7–8)

Qianlong, like Kublai, was known for his summer palace at Yuanming Yuan or "Garden of Perfect Brightness" near Beijing, as well as for the imperial palace at Jehol, both of which were described in detail in the Macartney accounts. Macartney commented, in his *Journal*, that Yuanming Yuan was said to be "eighteen miles round" and "laid out in all the taste, variety, and magnificence which distinguish the rural scenery of Chinese gardening." He commented on the "close arbours," "stupendous rocks," and "fairyland galleries" (95).

Leask has convincingly argued that "Kubla Khan" is indebted to earlier descriptions of the Gardens of Yuanming Yuan by the Jesuit missionary, Father Attiret in 1743 as disseminated by Sir William Chambers in his *A Dissertation upon Oriental Gardening* (1772) and the various constructs of the Anglo-Chinese garden that were fashionable since the 1730s (Leask 1998, 7–12). For instance, Chambers tells how in the gardens at Yuanming Yuan, there are "temples dedicated to the king of vengeance, deep caverns, and descents to subterranean habitations, overgrown with brushwood and brambles." Scenes of the supernatural also abound; according to Chambers, "flutes, and soft harmonious organs, impelled by subterraneous waters, interrupt, at stated intervals, the silence of the place, and fill the air with solemn melody." There are "colossal figures of dragons, infernal fiends, and other horrid forms, which hold in their monstrous talons, mysterious, cabalistic sentences, inscribed on tables of brass. The ears of men are struck with different sounds, some resembling cries of men in torment, the raging of the sea, the explosion of cannon, the sound of trumpets and all the noise of war" (27–29). A great deal of the topography of "Kubla Khan" is here in Chambers's account of the Anglo-Chinese garden—the pleasure houses, the romantic chasm with its "mighty torrent," the "caverns measureless to man," the monstrosity of the woman wailing for her demon lover, perhaps, as well as the "ancestral voices prophesying war." However Chambers transfers the Romantic sublime of terror from nature to art, in that, according to the theory of the Anglo-Chinese garden, the romantic chasm would be artificial, a product of human ingenuity, "a miracle of rare device" in which the miraculous is not supernatural but a compliment to the ingenuity of the gardener-emperor.

Leask argues that "Kubla Khan" belongs to the late eighteenth-century political discourse of the landscape garden and cites the Whig William Mason's devastating satirical riposte to Chambers, in which the architect is accused of designing a despotic garden state for George III in which the sublime of terror enforces political obedience (1998, 9). For Leask the poem belongs to the period of Coleridge's radical Unitarian dissenting politics and is, to some extent consistent with Coleridge's political program of the 1790s. Though this is an informed and ingenious reading of the poem, I would argue that "Kubla Khan" rejects an obviously domestic political reading, coded or otherwise, to partake in a larger imaginative discourse about China, Tartary, and human difference in general. The "deep romantic chasm" that is described as "a savage place," both holy and enchanted with its "woman wailing for her demon-lover" and its destructive fountain, relates more to the necessary antithesis of savage Tartary that defines and confirms the civilization of China represented by the pleasure dome.

Polo, Purchas, Bell, and many others had detailed at length the Tartar reliance on astrologers, magicians, necromancers, and shamans. For instance, Purchas describes how Kublai at the behest of his astrologers "pour[ing] forthe with his owne hands the milke of the royal Mares in the ayre, and on the earth, to give drinke to the Spirits and Idols which they worship." He describes how the necromancers or "Bachsi," are "exceedingly expert in their devilish art" raising storms, threatening "plagues or other misfortunes from their Idols." Purchas also claims the Bachsi are addicted to usury, sodomy, and cannibalism (418–19). Savage Tartary is thus a place of idols, demons, magicians, and unnatural practices, antithetical to the rational, Confucian civilization of China, which over its history has assimilated both the Mongul Kublai Khan and the Manchu Qianlong Emperors, though ambivalently and problematically. In the same way that the civilized but effeminate Song (conquered by Kublai Khan) and Ming (conquered by the Manchu) cultures refined their Mongul and Tartar conquerors, Kublai and the visionary speaker of the poem are also civilized by contact with a feminine presence. In the poem's concluding lines the civilizing and inspirational figure is female:

> A damsel with a dulcimer
> In a vision once I saw:
> It was an Abyssinian maid,
> And on her dulcimer she played
> Singing of Mount Abora.   (2: 37–44)

The damsel's agency is, of course, one that the Visionary of the poem wishes to assimilate to enable him to build "that dome in air," (1: 46) which Kublai has built on land; yet the process of civilizing in the poem is imaged as feminine, as the Mongul trajectory from savage conqueror to settled ruler accomplished by the influence of a feminine presence is congruent with the received discourse of China. Nevertheless the civilizing presence in the poem is clearly not Chinese but Abyssinian. One could resort here, as Elinor Shaffer does, to the notion that the poem is about Orientalist syncretism so that all of Asia is present in one spot and that Abyssinia can effortlessly double for China and be a synecdoche for the East in general; however, it may be that for Coleridge the civilizing agency, though feminine, must ultimately be Christian and involve a rejection of a Confucian rationalism unaided by Revelation. Leask has persuasively argued that Abyssinia, in contrast to Tartary, connoted for Coleridge's age an ancient Christian culture compatible with his then Unitarian belief which Confucian China could not. Such customs and belief had been evoked by James Bruce in his *Travels to Discover the Source of the Nile* (1790) which was widely read (Leask 1998, 12–18). In any case the paradigm of the discourse of China in the eighteenth century, underlying the series of histories, accounts, and fictions that I have outlined provides the informing structure for the poem, a poem deeply imbricated in the ways of viewing China and its Tartar others that derive from at least the times of Samuel Purchas.

If Coleridge's Kublai is either a conflation or, indeed, a displacement of Qianlong, the Son of Heaven of the Celestial Empire, it is tempting to think that those puzzling "ancestral voices" might be proleptic of the approaching Anglo-Chinese conflicts realized in the form of the later nineteenth-century Opium Wars. To allow the young Coleridge this degree of prescience might not be to claim too much. Although it is hard to image the elderly Qianlong Emperor as the postcolonial albatross, nevertheless Coleridge might envisage China as a potential victim of the commercial aggression and expansion of Georgian imperial Britain, a process of which Coleridge was very much aware. A reading of the poem in which China figures as a rational and civilized, yet flawed, empire was still available to late eighteenth-century Britain. There still existed the possibility, despite the contemporary researches of Sir William Jones, that the Chinese Empire was possessed of a greater authenticity at this time for Coleridge because its language and culture corresponded more closely to a universal and unmediated knowledge predating the Deluge and Babel. Certainly, Coleridge's "Kubla Khan" demonstrates none of the racial antipathy to the Chinese or other Eastern peoples that came to dominate the works of Thomas De Quincey in the lead-up to the Opium Wars of the nineteenth century to which we will now turn.

TARTARS, CHINESE, AND MALAYS IN DE QUINCEY'S WRITINGS

This chapter concludes with a discussion of the writing of Thomas De Quincey about the Far East. De Quincey's representation of Oriental figures takes us from the Sinopolitanism and cosmopolitanism of the late eighteenth century to the avowedly physical racism of the nineteenth. It would be inappropriate, however, to see De Quincey's writings as those of a representative voice for the nineteenth century and care must be taken in extrapolating from his views to those of a consensus position. Though influential, De Quincey's viewpoint is idiosyncratic and heavily involved in a unique psychobiographical project; nevertheless his presence as a major writer and personality of the British Romantic period necessitates a serious consideration of his ideas. De Quincey's encounter with the Eastern person he refers so as a "Malay" in the *Confessions of an English Opium Eater* (1821) is probably the most notorious. This encounter has been much discussed, notably in the context of the psychopathology of imperialism by John Barrell and Nigel Leask. Barrell traces De Quincey's fears, which run back and forth between the "private space of his own childhood and the most public terrain of the British Empire in the East." At one level De Quincey's fears of the Oriental function as a displacement of his anxieties about the Jacobinical tendencies of "mass society" and the British working classes, or "urban poor," of the early nineteenth century, a "dream dictatorship of the proletariat" (vii, 4–5, 19). However, in Barrell's argument, De Quincey's displacements are more complex than this in that they posit something antithetical to the self but which is assimilated into the self when confronted by something which lies beyond both, something inextricably Other: "[T]here is a 'this,' and there is something hostile to it, something which lies, almost invariably, to the east: but there is an East beyond that East, where something lurks which is equally threatening to both, and which enables or obliges them to reconcile their differences" enabling some form of solidarity to emerge to buttress British imperial power (11, 20). More than this, Barrell argues that De Quincey's Oriental fears are displacements of "some primal and private terror." As I outlined in chapter 1, De Quincey envisages race in terms of bloodlines, but understands that all races in the modern world, with the possible exceptions of Arabs and Jews, are mixed and hybrid. It is this state of hybridity and the fear and loathing it occasions in De Quincey that Barrell so brilliantly explores. For Leask, De Quincey's writings manifest a complex class- and race hatred. De Quincey's "apologia for opium is also an apologia for imperialism as a means of stimulating a torpid and internally fissured national culture, and of displacing domestic anxieties onto the oriental Other." De Quincey's self is plagued by a return of these "displaced anxieties magnified fourfold" (1992, 171). My own argument about De Quincey's representations of the East is less involved with the psychopathology of its originator, and more concerned to view them as an idiosyncratic and personalized intensification of a increasingly biological nineteenth-century racial discourse about the East, one which homogenizes and alienates.

In his *Confessions* (1821) De Quincey describes how in 1816 "a Malay" called at Dove Cottage in Grasmere where he was living. His servant, Barbara Lewthwaite, answers the door. She is immediately confounded by the "impassable gulf" between the Malay and the household and seeks out De Quincey to "exorcise" the "demon below." De Quincey fixes the Malay against the "native spirit of mountain intrepidity of the girl":

> And a more striking picture there could not be imagined, than the beautiful English face of the girl, and its exquisite fairness, together with her erect and independent attitude, contrasted with the sallow and bilious skin of the Malay, enameled or veneered with mahogany, by marine air, his small fierce restless eyes, thin lips, slavish gestures and adoration. Half hidden by the ferocious-looking Malay was a little child from a neighbouring cottage who had crept in after him and was now in the act of reverting its head, and gazing upwards at the turban and the fiery eyes beneath it, whilst he caught at the dress of the young woman for protection. (2: 57)

Leask writes of this passage that De Quincey here "mobilizes the full armoury of racial discrimination, 'racial typology,' the analytics of blood, ideologies of racial and cultural dominance or degradation" (1992, 210). This statement is essentially fair, although it depends on a later nineteenth-century articulation of racial hierarchies for its force. Rather than articulating racial thinking as it is developed, one must allow that De Quincey is also an innovator in the field of race thinking, capable of pushing further those nascent trends of biological determinism found in Linnaeus, Blumenbach, Kant, and others in extreme and violent directions. Although there is an increasing tendency to homogenize different peoples under typological headings, characteristically the Mongolian, De Quincey's lumping together of radically different eastern peoples is at one with the more extreme, later racialist thinkers, such as Knox, Nott, Gliddon, Gobineau (and later even more extreme racists), but not, in my view, typical of the majority discourse of China in the Romantic period, unstable as it was, and certainly some distance from Staunton, Ellis, or even Barrow. Similarly De Quincey's focusing on the blood as a marker of the "purity" of race marks him out as a very different thinker from some of those of his contemporaries and as an "ultraracist" of the period in terms of the violence and extremism of his writing. Additionally one must take account, following John Whale, of the impact of Protestant missionary discourse and De Quincey's particular religious mind-set on his ideas of the East (4–9).

In accordance with the idea of race derived from Kant, De Quincey's Malay is not Europeanized in any way but is irremediably Other and hardly human. He becomes a synecdoche for the Orient as a whole to be epitomized in a series of epithets and is inscribed alternately as either animalistic or demonic. He is a "tiger-cat," a "demon" with "fierce restless eyes" both "ferocious-looking," and slavish (57–8). The main signs of difference here are somatic or physical: the bilious and sallow complexion, the epiphanically yellow skin, and the rodentlike, ferocious eyes. Here we see in the fabled yellowness of the Oriental complexion an important and imaginary sign of difference. The figure has an uncanny otherness, which haunts De Quincey's dreams and is symbolized by the gift of opium to which both figures are addicted (Barrell 75–76; Leask 1992, 209). De Quincey's depiction of the Malay is also devoid of any real attempt to specify the geographic, linguistic, or cultural differences of his subject. Despite the homogenizing tendency of much nineteenth-century racial discourse, as the century progressed, there was a concurrent attempt to collect and establish data about local variations of peoples, evidenced in the vastly expanding tomes of Prichard's ethnological work. De Quincey's Malay brings with him other Asians from whom he is only differentiated by the fact that they are even more terrifying. De Quincey recounts how these figures haunted his dreams and "ran amuck at me, and led me into a world of troubles" (58).

When describing his Oriental opium dreams, De Quincey presents the Celestial Empire in terms of the most extravagant Oriental fantasy. He claims that to live in China would drive him insane; it is the seat of "awful images and associations"; a "young Chinese seems" to him "an antediluvian man"; Southern Asia, is the part of the earth "most swarming with human life." De Quincey tells how "in China, over and above what it has in common with the rest of southern Asia" he is "terrified by the modes of life, by the manners, and the barrier of utter abhorrence and want of sympathy placed between us by feelings deeper" than he can analyze, but he would sooner live with "lunatics or brute animals." In his Oriental dreams, as is well known, De Quincey brings all Asia under his nightmarish vision. Egypt, India, China, all provide images for these tormenting and horrific dreams (2: 70–72). De Quincey later wrote a series of virulently anti-Chinese articles inspired by the Opium Wars of 1839 and 1859. In "The Opium and the China Question" (1840), he declares, among other things, that the Chinese are "incapable of a true civilization, semi-refined in manners and the mechanic arts, but incurably savage in the moral sense," they are "conceited," "rascally," "inorganic," "stagnant," "improgressive," "lazy," "torpid," "sedentary," "wicked," "vindictive," "cruel," "bestial," "full of insolence, full of error, needing to be enlightened," and, above all, "something to be kicked." They are "ultrapusillanimous," "the vilest and silliest among nations" (11: 554, 541, 542, 546, 550, 552, 553, 554, 557, 559, 561,

562). De Quincey's arguments against the Qing Empire are couched in the language of Ricardian economics and the conventions of trade and diplomacy, but ultimately for him, China is an aberrant state, "a vast callous hulk":

> It is defended by its essential non-irritability, arising out of the intense non-development of its resources. Were it better developed, China would become an organized mass—something to be kicked, but which cannot kick again—having no commerce worth counting, no vast establishments of maritime industry, no arsenals, no shipbuilding towns, no Portsmouths, Deals, Deptfords, Woolwiches, Sunderlands, Newcastles, Liverpools, Bristols, Glasgows—in short, no vital parts, no organs, no heart, no lungs. (11: 542–43)

De Quincey represents China as a body possessing no nervous system, or possessing at least a system which is physiologically coarser and less developed than that of the European. De Quincey's discussion of the Chinese Empire as a "callous hulk" defended by "its essential non-irritability" and requiring to be kicked into action uses a bodily metaphor for a political entity. The symptoms of imperial torpor consist in its having no commerce and participation in free trade. De Quincey racializes commerce here, arguing that China's lack of commercial activity results not from the stage of society that it has reached but from the moral characteristics associated with Oriental races. The metaphor of the body politic is easily applied to the individual case. That the Chinese were less subject to pain because their nervous system was less sensitive than white Europeans became a cliché of nineteenth-century racist discourse.

De Quincey's discussion of China, however, is not conducted in entirely bodily terms. In the essays on the Opium Wars, he also evokes a model of social progress conforming to the Enlightenment stadial model of a progression from savagery, barbarism, and civilization and that his attacks on China relate to the forms of Oriental government, which he terms as barbaric. Although eighteenth-century writing about China almost always accorded the Chinese a high degree of civilization, De Quincey's relegation of China to the state of barbarism may allow for the possibility of improvement, cutting across the biological determinism apparent elsewhere in the essays. In his essay of 1840 on "The Opium and the China Question," De Quincey defines the term barbarian in its classical sense "equivalent to *alien* or *non-Grecian*" (9: 558). However it is clear that he has a model in his mind of development from savage, to barbarian, and thence to civilization. Earlier in the essay he has indicated that the nascent colonies of Australia and New Zealand would, anticipating Robert Knox, change the balance of power in the Far East. New Zealand, in particular, with its combination of the "noblest children of civilization" and the "noblest savages in the world" would have a special role to play. The growth of such colonies combined with increasing missionary endeavor will further tip the balance in Britain's favor. De Quincey sees China as ambivalently barbaric, in that it has degenerated from civilization and is morally savage. He identifies, in particular, "this horrible Chinese degeneration of moral distinctions." China is poised somewhere between savagery and barbarism, "incapable of a true civilization, semi-refined in manners and mechanic arts, but incurably savage in the moral sense" (9: 552, 554). In his essay "On the True Relations to Civilisation and Barbarism of the Roman Western Empire" (1839), De Quincey had argued that the later Roman Empire descended into barbarism as a result of forces that operated internally within its own political logic, and not as the result of the invasion of Barbarians from without. In fact, De Quincey argues that the Barbarians were in reality "the restorers and regenerators of the effete Roman intellect" (11: 388). Barbarism thus is a retreat or rejection of the principles of civilization demonstrated in the degradation or lack of taste and literature, the growing ignorance of the Romans, their "brutal, bloody and Tartar style of their festal exultations," and "the fearful scene of Turkish murder and bloodshed going on for ever in high places" (11: 388, 389, 392, 393). De Quincey's writing on China is thus somewhat conflicted. The model of stadial development to civilization is combined with a biological determinism that would belie any such movement to progression. Throughout the essays De Quincey treats China as a Tartar Empire eschewing the Tartar and Chinese distinction in a homogenized and monolithic concept of Oriental racial character.

De Quincey's writing about the Chinese would lead us to think that he constructed an imaginary and savage Oriental people by vast numbers of indistinguishable Asiatics. This position is complicated by a quite extraordinary, and seldom discussed, essay he published in 1837 that presented a quite different view of both China and Central Eurasian peoples. De Quincey's "The Revolt of the Kalmuck Tartars; Or, Flight of the Kalmuck Khan and His people from the Russian Territories to the Frontiers of China," describes the "flight eastwards of a principal Tartar nation across the bondless steppes of Asia."[8] The Torghuts people, known to the Russians as Kalmuck (or Kalmyck), were a western Mongol people who had moved from western Mongolia to the region around the lower Volga in southeast Russia in the seventeenth century. During the course of the succeeding century they became increasingly assimilated into the Russian Empire, which was expanding to the south and the east, thus losing their autonomy. In 1771, those Kalmucks living on the left or east bank of the Volga (known as Torghuts or Volga Kalmucks) returned to their ancient homeland near China (Zhungaria). This migration was of truly biblical proportions and was the last known exodus of a nomadic people in the history of Asia. For Purdue "when these last free nomads came under domination from the great agrarian empires that surrounded them, the steppe ended, and a great chapter in world history closed" (299). De Quincey's essay, based mainly on a single source, presents an imagined recreation of the exodus of the Kalmuck Tartars, their migrations and extensive sufferings, to their arrival in China. The essay is full of sublime scenery and dramatic events, "the steppes, the camels, the tents, the snowy and sandy deserts" acting as a backdrop to "the general conflagration on the Wolga," "the disastrous scene of the flight," "the Tartar siege of the Russian fortress Koulagina," and "the bloody engagement with the Cossacks in the mountain passes at Ouchim," all these things function to create the wildest of "wild romance." For De Quincey this event is combined with the "higher and philosophic interest," which belongs to "a case of authentic history, commemorating a great revolution for good or for evil, in the fortunes of a whole people—a people semi-barbarous, but simple-hearted, and of ancient descent" (9: 172–73). De Quincey's essay is an intriguing and powerful tour de force of political, historical, and racial narrative.

De Quincey presents the motivation for the flight as a result of the sense of injured merit and satanic pride of one of the Kalmuck princes, Zebek-Dorchi (Tsebek-Dordži or Tsebek Dorji Tayishi). Zebek, whose claim to be Khan of the Kalmucks had been passed over, like Satan with his sense of injured merit, seeks his revenge on the Russian court by removing their key subjects to China. Zebek is described in terms of a Gothic villain; he has the "dark intellectual qualities of Machiavellian dissimulation, profound hypocrisy, and perfidy which knew no remorse" (174). The tremendous suffering that is inflicted on his people during the exodus is thus not, in De Quincey's formulation, a necessary or essential sacrifice. By a series of intrigues, involving the support of the religious lamas, Zebek persuades the good-natured but naïve young Khan, Oubacha (Ubaši or Ubashi), that it is in the interests of the people to remove from a state of growing dependency on Russia, to the uncertain freedoms of the Qing Empire. Certainly, the Kalmucks resent the "galling assumption of authority" assumed by what they see as "a nation of ugly, stupid, and filthy barbarians" over "the freeborn Tartar" (180). De Quincey thus presents his Tartars, caught between the two empires of Russia and China, again as kind of in-between people, neither European nor fully Asian, to adapt Barrell's formulation, neither this, not that, nor the other but often all three. As Whale argues, De Quincey's "configuration of the pagan, often Orientalist Other is not only predictably imbricated with the self, but also provocatively mobile.... caught between 'East' and 'West' in De Quincey's imagination" (12). Discussing Zebek, De Quincey comments:

> He, a worm as he was, could he venture to assail the mighty behemoth of Muscovy, the potentate who counted three hundred languages around the footsteps of his throne, and from whose "lion ramp" recoiled alike "baptized and infidel"—Christendom on one side, strong by her intellect and her organization, and the "barbaric East," on the other, with her unnumbered numbers? The match was a monstrous one; but in its very monstrosity there lay this germ of encouragement, that it could not be suspected. (9: 176)

While the East is barbaric, the Kalmucks are only semibarbarous, not European and Christian; but neither Asiatic and barbarous, sharing in the masculinity of the Russian, and opposed to the femininity of the East with its swarms of "unnumbered numbers." The Kalmucks are not a part of Christendom, but neither are they part of Christendom's antithesis, Islam, but actually fighting for the Russians with great honor in one of the many wars then ongoing between Czarina and the Sultan.

The presentation of the Kalmuck peoples, in this essay, is something different from what one might expect after reading De Quincey's *Confessions* and his essays on China and the Opium Wars. Overall, "Revolt of the Kalmuck Tartars" treats them very sympathetically with admiration and empathy for their suffering. Their flight is compared to the great military expeditions, such as the Parthian expeditions of the Romans and that of Napoleon's advance and retreat from Russia. In religious terms the movement is "an Exodus...in so far resembling the great Scriptural Exodus of the Israelites, under Moses and Joshua." Their flight is described in sublime Miltonic terms. In "the gloomy vengeance of Russia and her vast artillery," De Quincey is reminded of "the solitary hand pursuing through desert spaces and through ancient chaos a rebellious host, and overtaking with volleying thunders those who believed themselves already within the security of darkness and of distance" (9: 172)

Yet nevertheless there is something which seems almost subhuman or primitive in the Kalmuck psychology and which reminds us of the depictions of Asiatic people in De Quincey's other works. De Quincey argues that in the "abruptness of its commencement, and the fierce velocity of its execution, we read an expression of the wild barbaric character of the agents." In both "the unity of purpose connecting this myriad of wills, and in the blind but unerring aim at a mark so remote," De Quincey recognizes "the Almighty instincts that propel the migration of the swallow, or the life-withering marches of the locust" (171–72). The Kalmucks have a "native ferocity" exasperated by "debasing forms of superstition," their natural disposition is "unamiable" (173). Their religion, a mixture of Buddhism and indigenous Shamanistic practices, is described as "dark and mysterious" (181). But more than this, the essay presents a series of almost unrelieved hardships and sufferings, starvation, the torture of extreme cold and heat, insufferable thirst, massacres, and bloodshed, "the most awful series of calamities, and the most extensive, which is any where recorded to have visited the sons and daughters of men" (187). We are reminded of the Malay who has a physiology which can survive a dose of opium sufficient to kill three dragoons and their horses. De Quincey compares the Kalmuck sufferings with those of other historical tragedies to find that theirs must surely rank foremost in length of duration as well as of intensity of pain and misery. It is in this aestheticization of suffering, this distillation of the "romantic misery peculiar" to the event that De Quincey reveals the source of his interest in the Kalmuck flight. He comments how "it is remarkable that these sufferings of the Tartars, though under the moulding hands of accident, arrange themselves almost with a scenical propriety." It as if they

combined, as with the skill of an artist; the intensity of the misery advancing regularly with the advances of the march, and the stages of calamity corresponding to the stages of the route; so that upon raising the curtain which veils the great catastrophe, we behold one vast climax of anguish, towering upwards by regular gradations, as if constructed artificially for picturesque effect. (188)

De Quincey takes his Kalmucks to the limits of human suffering, to the point at which "the bloody desperation of the miserable fugitives had reached its uttermost extremity" (188).

The final catastrophe occurs when the Kalmucks reaching Lake Tengis on the frontiers of China are overtaken by their pursuers and ancient enemies the Bashkirs and the Kirghises (Kirgiz), who are equally as miserable as they. Both parties run to the lake to quench their torturing thirst, before indulging in a mutual slaughter, which makes the lake run red. The hostility of both sides "assumed the appearance much more of a warfare amongst wild beasts than amongst creatures acknowledging the restraints of reason or the claims of human nature. The spectacle became too atrocious; it was that of a host of lunatics pursued by a host of fiends" (200). "Forgetful" of everything but that "one almighty instinct" both nations rush to slake their thirst before turning on each other: "Every moment the water grew more polluted: and yet every moment fresh myriads came up to the lake and rushed in, not able to resist their frantic thirst, and swallowing large draughts of water, visibly contaminated with the blood of their compatriots" (204). Whale discusses how De Quincey's representation of landscape here reveals a disturbed mixture of history and Christianity and how his militant vision of Christian civilization secured by the apocalyptic battle of Waterloo is questioned by his construction of such "Eastern" Others. Certainly the final battle is here imaged as an apocalypse, with the cannibalistic imagery further debasing the Kalmuck, essentially creatures of instinct, such as wild beasts or "enraged hornets" (199). Their ability to withstand suffering is almost beyond imagination, and here once again De Quincey preempts later-nineteenth-century racist notions that the nervous systems of Asian people are physiologically better able to withstand pain.

Thus I would argue that, albeit in a different way, De Quincey's construction of the Tartar, is equally a product of fantasy, a nation fit to paint the extremities of suffering and vengeance upon, a nation that acts as a collective, upon instinct, like the locust, hornet or swallow. His Tartar is also an in-between category, not European, not Asian, not Christian, not Muslim, neither Russian, Chinese, nor Turk, inhabiting the fantastic space of the imaginary land of Tartary with its endless deserts, sublime mountains, and extremes of cold and heat, present in both Jones's and Coleridge's debatable land of Tartary. The essay has one further surprise that returns it to the place from which these two chapters on the East began, the Qing Empire. Despite De Quincey's other degrading remarks about China elsewhere, his presentation of the Chinese Emperor Qianlong at the close of the essay, is almost wholly positive. Like Sir William Jones who describes the Emperor as "a man of the brightest genius and the most amiable affections" ("On China" 1807, 367), De Quincey does not mention that Qianlong was not ethnically Han Chinese but an alien ruler. As we have seen other commentators on the Qing Empire confusingly conflate the Mongul and Manchu peoples under the heading Tartar, but De Quincey's emperor has little in common with his returning Tartar subjects. Qianlong witnesses the catastrophe of the Kalmucks during one of his hunting trips where he situated "on the very margin of the vast central deserts of Asia" (11: 201). He sends his cavalry to aid the Kalmucks as "an act of fatherly care for these erring children (as he esteemed them) now returning to their ancient obedience" (202). Under Qianlong's tutelage, the Kalmucks are transformed from a "purely pastoral and vagrant people" to one "essentially dependent upon agriculture; and thus far raised in the social rank." They are "reclaimed from roving and from the savage customs connected with so unsettled a life" (206). Thus ends the great Mongul adventure, originating with Genghis and further by his grandson, Kublai, to rule the world, an epochal end to an era of enormous imperial aspiration and achievement. It is a bitter-sweet moment, nostalgic, and final. All the advantages, if such they were, gained from the domestication of the Qing Empire are overbalanced by the increasing remoteness of their "conversion to Christianity, without which in these times there is no absolute advance possible on the path to true civilization," (206) an authentically De Quincian note sounding discordantly.

De Quincey's Kalmucks bring this study to a conclusion. In racial discourse the Mongolian came to stand for all the Far Eastern peoples and the Kalmuck became the typical representative of that grouping. For Buffon, Blumenbach, Camper and others, the Kalmuck was a racial type equal with the African and generally regarded as having degenerated just as far. The Kalmuck, in the aesthetic hierarchy of racial science was also deemed the ugliest and furthest away from the European norm. In the nineteenth century the "Yellow Peril" subsumed Mongols, Tartars, and Chinese in an homogenizing racial discourse, summed up by the early twentieth century in that character of popular racist romance, Dr. Fu Manchu, a Manchu or Tartar who stood for all the peoples of China. The conflation of Tartar, Mongol, and Chinese in De Quincey shows the extent to which a fully biological and essentializing racial belief has achieved a dominance over other religious, economic, and commercial discourse in his writing. The eighteenth-century construction and exploitation of the distinction between savage Tartar and civilized Chinese that defined difference through a stadial notion of social progress was increasingly racialized and, in the end, abandoned in favor of a monolithic and physical categorization of the peoples of the Far East. In De Quincey's extraordinary essay we hear the death knell of the Tartar as a fictional construct.

NOTES

INTRODUCTION

1. This issues of the fabrication of race as a rationalization for slavery and colonialism is discussed by Bernard Boxhill (19, 1–42).
2. The literature in this area is now substantial but the following are especially notable: Augstein, (1999) and her invaluable selection of writings (1996); Banton; Bernasconi, *Concepts of Race* (2001) and "Who Invented the Concept of Race" (2001); Bernasconi and Lott; Boxhill; Brantlinger (2003); Bulmer and Solomos; Eze, *Race and the Enlightenment* (1997); Fredrickson (2002); Gossett; Lyon; MacDougall; McClintock; Malchow; Niro; Nussbaum (1995; *Limits of the Human*, 2003); Poliakov; Schiebinger, *Nature's Body* (1994); Stanton; Voeglin; Ward and Lott; Wiegman; Zantop, *Colonial Fantasies* (1997).
3. Thomas's work has been widely influential on criticism about the cultures of colonialism and exploration, especially 1991, 1994, and 1997.
4. Kim F. Hall is also important for discussions of early modern theories of difference.
5. For an account of this semiotic association of white and black, see Fryer.
6. A similar thesis is developed by Stuart Hall 225–78.

1   THE RACE IDEA AND THE ROMANTICS: COLERIDGE AND DE QUINCEY

1. Goldberg 1993; Livingstone; and Van Den Berghe 101–13.
2. Bernier's "A new division of the earth according to the different species or races of men who inhabit it, sent by a famous traveller to Mons * * * * *, nearly in these terms" is reprinted in Bernasconi and Lott, 1–4. Bernier is discussed by Hannaford (191, 202–3) and Wheeler 2000 (96, 160).
3. Schiebinger 1994 (119); for the fourfold humoral basis of eighteenth-century racial classification, consult Wheeler 2000 (22–28).

4. Important discussions of Linnaeus's ideas include Banton 2–5; Eze, *Race and Enlightenment* 1997 (10–14); Pratt 32–33; Schiebinger 1994 (28–39, 40–74); Larson 1971 and 1974; and Koerner.

5. Kames in Kitson, *Theories of Race* 1999 (51–52).

6. This debate is authoritatively summarized in Augstein, *Prichard's Anthropology* 1999 (58–92).

7. Wheeler 2000 (209–33) discusses the complexity of Long's thought. Although Wheeler stresses Long's nonbiological racism, I focus on the somatic aspects of his work, because these were elements of his work that most influenced his contemporaries. Long also distinguished between the African-born and the Creole slave, Long 1774 (2: 410–14).

8. Virey's work was translated as *Natural history of the Negro Race. Extracted from the French* by J.H. Guenebault and published in America in 1837, where it proved influential in the debates about race and slavery. Fredrickson 2002 (67–268, 179n); Augstein 1994 (163–80).

9. George Fredrickson 1971 argues that for this reason polygenesis remained unpopular as a theory of race even in the antebellum South; Peterson argues for the importance of the curse of Ham as a more popular, Christian justification of slavery. Gosset 54–83 and Stanton also discuss this issue in the American context.

10. Lively 99–124 provides an excellent discussion of the racist implications of Darwin's theory of natural selection.

11. Brantlinger 2003 (164–88) discusses Darwin's notions of extinction theory. Also relevant are Stepan 1982 (47–139) and Stocking 128–273.

12. Important discussions of Buffon's ideas about racial theory include Roger and Bonefoi (especially 174–84, 288–335; Sloan 1976, 356–75; Farber 259–84; Popkin 1973, 245–62; Eddy 1994, 644–61) provides a useful overview of the debate. See also Reill 33–70.

13. Buffon *Histoire naturelle* 1: 38–40; 4: 386. Quoted in Eddy 1994 (646).

14. Buffon's concept of degeneration is discussed in Roger and Bonnefoi 299–38; Sloan 1973 (302–11) and 1976 (370); Hannaford 203–7; and Eddy 1994 (651–54).

15. Buffon "Variétés dans l'espèce humaine" (1749); *Histoire naturelle* 3: 523–24; Eze, *Race and the Enlightenment* 1997 (26); and Eddy 1984 (1–45).

16. Maupertius's ideas about race are discussed by Bowler 1983 (70–73).

17. Sloan 1979 (109–53) argues this.

18. The debate about Kant's theories of race is now substantial and complex. Important discussions include Eze, "The Colour of Reason" 1997; Larrimore 1999 (99–125); Bernasconi, "Who Invented the Concept of Race?" 2001; 2002 (145–66); Bindman 2002 (155–60, 169–89, 245n); Zammito; Armstrong 213–36. Those defending

Kant include Hill and Boxhill 448–71; Muthu 122–210. Essays by Zammito, Shell, and Larrimore on Kant and race are contained in Eigen and Larrimore 35–54, 55–72, 73–90, 91–120.

19. I cite from the translation of Kant's "On the Different Human Races," by Jon Mark Mikkelsen from Bernasconi and Lott 8–22. Kant restated these ideas in his essay of 1784 *Bestimmung des Begriffs der Menschenrasse* though he is unclear whether the discoveries made just around that time in Oceania indicate the existence of a fifth, additional race. This subject is discussed by Bindman 2002 (169–73).

20. Banks's traffic in skulls and the networks he established are discussed by Carter 274–77; Gascoigne 149–59; Turnbull 215–221; Bindman 2002 (123–50, 173–81); and Fulford, Lee, and Kitson 127–48. Later scientific bone collecting is discussed by Macdonald 96–135.

21. For a fascinating discussion of the shifting origins of the human race and the construction of the Caucasian, see Augstein, "From the land of the Bible to the Caucasus" 1999 (58–79).

22. Bindman 2002 (190–201) discusses the aesthetic implications of Blumenbach's racial ideas.

23. Smith's ideas were challenged in the United States by the polygenist John Augustine Smith, "A Lecture introductory to the second Course of Anatomical Instruction in the College of Physicians and Surgeons for the State of New-York," *New York Medical and Philosophical Journal and Review* 1 (1809): 32–48.

24. Important discussions of Cuvier's work include William Coleman; Outram; and Augstein, *Prichard's Anthropology* 1999 (57–104).

25. As with Camper, Blumenbach, and others the human skull was to exert its uncanny fascination on the Frenchman. Cuvier's brief *Instructive note on the researches to be carried out relative to the anatomical differences between the diverse races of man* counseled his fellow researchers to collect specimens everywhere, but chiefly of the skulls of different races, not failing to "visit places where the dead are deposited" (quoted in Stocking 30).

26. In 1994, Nelson Mandela requested that France release Baartman's remains. When the remains were eventually returned in April 2002, the funeral service was a national event. S.J. Gould 1982 (20–27); Gilman 223–63; and Wiegman 56–59.

27. The impact of the Saint Domingue revolution on discourses of race is discussed by Geggus.

28. Wollstonecraft's reviews are collected in Wollstonecraft vol. 7. Her ideas about race are discussed in Juengel 897–927 and Ferguson 1993 (8–33).

29. This passage is quoted in Wood 2002 (168). My discussion of Cobbett's racial thought is indebted to Wood 2002 (152–69).

30. Earlier discussions of Coleridge's notions of race include Haegar 333–57; Keane especially, 57–66; and most recently, Wood 2002 (218–29).

31. The racial implications of the work of the German *Naturphilosophie*, especially Fichte, Oken, and Schelling, are discussed by Poliakov 238–54.

32. Levere contains an excellent discussion of Coleridge's theories of life and organization.

33. "Various have been the disputes of antiquarians concerning the origin of nations. I have found no reason whatsoever to differ in the least from the plain and simple account given us in our Scriptures." Coleridge 1949 (254, 430).

34. The note is cited in Levere 115. The neatest version of Coleridge's attempt to combine Blumenbach's pentad of races with Noah's three sons is given in an entry for February 24, 1827 in Coleridge 1990 (2: 55).

35. Cullingworth 18 reports that White's collection was presented to St. Mary's Hospital in Manchester and mostly destroyed by fire in 1847. The body of Hannah Beswick, however, was obtained by a Dr. Ollier on White's death and then left to the Manchester Natural History Museum and later buried in an unmarked grave in Manchester cemetery in 1868. The politics of Manchester medicine are discussed by Pickerstone and Butler 227–49 and Sarafianos 102–18.

2   ROMANTIC ANATOMIES OF RACE: THE NEW COMPARATIVE ANATOMY AND THE CASE OF VICTOR FRANKENSTEIN

1. Tyson's anatomy is discussed by Cole 198–221 and S.J. Gould 1983 (18–25).

2. Linnaeus to John George Gmelin, February 14, 1747, quoted in Koerner 87.

3. Linnaeus "Markattan Diana" 1754 (210). Quoted in Koerner 87.

4. Linnaeus "Anthropropmorpha" (1760). Quoted in Schiebinger 1994 (80).

5. Important discussions of this concept include, Lovejoy; Bynum 1984 (1–28); Bowler 1983 (59–62); Woodard 1–30 and Jordan 482–511.

6. That White has his friend John Hunter in mind is made clear by note 7 to his essay which refers to both Hunter's collections and William Sharp's engraving of the Reynolds portrait of Hunter. White also refers to Home's "Life of Hunter" describing the arrangement of the museum (144, 141–42). However in the Preface to his essay White writes that he was "insensibly led to the present consideration, from hearing Mr. John Hunter's Remarks on the Gradation of Skulls, as he stated in the introduction to a Course of Lectures on Midwifery, which he delivered last winter at the Lying-in Hospital in Manchester" (iii). W.D. Ian Rolfe argues that this must therefore be Dr. John Hunter (1730–1809), as Hunter

died in 1793 several years before the publication of White's essay (316 n.87). The reference is more likely to be a corruption of a comment about White's own lectures in Manchester (Sarafianos 102–18).

7. Meijer is the most recent and authoritative account of Camper's ideas of race and aesthetics. Also important are Bindman 2002 (201–9); S.J. Gould 1991 (23–28, 34, 36) and 1985 (210–14); Bynum 1975 (1–28).

8. Camper was the first to separate the African chimpanzee from the Asian orangutan (Meijer 10).

9. Anon newspaper cutting (n.d) penciled 1788. Quoted by Moore 473.

10. The portrait is discussed by Taylor 1–4 and Turnbull 202–25.

11. I am indebted for this suggestion and for the following reference from Camper's diary to Simon Chaplin, Senior Curator of the Hunterian Museum, London, who generously shared his thoughts and the fruits of his recent research with me.

12. "Petri Camperi Itinera in Anglia 1748–1785." *Opuscula selecta Neerlandicorum de arte medica.* Vol. 15 (Amsterdam: Nederlandisch Tijdschrift voor Geneeskunde, 1939).

13. The notes of these lectures have been published by Kemp. They contain no passage similar to that described by Ramsay.

14. Discussions of Geoffroy's ideas include, Le Guyader; Appel 69–105; and Amundsen 153–77.

15. John Hunter also anticipated the theory of "recapitulation," although his speculations on the subject were probably not known (Meyer 381–82).

16. The standard accounts of this debate see Goodfield-Toulmin, Temkin; Jacyna; and Ruston 24–109.

17. The racial implications of Cabanis and the Ideologue's science are discussed by Poliakov 218–20.

18. Notable such accounts include Morretti; Baldick; Botting; Veeder; Gilbert and Gubar.

19. The novel's relationship to the literature of grave-robbing and anatomy is discussed by Marshall. The issue is discussed in general terms by Linebaugh.

20. Paul Youngquist identifies Frankenstein with Hunter 53–56.

21. Mary Shelley 1987 (174) read Buffon in June–July 1817.

22. For general discussions of the subject see T. Marshall; R. Richardson; and S. Wise. MacDonald discusses the racial implications of this subject in nineteenth-century Tasmania.

23. The racial and gender implications of anatomy are discussed by Fee 415–33; Schiebinger 1989; and Jordanova. Robyn Wiegman argues for the "analogic wedding of blacks and women" in racial discourse. "Through analogies between the smaller brain capacities and the perversely developed sexuality of black and female bodies, comparative anatomy read the African's difference through the twin registers of

sexual difference: as both a stereotypically feminized category and the preeminently sexual" (44, 2, 23–24, 29–35, 43–78).

24. "The presence or absence of a beard not only drew a sharp line between men and women, it also served to differentiate the varieties of men" (Schiebinger 1990, 120, 120–26).

3   "Candid Reflections:" The Idea of Race in the Debate over the Slave Trade and Slavery in the Late Eighteenth and Early Nineteenth Centuries

1. This debate is now substantial but the following have been of especial use: Blackburn 517–18; Eltis; Drescher 1977; Fields 99; Solow and Engerman. In 2003 Phillip Gould challenged the premise that objections to the slave trade were rooted in modern laissez-faire capitalism, Gould's work revises our understanding of antislavery literature as a form of cultural criticism in its own right.

2. Recent theories of "whiteness" are discussed by M. Hill.

3. Other relevant discussions include Alastair Bonnet 200–218 and Drescher (1992) who argues that scientific racism was a consequence of the abolitionist campaign rather than a cause.

4. Important works on this subject include Anstey; Hugh Thomas; and D. Richardson 440–63. Our understanding of the historical workings of the slave trade has been greatly enhanced by William St Clair's 2006 history of the British slaving fort of Cape Coast Castle.

5. Somerset won the case, which was widely seen as proclaiming the illegality of slavery in England. The ruling of Lord Chief Justice Mansfield, however, merely denied that the owners of slaves resident in England had the legal right to compel them to return to the colonies. The case is described in Shyllon and retold in Schama 44–63 Hochschild 48–52 and Wise 2006.

6. Davis however, warns that we must not presume that Long "was totally unrepresentative of his time" (461) and Fryer claims that Long's ideas "were shared by many and that racism had more than a foothold in England" (161).

7. George Foster, "Noch etwas über die Menschenrassen," *Werke* 8, ed. Siegfried Scheibe (Berlin: Akadmi, 1991), 150–53. Quoted in Bernasconi 2002 (161).

8. This was argued by Edwards in his "A Speech delivered at a Free Conference between the Honorable Council and assembly of Jamaica (Kingston, Jamaica, 1789)," in Kitson, *The Abolition Debate* 1999 (325–47).

9. Gates 1986 (127–69) discusses the importance of literacy as a technology, as does Aravamudan 269–88.

10. Smith 1789 in Kitson, *Theories of Race* 1999 (78, 356n). Smith 1965 (32) repeated this comment in the expanded version of his Essay of 1810.
11. Important discussions include Hair 43–68; A. Richardson 1994 (153–66); Brantlinger 1998; and Hammond and Jablow.
12. The most recent biography of Clarkson is E. G. Wilson 1989.
13. Recent collections of such writing include Kitson and Lee; Basker; and Wood 2003. Important recent criticism of literature and abolition includes Boulukos 2007; Carey; D. Coleman 2005; M. Ellis; Ferguson 1992; P. Gould; Lee; Helen Thomas; and Wood 2002.
14. Hannah More, *Slavery: A Poem* (1788). The text is taken from Wood 2003, 103, 101–10.
15. Representations of cannibalism are discussed by Barker, Hulme, and Iversen; Hulme 1986 (1–12); Boucher; and Brantlinger 1988 (184–86). Allegations of cannibalism among the Africans had been made in the eighteenth century in William Snelgrave's proslavery *A New Account of some Parts of Guinea, and the Slave-Trade* (London, 1734). Snelgrave's claims were challenged by John Atkins's *A Voyage to Guinea, Brasil, and the West-Indies in His Majesty's Ships, the Swallow and the Weymouth* (London, 1735). The texts are discussed by Philip Edwards 147–49.
16. A less positive reading of this passage that sees it as repeating stereotypically racist fears of miscegenation is provided by D. Coleman 1994 (349).
17. Nussbaum 2003, 196. Nussbaum argues that black men, such as Equiano and Sancho attempted to compete against the racialized expectations of black masculinity and establish sufficient personal authority to mould their own destinies, 189–212.
18. Important criticism on Cugoano includes Caretta 1999; Wheeler 1999 (259–60) and 2001 (17–38).
19. Carretta identifies this quotation as imaginary.
20. Carretta 2005 (347). Equiano 109–10.
21. Recently Srinivas Aravamudan 284, 269–88 has argued that for Equiano "the twin cultural entities of Christian religion and British nation are what he recognizes as emancipatory." Most critics do not situate the *Narrative* in the context of race. Wheeler, 1999 (260–87) and Gautier 161–79 are exceptions. This discussion of Equiano is confined to the subject of the race idea in his writing. Influential criticism of Equiano's *Narrative* includes Caretta 2005; Sandiford; Edwards 1992; Ogude 31–43; Potkay 677–92; Gates 152–58; Marren, 94–105; Helen Thomas 226–25; and Hofkosh, 330–43.
22. Wheeler 1999 (235). Wheeler 257–70 also discusses Equiano's use of the stadial model of difference in which the attainment of civil society is the crucial distinguishing feature of British preeminence.
23. Wheeler 1999 discusses the influence of the theories of the Virginian physician John Mitchell on Equiano 264–65.

24. This scene is discussed in Carretta 2005 324–25.
25. Colonialism as an alternative to slavery is discussed by D. Coleman 2005; Curtin 88–113; and Brown 273–306.

4 ROMANTICISM, RACE, AND CANNIBALISM IN THE "SOUTH SEAS"

1. In addition to Rennie, the following are especially important: P. Edwards; Edmond; N. Thomas 1997; V. Smith; Calder, Lamb, and Orr; Lamb, Smith, and N. Thomas 2000.
2. Important discussions of the construction of the cultural representations of cannibalism include Arens; Hulme; Kitson 2001 (204–25); Lestrignant; Barker, Hulme, and Iversen 1992; Obeyesekere 1992; Sanbourn; and King.
3. Other critical discussions of this incident include Barber 241–92; Rawson 168–97; N. Thomas 2003, 104–8; and Salmond 2003, 220–44.
4. Carl Solander to Joseph Banks, August 14, 1775; Mitchell Library, Banks Papers, MS as 24, quoted in Beaglehole 444–45.
5. The Hunterian Museum held at the Royal College of Surgeons contains three crania described as "Maori," all mutilated and probably subjected to violent death in warfare. One is female and the dentition of the other two reveals an age more than twenty. All three are complete with mandibles, unlike Pickersgill's head that lacked this part of the skull. The Hunterian Museum at the University of Glasgow originating from William Hunter's collection also does not contain this head, although it is most likely the Hunter referred to by Solander was John. The crews of Cook's three voyages were often in search of curiosities, especially human remains that were in great demand by the new proponents of comparative anatomy. J.F. Blumenbach frequently requested crania from Joseph Banks. In a letter of June 20, 1787, Blumenbach requested one of the South Sea skulls of Banks, but on this occasion was unsuccessful as Banks had already given away both the skulls he then had, one to Peter Camper and the other to John Hunter (British Museum Additional MS. 8096. 383–84). For this aspect of Banks's career as a collector and disseminator of exotic skulls, see Fulford, Lee, and Kitson 108–26; Gascoigne 119–83; Moore 355, 247, 278, 285–86; Turnbull 202–25.
6. Discussions of Byron's *The Island* include Addison 687–706; McKusick 1992 (839–56); Leask 1992 (63–67); Kenyon-Jones 132–34; and Edmond 63–97.
7. A similar point was made in Southey's "Review of William Ellis's Polynesian Researches," in *Quarterly Review* 43 (1830): 1–54.
8. I am grateful to Tim Fulford for drawing my attention to this letter.

5 ROMANTIC SINOPOLITANS: NATURAL PHILOSOPHERS, TRAVELERS, DIPLOMATS, AND MISSIONARIES

1. Said 1985 (1, 2, 17, 42, 51, 73–74, 117, 251, 254 120, 285) in *Orientalism* argues that China and Japan only become a part of Orientalism once the West (especially the United States) becomes interested in establishing a political and economic hegemony over them in the nineteenth and twentieth centuries, thus demonstrating his elasticity of the concept.

2. Important studies in this area are Marshall and Williams; Mackerras; Cameron; Ch'en, Ching and Oxtoby; Chung-shu 1940 and 1941 Aldridge; Hsia *Vision of China* 1998; Foss and Lach; and Gelber.

3. The complex translation and publication history of Du Halde's work is discussed by Fan Cunzhong.

4. Jones's writings are discussed by Fan Cunzhong in Hsia, ed. *Vision of China* 1998 (325–38).

5. For the background to this event, the following are exceptionally useful: Rawski 2006 (22–40). For the historiographical debates about the Qing dynasty see, Guy 151–64; Mote; Perdue; Crossley 1999; Spence 1990.

6. Perdue 5, 8, argues that "[p]lacing China in world history should be a priority today, and study of the frontier is a promising way to integrate China with the wider Eurasian world." In its way this study attempts to reinscribe the Qing Empire into the world of Romantic writing.

7. The impact of the tea trade is discussed by Porter 193; Forrest 27, 284; Hobhouse 133; and Kowalski-Wallace 19–36.

8. The background to this crisis is discussed in Hobhouse 117–74; Hsü 139–67; and Morse.

9. The prevailing view is that Macartney never performed the koutou; however, Liu Jiaju suggested in 1998 that he might have performed the ritual in private for the emperor. Certainly this was the view of the Jiaqing Emperor during Amherst's mission of 1816. Zhang Shunhong 31–43 (especially 36–37, 37n).

10. The traditional view of British historians is demonstrated in Cranmer Byng 117–87; Pritchard; Bickers 7–10; and Singer.

11. The Edict was transmitted to Macartney on October 3 in Latin. A translation of is included in Macartney's *Journal* 336–41. Hevia 1995 (238–48) discusses the historiography of the letter.

12. This example of Austen's interest in China has received surprisingly little comment. One of the few exceptions to this is Peter Knox-Shaw's insightful discussion (Knox-Shaw 212–21).

13. James Wathen, for instance criticizes Barrow: "This traveller, with a stroke of the pen, boldly consigns to infamy and contempt a nation

whose population is said to be more than three hundred millions, or nearly *one third of the whole existing human species!* A nation, who had arrived at great perfection in sciences and literature, who had discovered and practiced the divine art of printing, at a time when Europe was wrapped up in the thick cloud of ignorance and barbarism, and had not even learnt that such a nation had an existence! For my part, I have no complaints to make against the Chinese. The merchants of Canton are spoken of as honourable men, by those who have dealt with them upon the largest scale for many years. The gentleman of the Company's Factory are in habits of friendship and confidence with them, and they appeared to me to deserve that friendship and that confidence" (220). Wathen also attacks Barrow's discussion of infanticide as fanciful (229). Such views are repeated in Clarke Abel's *Narrative of a Journey in the Interior of China:* "That infanticide is practiced in China, especially in times of dreadful scarcity, to which, from the nature of the government, and the corruption of local officers, that country is particularly subject, the concurring testimony of many authors scarcely admits of a doubt; but that it ever materially affects the amount of population, and still less that it ever depends on any general want of that divine and uncontrollable principle which guards the safety of offspring, the entire absence of all evidence, within our experience, even of its mere existence, does not allow me to believe. From all that I was capable of observing, and from all that I was enabled to learn, I am quite of the opinion expressed by an eloquent writer, 'That when the parent has any possible means of supporting his offspring, there is no country where maternal affection is stronger that in China'" (235).

14. Protestant missionary activity in China is discussed by Neill 261–322; Cary-Elwes, 209–17; and Hiney 2, 26–30.

6   Tartars, Monguls, Manchus, and Chinese

1. Other important studies of the Manchu include Wakeman; Elliot; Rawski 1998; Crossley 1999; Millward, Dunnell, Elliot and Forêt, and Rawski and Rawson.
2. This subject is discussed in Kaul 85–130, 121–30, 259–65.
3. Settle's drama is discussed by Hsia, *Chinesia* 1998, 24–39; Qian Zhongshu 29–68; and Ballaster 201–2.
4. Important criticism of Goldsmith's novel includes Hamilton Jewett Smith; Conant 157, 184–199; Booth 585–96; Charles Knight 347–64; Brooks 124–44; Porter 138–42; and Ballaster 202–8, 242–53.
5. The Mongols did have a written language introduced by Genghis Khan from his vassals the Uighurs. Kublai, however, instructed his spiritual adviser Phags-pa to design a common script for his empire

(Man 148–51). In November 1802 Coleridge wrote in his Notebook that "Kubla Khan ordered letters to be invented for his people—" (1957–73, 1: 1281). Jones's influence on Coleridge is discussed by Drew 196–97.

6. Important discussions of "Kubla Khan" include Beer; Butler 1992 (133–57); and Shaffer.

7. The arguments for the dating of "Kubla Khan" are discussed by Schneider.

8. The background of this event is discussed by Barkman, 89–115, Millward, and Perdue 293–99. Little has been written on De Quincey's essay. Notable exceptions are De Luca 95–108 and Whale 4–19.

BIBLIOGRAPHY

PRIMARY

Abel, Clarke. *Narrative of a Journey in the Interior of China, and of a Voyage from That Country in the Years 1816 and 1817.* London: Longman, Hurst, Rees, Orme, and Brown, 1818.

Abernethy, John. *An Enquiry into the Probability and Rationality of Mr Hunter's "Theory of Life."* London: Longman, 1814.

Alexander, William. "Journal of a Voyage to Pekin in China on board the Hindostan E I M Which Accompanied Lord Macartney on His Embassy to the Emperor." British Library. n.d.

Anson, George. *A Voyage Round the World in the Years MDCCXL, I, II, III, IV.* Ed. Glyndwr Williams. London: Oxford University Press, 1974.

Atkins, John. *A Voyage to Guinea, Brasil, and the West-Indies in His Majesty's Ships, the Swallow and the Weymouth.* London: C. Ward & R. Chandler, 1735.

Austen, Jane. *Mansfield Park.* Ed. Kathryn Sutherland. Penguin: Harmondsworth, 2001.

Bacon, Francis. *The Advancement of Learning and New Atlantis.* Ed. Arthur Johnston. Oxford: Clarendon Press, 1974.

Barrow, John. *Some Account of the Public Life, and a Selection from the Unpublished Writings of the Earl of Macartney.* 2 vols. London: T. Cadell & W. Davies, 1807.

———. *Travels in China.* London: T. Cadell and W. Davies, 1804.

Beckford, Jr. William. *A Descriptive Account of the Island of Jamaica.* 2 vols. London: T. and J. Egerton, 1790.

———. *Remarks upon the Situation of Negroes in Jamaica.* London: T. and J. Egerton, 1788.

Bell, Charles. *The Anatomy and Philosophy of Expression as Connected with the Fine Arts.* 1806; London: George Bell and Sons, 1886.

Bell, John. *A Journey from St. Petersburg to Pekin, 1719–22.* Ed. J.L. Stevenson. Edinburgh: Edinburgh University Press, 1966.

Benezet, Antony. *Some Historical Account of Guinea Its Situation, Produce, and the General Disposition of Its Inhabitants with an Inquiry into the Rise and Progress of the Slave-Trade Its Nature and Lamentable Effects.* London, 1771; 2nd ed. 1788. London: Frank Cass, 1968.

Bernier, François. "A New Division of the Earth According to the Different Species or Races of Men Who Inhabit It, Sent by a Famous Traveller to Mons * * * * *, Nearly in These Terms." *Journal des Scavans,* April 24,

1684. Trans. T. Bendyshe in *Memoirs Read before the Anthropological Society of London*. Vol. 1. London: Anthropological Society. 360–64. Reprinted in Bernasconi and Lott. 2000. 1–4.

Blake, William. *The Complete Poems*. Ed W. H. Stevenson. 2nd ed. Harlow: Longman, 1989.

Blumenbach, Johann Friedrich. *De Generis Humani Varietate Nativa*. 3rd edn. Göttingen: Apud Vandenhoek et Ruprecht, 1795. In *The Anthropological Treatises of Johann Friedrich Blumenbach*. Translated and edited by Thomas Bendyshe. London: The Anthropological Society, Longman, Green Longman, Roberts & Green, 1865.

Bonnet, Charles. *Contemplation de la nature*. In *Oeuvres Complètes*. Neuchâtel, 1779–83.

———. *Palingénésie philosophique*. 2 tomes. 1769. In *Oeuvres Complètes*. Neuchâtel, Geneva. 1779–83.

Bougainville, Louis de. *A Voyage Round the World*. Trans. Johann Reinhold Forster. London: J. Nourse, 1772.

Bowles, William Lisle. *The Poetical Works of William Lisle Bowles*. Ed. George Gilfillan. 2 vols. Edinburgh: James Nichol, 1855.

Brown, George. *Melanesians and Polynesians: Their Life-Histories Described and Compared*. Macmillan: London, 1910.

Buffon, George Louis Le Clerc. *Barr's Buffon: Buffon's Natural History, Containing a Theory of the Earth, a General History of Man, of the Brute Creation, and of Vegetables, Minerals, &c. from the French with Notes by the Translator*. 10 vols. London: J. S. Barr, 1792.

———. *Natural History, General and Particular*. Trans. William Smellie. Edinburgh: William Creech, 1780.

———. "Variétés dans l'espèce humaine." *Histoire naturelle* 3 (1749): 523–24.

Burney, James. *With Captain James Cook in the Antarctic and Pacific: The Private Journal of James Burney Second Lieutenant of the Adventure on Cook's Second Voyage*. Ed. Beverley Hooper. Canberra: National Library of Australia, 1975.

Byron, George Gordon, Lord. *Lord Byron: The Complete Poetical Works*. Ed. Jerome J. McGann. 7 vols. Oxford: Clarendon Press, 1980–93.

Camper, Pieter. *Natuurkundige verhanelingen van Petrus Camper over den orang Outing*. Amsterdam: Erven and Meyer, 1782.

———. *Neerlandicorum de arte medica*. Vol. 15. Amsterdam: Nederlandisch Tijdschrift voor Geneeskunde, 1939.

———. "Petri Camperi Itinera in Anglian 1748–1785." *Opuscula Selecta*. Amsterdam: Volcher Coiter, 1936.

———. *The Works of the Late Professor Camper, on the Connexion between the Science of Anatomy and the Arts of Drawing, Painting, Statuary, &c &c*. Trans T. Cogan. London: C. Dilly, 1794.

Chambers, William. *A Dissertation on Oriental Gardening*. London: W. Griffin, 1772.

Chaucer, Geoffrey. *The Riverside Chaucer*. 3rd ed. Oxford: Oxford University Press, 2007.

Clarkson, Thomas. *An Essay on the Impolicy of the African Slave Trade.* London: J. Phillips, 1786; 2nd edn, 1788.

————. *An Essay on the Slavery and Commerce of the Human Species, Particularly the African, translated from a Latin Dissertation.* 2nd ed. London: J. Phillips, 1786.

Cobbett, William. *Political Register.* July 28, 1804.

————. *Political Register.* August 4, 1821.

Coleridge, S.T. *Biographia Literaria.* Ed. James Engell and Walter Jackson Bate. 2 vols. London and Princeton: Princeton University Press, 1983.

————. *The Friend.* Ed. Barbara Rooke. 2 vols. London and Princeton: Princeton University Press, 1969.

————. *Lectures 1795: On Politics and Religion.* Ed. Lewis Patton and Peter Mann. London and Princeton: Princeton University Press, 1974.

————. *Marginalia.* Vols. 1 and 2. Ed. George Whalley; Vol. 3. Ed. H.J. Jackson and George Whalley. London and Princeton: Princeton University Press, 1980–84.

————. *The Notebooks of Samuel Taylor Coleridge,* I–III. 1794-1818. Ed. Kathleen Coburn. London and Princeton: Princeton University Press, 1957–73.

————. *The Notebooks of Samuel Taylor Coleridge,* IV. 1819–26. Ed. Kathleen Coburn and Merton Christensen. London and Princeton: Princeton University Press, 1990.

————. *The Philosophical Lectures of Samuel Taylor Coleridge.* Ed. Kathleen Coburn. London: The Pilot Press, 1949.

————. *Poetical Works.* Ed. J.C.C. Mays. 6 vols. London and Princeton: Princeton University Press, 2003.

————. *Shorter Works and Fragments.* Ed. H.J. Jackson and J.R. de J. Jackson. 2 vols. London and Princeton: Princeton University Press, 1995.

————. *Table Talk Recorded by Henry Nelson Coleridge.* Ed. Carl Woodring. 2 vols. Princeton: Princeton University Press, 1990.

Cook, James. *The Journals of Captain Cook on his Voyages of Discovery. II: The Voyage of the Resolution and Adventure 1772–1775.* Ed. J.C. Beaglehole. Cambridge: Hakluyt Society and Cambridge University Press, 1961.

————. *The Journals of Captain James Cook on his Voyages of Discovery. III: The Voyage of the Resolution and Discovery 1776–1780.* Ed. J.C Beaglehole. 2 vols. Cambridge: Hakluyt Society and Cambridge University Press, 1967.

————. *A Voyage towards the South Pole, and Round the World. Performed in His Majesty's Ships the Resolution and Adventure, in the Years 1772, 1773, 1774, and 1775, ... In which is Included, Captain Furneaux's Narrative of His Proceedings in the Adventure during the Separation of the Ships.* 2 vols. London: W. Strahan and T. Cadell, 1777.

Cowper, William. *The Poems of William Cowper.* Ed. John D. Baird and Charles Ryskamp. 3 vols. Oxford: Clarendon Press, 1980–95.

Cugoano, Quobna Ottobah. *Thoughts and Sentiments on the Evil of Slavery.* Ed. Vincent Carretta. Harmondsworth, Penguin, 1999.

Cuvier, Georges. *Cuvier's Animal Kingdom: Arranged according to Its Organization, Translated from the French...by H. McMurtie.* London: Orr and Smith, 1834.

———. *Leçons d'anatomie comparée de G. Cuvier: Lectures on Comparative Anatomy.* Translated by William Ross. 2 vols. London: T.N. Longman and O. Rees, 1802.

Darwin, Charles. *The Descent of Man and Selection in Relation to Sex.* London: John Murray, 1901.

Davies, John. *The History of the Tahitian Mission, 1799–1830.* Ed. C.W. Newbury. Cambridge: Hakluyt Society, 1961.

Defoe Daniel. *The Farther Adventures of Robinson Crusoe,.. Written by Himself.* London: William Clowes, 1974.

D'Oyly, George. "An Enquiry into the Probability of Mr. Hunter's Theory of Life." *Quarterly Review* XLIII (1808): 1–34. Reprinted in Butler. Ed. *Frankenstein.* 1993. 231–51.

De Pauw, Cornelius. *Philosophical Dissertations on the Egyptians and Chinese. Translated from the French of Mr. De Pauw, Private Reader to Frederic II. King of Prussia, By Capt. J. Thomson. In Two Volumes.* London: T. Chapman, 1795.

De Quincey, Thomas. *The Works of Thomas De Quincey.* 21 vols. London: Pickering & Chatto, 2000–03.

Du Halde, Jean-Baptiste. *The General History of China, Containing a Geographical,.. and Physical Description of the Empire of China, Chinese Tartary, Corea and Thibet,.. with Maps and Copper Plates. Done from the French of Du Halde.* 4 vols. R. Brookes: London, 1736.

Edwards, Bryan. *The History, Civil and Commercial, of the British Colonies in the West Indies.* 3rd ed. London: J. Stockdale, 1801.

———. "A Speech Delivered at a Free Conference between the Honorable Council and Assembly of Jamaica. Kingston, Jamaica, 1789." In Kitson. Ed. *The Abolition Debate.* 1999. 325–47.

Ellis, Sir Henry. *Journal of the Proceedings of the Late Embassy to China.* London: John Murray, 1818.

Ellis, William. *Polynesian Researches in the South Seas Islands.* 2 vols. 1829. 2nd ed. 4 vols. London: Fisher and Jackson, 1832.

Equiano, Olaudah. *The Interesting Narrative and Other Writings.* Ed. Vincent Carretta. Harmondsworth: Penguin, 1995.

Forster, George. *A Voyage Round the World.* 2 vols. London: White, Robson, Elmsly, and Robinson, 1777.

———. *Georg Forsters Werke, Sämtliche Schriften, Tagebücher, Briefe, Akademie der Wissenschaften der DDR.* Berlin: Akademie-Verlag, 1977–90.

Forster, John Reinhold. *Observations Made during a Voyage Round the World, on Physical Geography, Natural History, and Ethic Philosophy.* London: G. Robinson, 1778.

Geoffroy Saint-Hilaire, Etienne. *Philosophie anatomique.* 2 vols. Paris, 1818–22.

Gobineau, Arthur, de. *The Inequality of the Human Races*. New York: Howard Fertig, 1999.

Goldsmith, Oliver. *Collected Works of Oliver Goldsmith*. 6 vols. Ed. Arthur Friedman. Oxford: Clarendon Press, 1966.

———. *History of the Earth and Animated Nature*. London: J. Nourse, 1774.

Grosier, Jean Baptiste Gabriel Alexandre. *A General Description of China, Containing the Topography of the Fifteen Provinces Which Compose This Vast Empire, That of Tartary, the Isles, etc. Translated from the French*. 2 vols. London, 1788.

Haweis, Thomas. Preliminary Discourse. In William Wilson. *A Missionary Voyage to the Southern Pacific Ocean*. London: T. Chapman, 1799.

Hegel, G.W.F. *Lectures on the Philosophy of World History*. Trans. H.B. Nisbet. Cambridge: Cambridge University Press, 1975.

Holmes, C. Ed. *Captain Cook's Second Voyage: The Journals of Lieutenants Elliot and Pickersgill*. London: Caliban Books, 1984.

Home, Everard. "A Short Account of the Life of the Author." In John Hunter. *A Treatise on the Blood, Inflammation, and Gunshot Wounds*. London: George Nicol, 1794.

Hunter, John. *Essays and Observations on Natural History, Anatomy, Physiology, Psychology and Geology*. Ed. Richard Owen. 2 vols. London: Van Voorst, 1861.

———. *The Natural History and Diseases of the Human Teeth*. London: J. Johnson, 1771.

Jones, Sir William. "Fifth Anniversary Discourse, delivered 21 February, 1788. On the Tartars. *The Collected Works of Sir William Jones*. 13 vols. London, 1807. Vol. 1.

———. Seventh Anniversary Discourse delivered 25 February, 1790. On China. *The Collected Works of Sir William Jones*. 13 vols. London, 1807. Vol. 1.

Kames, Henry Home, Lord. *Sketches of the History of Man*. 2 vols. London and Edinburgh, 1774.

Kant, Immanuel. "On the Different Human Races." Trans. Jon Mark Mikkelsen. In Robert Bernasconi and Tommy L. Lott. Eds. *The Idea of Race*. Indianapolis: Hackett Publishing Company, Inc. 2000. 8–22.

Keats, John. *The Complete Poems*. Ed. Miriam Allott. Harlow: Longman, 1970.

Kemeys, John. *Free and Candid Reflections Occasioned by the Late Additional Duties on Sugar and on Rum*. London, 1783.

Knox, Robert. *The Races of Men: A Fragment*. Philadelphia: Lea & Blanchard, 1850.

Lambe, William. *Reports of the Effects of a Peculiar Regimen on Scirrhous Tumours and Cancerous Ulcers*. London, 1809.

Lavater, Johann Casper. *Essays on Physiognomy*. Trans. Henry Hunter. 3 vols. London, 1789–98.

Lawrence, William. *An Introduction to Comparative Anatomy, Being Two Introductory Lectures Delivered at the Royal College of Surgeons.* London: J. Callow, 1816.

———. *Lectures on Physiology, Zoology, and the Natural History of Mankind.* 1819. 3rd ed. London: James Smith, 1823.

Leigh Hunt, James Henry. *Account of the Remarkable Rise and Downfall of the Late Great Kan of Tartary: With the Still More Remarkable Fancies That Took Possession of the Heads of Some of His Antagonists.—Very Curious and Necessary to Be Known, in order to a Complete History of the Present Marvellous Times.—By the Editor of the* Examiner. London, 1817.

Ligon, Richard. "A True & Exact History of the Island of Barbados. 1657." In Thomas W. Krise. Ed. *Caribbeana: An Anthology of English Literature of the West Indies, 1657–1777.* Chicago: University of Chicago Press, 1999. 16–30.

Linnaeus. *Caroli Linnaei Systema naturae: Regnum animale.* A Photographic Facsimile of the First Volume of the Tenth Edition (1758). London: British Museum, 1939.

Long, Edward. *Candid Reflections upon the Judgement Latterly Awarded by the Court of the King's Bench on What is Commonly Called the Negroe-Cause.* London, 1772.

———. *History of Jamaica.* 3 vols. London: T. Lowdnes, 1774.

Macartney, George. *An Embassy to China: Being the Journal Kept by Lord Macartney during his Embassy to the Emperor Ch'ien-lung, 1793–94.* Ed. J.L. Cranmer-Byng. London: Longman, 1962.

Mack, Robert L. Ed. *Arabian Nights' Entertainments.* Oxford: World's Classics, 1995.

Marra, J. *Journal of the Resolution's Voyage, in 1772, 1773, 1774, and 1775.* London: F. Newberry, 1775.

Martin, John. *An Account of the Natives of the Tonga Islands in the South Pacific Ocean with an Original Grammar and Vocabulary of Their Language.* 2 vols. London: John Murray, 1817.

Martini, Martinus. *Bellum Tartaricum, or the Conquest of the Most Renowned Empire of China, by the Invasion of the Tartars.* London 1654.

Maupertius, Pierre-Louis Moreau de. *The Earthly Venus Translated from the Venus Physique by Simone Brangier Boas.* New York and London: Johnson Reprint Corporation, 1968.

Milne, William. *A Retrospect of the First Ten Years of the Protestant Mission in China.* Malacca, 1820.

Montesquieu. *The Spirit of the Laws.* Ed. Anne Cohler, Basia Miller, and Harold Stone. Cambridge: Cambridge University Press, 1989.

More, Hannah. *Slavery: A Poem,* London: T. Cadell, 1788. In Wood 2003, 101–10.

Morrison, Robert. *A Memoir of the Principal Occurrences during and Embassy from the British Government to the Court of China in the Year 1816.* London, 1819.

Morse, H.B. *The Chronicles of the East India Company Trading to China, 1635–1834.* 5 vols. Taipei: Ch'eng-wen Publishing Company, 1975.

Murphy, Arthur. *The Orphan of China. A Tragedy by Arthur Murphy, Esq as Performed at the Theatre-Royal, Drury Lane.* London: P. Vaillant, 1797.

Nickolls [Nichols], Robert Boucher. *Letter to the Treasurer of the Society Instituted for the Purpose of Effecting the Abolition of the Slave Trade.* London, 1787.

Nott, Josiah and George Gliddon. *Types of Mankind or Ethnological Researches Based upon the Ancient Monuments, Paintings, Sculptures, and Crania of Races.* 10th ed. Philadelphia: J.B. Lippincott, 1871.

Nugent, Maria. *Lady Nugent's Journal of Her Residence in Jamaica from 1801 to 1805.* Ed. Philip Wright. Institute of Jamaica: Kingston, Jamaica, 1966.

Oken, Lorenz. *Lehrbuch de Naturphilosophie.* Third Part. Jena, 1811.

Palafox. *The History of the Conquest of China by the Tartars.* London, 1676.

Pereira, Galeote. *South China in the Sixteenth Century. Being the Narratives of Galeote Pereira, Fr. Gaspar da Cruz,.. Fr. Martín de Roda,.. 1550–1575.* Ed. C.R. Boxer. London: Hakluyt Society, 1953.

"Philo-Xylon". *Letters of Philo-Xylon, First Published in the Barbadoes Gazette, during the Years 1787 and 1788.* Barbadoes, 1789. No. VIII.

Polidori, John William. *Diary of J.W. Polidori, 1816.* Ed. W. M. Rossetti. London: Elkin Mathews, 1911.

Polo, Marco. *The Travels.* Trans. Ronald Latham. Penguin: Harmondsworth, 1958.

Prichard, James Cowles. *The Natural History of Man.* 1843. 2nd ed. London: Hippolyte Bailliere, 1845.

———. *Researches into the Physical History of Man.* London: John and Arthur Arch, 1813. Ed. George W. Stocking. Chicago and London: University of Chicago Press, 1973.

———. *Researches into the Physical History of Mankind.* 1826. 2nd ed. 2 vols. London: John Arthur Arch, 1826.

———. *Researches into the Physical History of Mankind.* 3 vols. London: Sherwood, Gilbert, Piper, 1836–47.

Priest, Josiah. *Slavery, as It Relates to the Negro, or African Race Examined in the Light of Circumstances, History and Holy Scriptures.* Albany: C. Van Benthuysen and Co., 1843.

Purchas, Samuel. *Purchas His Pilgrimage: Or Relations of the World and the Religions Observed in All Ages and Places Discovered, from the Creation vnto This Present.* London: W. Stansby, for H. Fetherstone. 1613. 4th ed. 1626.

Ramsay, James. *An Essay on the Treatment and Conversion of African Slaves in the British Sugar Colonies.* London: J. Philips, 1784.

Ricci Matthew (Matteo). *China in the Sixteenth Century: The Journals of Matthew Ricci: 1583–1610.* Trans. Louis J. Gallagher. New York: Random House, 1953.

Russell, Michael. *Polynesia; or, An historical Account of the Principal Islands in the South of the Cannibal.* Edinburgh: Edinburgh Cabinet Library, 1842.

Settle, Elkanah. *The Conquest of China, By the Tartars: A Tragedy Acted at the Duke's Theatre. Written by Elkanah Settle, Servant to His Majesty.* London, 1676.

Seward, Anna. *Elegy on Captain Cook to which is added an Ode to the Sun.* London: J. Dodsley, 1780.

Shelley, Mary. *Frankenstein, or the Modern Prometheus.* Ed. Norah Crook. Vol. 1. *The Novels and Selected Works of Mary Shelley.* London: William Pickering, 1966.

———. *The Journals of Mary Shelley, 1814–44.* Ed. Paula R. Feldman and Diana Scott-Kilvert. Baltimore and London: Johns Hopkins University Press, 1987.

Smellie, William. *Philosophy of Natural History.* 2 vols. Edinburgh, 1790.

Smith, Charles Hamilton. *The Natural History of the Human Species.* Boston: Gould and Lincoln, 1851.

Smith, John Augustine. "A Lecture Introductory to the Second Course of Anatomical Instruction in the College of Physicians and Surgeons for the State of New York." *New York Medical and Philosophical Journal and Review* 1 (1809): 32–48.

Smith, Samuel Stanhope. *An Essay on the Causes of the Variety of Complexion in the Human Species to Which Are Added Strictures on Lord Kaims's Discourse on the Original Diversity of Mankind.* Philadelphia, 1787; Edinburgh, 1788; London: John Stockdale, 1789.

———. *An Essay on the Causes of the Variety of Complexion and Figure in the Human Species.* Ed. Winthrop D. Jordan. Cambridge, MA: The Belknap Press of Harvard University Press, 1965.

Snelgrave, William. *A New Account of Some Parts of Guinea, and the Slave-Trade.* London: J. J. & P. Knapton, 1734.

Southey, Robert. *The Life and Correspondence of Robert Southey.* 6 vols. London, 1849–50.

———. "Account of the Baptist Mission." *Annual Review for 1802,* 1 (1803): 207-18.

———. "Review of *Transactions of the Missionary Society in the South Seas.*" *Quarterly Review* 2 (1809): 24–61.

———. "Review of William Ellis's *Polynesian Researches.*" *Quarterly Review* 43 (1830): 1–54.

Staunton, George. *An Historical Account of the Embassy to the Emperor of China.* 3 vols. London: W. Bulmer and Co., 1797.

Stewart, John. *An Account of Jamaica and Its Inhabitants, by a Gentleman Long Resident in the West Indies.* London, 1823.

Tobin, James. *Cursory Remarks upon the Rev. Mr Ramsay's Essay on the Treatment and Conversion of African Slaves.* London, 1787.

———. *Farewel Address to the Rev. Mr. J. Ramsay [in reply to a letter from him]*. London, 1788.

———. *A Short Rejoinder to Mr Ramsay's Reply*. London, 1785.

Trelawny, Edward. *Essay concerning Slavery*. London: Charles Corbett, 1746.

Tyson, Edward. *Orang-Outang, sive Homo Sylvestris: Or, the Anatomy of a Pygmie*. Ed. Ashley Montagu. London: Dawsons, 1966.

Virey, Julien-Joseph. *Histoire naturelle du genre humain*. Paris, Year IX (1800–01).

Volney, Constantin. *The Ruins: Or a Survey of the Revolutions of Empires*. London: J. Johnson, 1792.

Voltaire. *The Orphan of China: A Tragedy Translated from the French of M. De Voltaire First Acted at Paris, on the 20th August, 1755*. 6th ed. London, 1761.

———. *Philosophical Dictionary*. Ed. Theodore Besterman. Harmondsworth: Penguin, 1972.

———. *Treaté du métaphysique*. Ed. W.H. Barber. *The Complete Works of Voltaire*. Vol. 14. Oxford: The Voltaire Foundation, 1989.

Wathen, James. *Journal of a Voyage in 1811 and 1812 to Madras and China… Illustrated with Twenty-four Coloured Prints and Drawings from the Author*. London: J. Nichols, Son, and Bentley, 1814.

White, Charles. *An Account of the Regular Gradation in Man, and in Different Animals and Vegetables; and the Former to the Latter*. London: C. Dilly, 1799.

Williams, Helen Maria. *Poems on Various Subjects*. London: G. and W.B. Whittaker, 1823.

Williams, Thomas. *Fiji and the Fijians. Volume 1: The Islands and Their Inhabitants*. London: Alexander Heylin, 1858.

Wollstonecraft, Mary. *The Works of Mary Wollstonecraft*. Ed. Janet Todd and Marilyn Butler. 7 vols. London: Pickering, 1989.

SECONDARY

Addison, Catherine. " 'Elysian and Effeminate': Byron's *The Island*." *SEL* 35 (1995): 678–706.

Aldridge, A. Owen. "The Perception of China in English Literature of the Enlightenment." *Asian Culture Quarterly* 14 (1986): 1–26.

Allen, Theodore, W. *The Invention of the White Race. Vol.1: Racial Oppression and Social Contract*. London: Verso, 1994.

———. *The Invention of the White Race. Vol. 2: The Origin of Racial Oppression in Anglo-America*. London: Verso, 1997.

Amundsen, Ron. "Typology Reconsidered: Two Doctrines on the History of Evolutionary Biology." *Biology and Philosophy* 13 (1988): 153–77.

Anderson, Lorin. "Bonnet's Taxonomy and the Chain of Being." *Journal of the History of Ideas* 37 (1976): 45–58.

Anderson, Lorin. *Charles Bonnet and the Order of the Known.* Dordrecht: D. Reidel, 1982.

Anstey, Roger. *The Atlantic Slave Trade and British Abolition.* New Jersey: Humanities Press, 1975.

Appel, Toby A. *The Cuvier-Geoffroy Debate: French Biology in the Decades before Darwin.* Oxford: Oxford University Press, 1987.

Appleton, William. *A Cycle of Cathay: The Chinese Vogue in England during the Seventeenth and Eighteenth Centuries.* New York: Columbia University Press, 1951.

Aravamudan, Srinivas. *Tropicopolitans: Colonialism and Agency 1688–1804.* Durham and London: Duke University Press, 1999.

Arens, William. *The Man-Eating Myth: Anthropology & Anthropophagy.* Oxford and New York: Oxford University Press, 1979.

Armstrong, Meg. " 'The Effects of Blackness': Gender, Race, and the Sublime in Aesthetic Theories of Burke and Kant." *Journal of Art and Aesthetics* 54 (1996): 213–36.

Augstein, H.F. "From the Land of the Bible to the Caucasus and Beyond: The Shifting Ideas of the Geographical Origin of Humankind." In Ernst and Harris. Eds. *Race, Science and Medicine.* London and New York: Routledge. 1999. 58–79.

———. *James Cowles Prichard's Anthropology: Remaking the Science of Man in Early Nineteenth Century Britain.* Amsterdam: Rodopi, 1999.

———. Ed. *Race: The Origins of an Idea, 1760–1850.* London: Thoemmes, 1996.

Baldick, Chris. *In Frankenstein's Shadow: Myth, Monstrosity and Nineteenth-Century Writing.* Oxford: Clarendon Press, 1987.

Ballaster, Ros. *Fabulous Orients: Fictions of the East in England 1662–1785.* Oxford: Oxford University Press, 2005.

Banton, Michael. *Racial Theories.* Cambridge: Cambridge University Press, 1987.

Barber, Ian. "Archaeology, Ethnology, and the Record of Maori Cannibalism before 1815: A Critical Review." *Journal of Polynesian Society* 101 (1992): 241–92.

Barker, Anthony J. *The African Link: British Attitudes to the Negroes in the Era of the Atlantic Slave Trade, 1550–1807.* London: Frank Cass, 1978.

Barker, Francis, Peter Hulme, and Margaret Iversen. Eds. *Cannibalism and the Colonial World.* Cambridge: Cambridge University Press, 1992.

Barkman, C.D. "The Return of the Torghuts from Russia to China." *Journal of Oriental Studies* 2 (1955): 89–115.

Barrell, John. *The Infection of Thomas De Quincey: A Psychopathology of Imperialism.* New Haven: Yale University Press, 1991.

Basker, James G. Ed. *Amazing Grace: An Anthology of Poems about Slavery 1660–1810.* New Haven and London: Yale University Press, 2003.

Batchelor, Robert "Concealing the Bounds: Imagining the British Nation through China." In Felicity Nussbaum. Ed. *The Global Eighteenth*

Century. Johns Hopkins University Press: Baltimore and London, 2003. 79–92.

Beaglehole, J.C. *The Life of Captain James Cook.* Stanford: Stanford University Press, 1974.

Beer, John. *Coleridge the Visionary.* London: Macmillan, 1959.

Bernal, Martin. *Black Athena: The Afroasiatic Roots of Classical Civilization.* London: Free Association Books, 1987. London: Vintage Books, 1991.

Bernasconi, Robert. Ed. *Concepts of Race in the Eighteenth Century.* 8 vols. Bristol: Thoemmes Press, 2001.

———. "Kant and Blumenbach's Polyps: A Neglected Chapter in the History of the Concept of Race." In Eigen and Larrimore. Eds. *The German Invention of Race.* 2006. 73–90.

———. "Kant as an Unfamiliar Source of Racism." In Ward and Lott. Eds. *Philosophers on Race,* 2002. 145–66.

———. "Who Invented the Concept of Race? Kant's Role in the Enlightenment Construction of Race." In Bernasconi. Ed. *Race,* 2001. 11–36.

Bernasconi, Robert and Tommy L. Lott. Eds. *The Idea of Race.* Indianapolis: Hackett Publishing Company, Inc, 2000.

Bickers, Robert A. Ed. *Ritual and Diplomacy: The Macartney Mission to China 1792–94.* London: British Association for Chinese Studies/ Wellsweep, 1993.

Biddiss, M.D. "The Politics of Anatomy: Dr Robert Knox and Victorian Racism." *Proceedings of the Royal Society of Medicine* 69 (1976): 245–50.

Bindman, David. *Ape to Apollo: Aesthetics and the Idea of Race in the 18th Century.* Ithaca: Cornell University Press, 2002.

———. "Blake's Vision of Slavery Revisited." *Huntington Library Quarterly* 58 (1996): 373–79.

Blackburn, Robin. *The Making of New World Slavery: From the Baroque to the Modern 1492–1800.* Verso: London and New York, 1997.

Bohls, Elisabeth. "Standards of Taste, Discourse of 'Race' and the Aesthetic Education of a Monster: Critique of Empire in *Frankenstein.*" *Eighteenth-Century Life* 18 (1994): 23–36.

Booth, Wayne. "'The Self-Portraiture of Genius': *The Citizen of the World* and Critical Method." *Modern Philology* 73 (1976): 585–96.

Bonnet, Alastair. "Constructions of Whiteness in European and American Anti-racism." In Torres, Mirón, and Xavier Inda. Eds. 1999. 200–18.

Botting, Fred. *Making Monstrous: Frankenstein, Criticism, Theory.* Manchester: Manchester University Press, 1991.

Boucher, Philip P. *Cannibal Encounters: Europeans and Island Caribs 1492–1763.* Baltimore and London: Johns Hopkins University Press, 1992.

Boulukos, George. *The Grateful Slave: The Emergence of Race in Eighteenth-Century British and American Culture.* Cambridge: Cambridge University Press, 2007.

———. "Maria Edgeworth's 'Grateful Negro' and the Sentimental Argument for Slavery." *Eighteenth-Century Life* 23 (1999): 12–19.

Bowler, Peter J. "Bonnet and Buffon: Theories of Generation and the Problem of Species." *Journal of the History of Biology* 6 (1973): 259–281.

———. *Evolution: The History of an Idea*. Berkeley: University of California Press, 1983.

Boxhill, Bernard. Ed. *Race and Racism*. Oxford: Oxford University Press, 2003.

Brantlinger, Patrick. *Dark Vanishings: Discourses on the Extinction of Primitive Races, 1800–1930*. Ithaca and London: Cornell University Press, 2003.

———. *Rule of Darkness: British Literature and Imperialism*. Ithaca: Cornell University Press, 1988.

Brockey, Liam Matthew. *Journey to the East: the Jesuit Mission to China, 1579–1724*. Cambridge, MA: The Belknap Press of Harvard University Press, 1965.

Brooks, Christopher. "Goldsmith's *Citizen of the World*: Knowledge and the Imposture of 'Orientalism.'" *Texas Studies in Language and Literature* 35 (1993): 124–44.

Brown, Christopher L. "Empire without Slaves: British Concepts of Emancipation in the Age of the American Revolution." *William and Mary Quarterly* 56.2 (1999): 273–306.

Bulmer, Martin and John Solomos. Eds. *Racism*. Oxford: Oxford University Press, 1999.

Butler, Marilyn. Introduction. *Frankenstein 1818 Text*. World's Classics. Oxford: Oxford University Press, 1993.

———. "Plotting the Revolution: The Political Narratives of Romantic Poetry and Criticism." In Kenneth Johnston, Gilbert Chaitin, Karen Hanson, and Herbert Marks. Eds. *Romantic Revolutions: Criticism and Theory*. Bloomington and Indianapolis: Indiana University Press, 1992. 133–57.

Bynum, W.F. "The Great Chain of Being." *History of Science* 13 (1984): 1–28.

———. "The Great Chain of Being after Forty Years: An Appraisal," *History of Science* 13 (1975): 1–28.

Calder, Alex, Jonathan Lamb, and Bridget Orr. Eds. *Voyages and Beaches, 1769–1840*. Honolulu: University of Hawai'i Press, 1999.

Cameron, Nigel. *Barbarians & Mandarins: Thirteen Centuries of Western Travelers in China*. New York and Tokyo: Weatherhill, 1970.

Carey, Brycchan. *British Abolitionism and the Rhetoric of Sensibility: Writing, Sentiment, and Slavery, 1760–1807*. Basingstoke: Palgrave Macmillan, 2005.

———, and Peter J. Kitson. Eds. *Slavery and the Cultures of Abolition*. Cambridge: Brewer, 2007.

Carretta, Vincent. *Equiano, the African: Biography of a Self-made Man*. Athens: University of Georgia Press, 2005.

———. Introduction. In Olaudah Equiano. *The Interesting Narrative and Other Writings*. Ed. Vincent Carretta. Harmondsworth: Penguin, 1995. ix–xxviii.

———. "Olaudah Equiano or Gustavus Vassa? New Light on an Eighteenth-Century Question of Identity." *Slavery and Abolition*, 20.3 (1996): 96–105.

———. "Questioning the Identity of Olaudah Equiano, or Gustavus Vassa, the African." In Felicity Nussbaum. Ed. *The Global Eighteenth Century*. 2003. 226–35.

Carter, H.B. *Sir Joseph Banks, 1743–1820*. London: British Museum, 1988.

Cary-Elwes, Columba. *China and the Cross: Studies in Missionary History*. London: Longmans, 1957.

Ch'en, Jerome. *China and the West: Society and Culture 1815–1937*. London: Hutchinson, 1979.

Ch'en, Shouyi. "The Chinese Orphan: A Yuan Play: Its Influence on European Drama of the Eighteenth Century." In Hsia. Ed. *Vision of China*. 1999. 359–82.

Ching, Julia and Willard G. Oxtoby. *Discovering China: European Interpretations in the Enlightenment*. New York: University of Rochester Press, 1992.

Cole, F.J. *A History of Comparative Anatomy from Aristotle to the Eighteenth Century*. London: Macmillan, 1949.

Coleman, Deirdre. "Conspicuous Consumption: White Abolitionism and English Women's Protest Writing in the 1790s." *ELH* 61 (1994): 341–62.

———. *Romantic Colonization and British Anti-slavery*. Cambridge: Cambridge University Press, 2005.

Coleman, William. *Georges Cuvier, Zoologist: A Study in the History of Evolutionary Theory*. Cambridge, MA: Harvard University Press, 1964.

Colley, Linda. *Britons: Forging the Nation 1707–1837*. London: Pimlico, 1994.

———. *Captives: Britain, Empire and the World 1600–1850*. London: Pimlico, 2003.

Conant, Martha Pike. *The Oriental Tale in England in the Eighteenth Century*. New York: Columbia University Press, 1908.

Cox, Oliver. *Caste, Class, and Race: A Study in Social Dynamics*. Garden City, NY: Doubleday, 1948.

Cranmer Byng, J. L. "Lord Macartney's Embassy to Peking in 1793, from Official Chinese Documents." *Journal of Oriental* Studies 4: 1–2 (1957–58): 117–87.

Crook, Nora and Derek Guiton. *Shelley's Envenomed Malady*. Cambridge: Cambridge University Press, 1986.

Cross, Stephen J. "John Hunter, the Animal Oeconomy, and Late Eighteenth-Century Physiological Discourse." In William Coleman and Camille Limoges. Eds. *Studies in History of Biology*. Baltimore and London: Johns Hopkins University Press, 1981. 1–110.

Crossley, Pamela Kyle. *The Manchus*. Oxford: Blackwell, 1979.

———. *A Translucent Mirror: the History and Identity in Qing Imperial Mythology*. Berkeley: University of California Press, 1999.

Crouch, Laura. "Davy, a Discourse: A Possible Scientific Source of *Frankenstein*." *Keats-Shelley Journal* 27 (1978): 35–44.

Cullingworth, Charles. *Charles White, FRS: A Great Provincial Surgeon and Obstetrician of the Eighteenth Century*. London: Heney J. Glaisher, 1904.

Cunzhong, Fan. "Sir William Jones's Chinese Studies." In Hsia. Ed. *Vision of China*, 1998. 325–38.

Curtin, Philip D. *The Image of Africa: British Ideas and Actions, 1780–1850*. London: Macmillan, 1964.

Darwin, John. *After Tamerlane: the Global History of Empire*. London: Allen Lane, 2007.

Davis, David Brion. *The Problem of Slavery in the Age of Revolution*. Ithaca: Cornell University Press, 1975.

Dawson, Raymond. *The Chinese Chameleon: An Analysis of European Conceptions of Chinese Civilization*. London and New York: Oxford University Press, 1967.

De Francis, John. *The Chinese Language: Fact and Fantasy*. Honolulu: University of Hawai'i Press, 1984.

De Luca, Vincent A. "Satanic Fall and Hebraic Exodus: An Interpretation of De Quincey's 'Revolt of the Tartars'" *Studies in Romanticism* 8 (1989): 95–108.

Deane, Seamus. "Goldsmith's The Citizen of the World." In Andrew Swarbrick. Ed. *The Art of Oliver Goldsmith*. London: Vision Press, 1984. 33-50.

Desmond, Adrian. *The Politics of Evolution: Morphology, Medicine and Reform in Radical London*. Chicago: University of Chicago Press, 1989.

Dobson, Jessie. *A Guide to the Hunterian Museum*. Edinburgh: E & S. Livingstone, 1958.

Douglas, Guthrie. "The Travel Journals of Peter Camper (1722–1789)." *Edinburgh Medical Journal* 55 (1948): 338–53.

Doyle, Laura. "Racial Sublime." In Richardson and Hofkosh. Eds. *Romanticism, Race and Imperial Culture, 1780–1834*. 1996. 15–39.

Drescher, Seymour. *Econocide: British Slavery in the Era of Abolition*. Pittsburgh: Pittsburgh University Press, 1977.

———. "The Ending of the Slave Trade and the Evolution of European Scientific Racism." In Joseph E Inikori and Stanley Engerman. Eds. *The Atlantic Slave Trade: Effects on Economies, Societies and Peoples in Africa and the Americas*. Durham: Duke University Press, 1992.

Drew, John. *India and the Romantic Imagination*. Delhi: Oxford University Press, 1998.

Dunmore, John. *French Explorers in the Pacific*. 2 vols. Oxford: Clarendon Press, 1965.

Eddy, John H. Jr. "Buffon's *Histoire Naturelle*: History? A Critique of Recent Interpretations." *Isis* 85 (1994): 644–61.

———. "Buffon, Organic Alterations and Man," *Studies in the History of Biology* 85 (1984): 1–45.

Edmond, Rod. *Representing the South Pacific: Colonial Discourse from Cook to Gaugin*. Cambridge: Cambridge University Press, 1997.

Edwards, Paul. *Unreconciled Strivings and Ironic Strategies: Three Afro-British Authors of the Georgian Era: Ignatius Sancho, Olaudah Equiano, Robert Wedderburn.* Edinburgh: Edinburgh University Press, 1992.

Edwards, Philip. *The Story of the Voyage: Sea-Narratives in Eighteenth-Century England.* Cambridge: Cambridge University Press, 1994.

Eigen Sara and Mark Larrimore. Eds. *The German Invention of Race.* Albany: State University of New York Press, 2006.

Elliot, Mark C. *The Manchu Way: The Eight Banners and Ethnic Identity in Late Imperial China.* Stanford: Stanford University Press, 2001.

Ellis, Markman. *The Politics of Sensibility: Race, Gender and Commerce in the Sentimental Novel.* Cambridge: Cambridge University Press, 1996.

Eltis, David. *Economic Growth and the Ending of the Transatlantic Slave Trade.* Oxford: Clarendon Press, 1987.

Ernst, Waltraud and Bernard Harris. Eds. *Race, Science and Medicine, 1700–1960.* London and New York: Routledge, 1999.

Eze, Emmanuel Chukwudi. "The Colour of Reason." In Emmanuel Chukwudi Eze. Ed. *Post Colonial African Philosophy: A Critical Reader.* Oxford: Blackwell, 1997.

———. Ed. *Race and the Enlightenment: A Reader.* Oxford: Blackwell, 1997.

Fan, Cunzhong. *Dr. Johnson and Chinese Culture.* London: The China Society, 1945.

Farber, Paul Lawrence. "Buffon and the Concept of Species." *Journal of the History of Biology* 5 (1972): 259–84.

Fee, Elizabeth. "Nineteenth-Century Craniology: The Study of the Female Skull." *Bulletin of the History of Medicine* 53 (1979): 415–33.

Ferguson, Moira. *Colonialism and Gender from Mary Wollstonecraft to Jamaica Kincaid.* New York: Columbia University Press, 1993.

———. *Subject to Others: British Women Writers and Colonial Slavery 1670–1834.* London and New York: Routledge, 1992.

Fields, Barbara J. "Slavery, Race and Ideology in the United States of America." *New Left Review* 181 (1990): 99.

Forrest, Denys. *Tea for the British: The Social and Economic History of a Famous Trade.* London: Chatto & Windus, 1978.

Foss, Theodore and Donald Lach. "Images of Asia and Asians in European Fiction, 1500–1800." In Thomas Lee. Ed. *China and Europe: Images and Influences in the Sixteenth to the Eighteenth Centuries.* Hong Kong: Chinese University Press, 1991.

Frank, André Gunder. *ReOrient: Global Economy in the Asian Age.* Berkeley: University of California Press, 1998.

Frankenberg, Ruth. *The Social Construction of Whiteness: White Women, Race Matters.* New York and London: Routledge, 1993.

Frayling, Christopher and Robert Wokler. "From the Oran-utan to the Vampire: Towards an Anthropology of Rousseau." In R.A. Leigh. Ed. *Rousseau After 200 Years.* Buffalo: State University of New York Press: Buffalo, 1978.

———. *Vampyres: From Byron to Count Dracula.* London: Faber and Faber, 1991.

Fredrickson, George. *The Black Image in the White Mind: The Debate on Afro-American Character and Destiny, 1817–1914.* New York: Harper, 1971.

———. *Racism.* Princeton: Princeton University Press, 2002.

Fryer, Peter. *Staying Power; The History of Black People in Britain.* London: Pluto Press, 1984.

Fulford, Tim, Debbie Lee, and Peter J. Kitson. *Literature, Science and Exploration in the Romantic Era: Bodies of Knowledge.* Cambridge: Cambridge University Press, 2004.

Fulford, Tim and Peter J. Kitson. Eds. *Romanticism and Colonialism: Writing and Empire, 1780–1830.* Cambridge: Cambridge University Press, 1998.

Gascoigne, John. *Joseph Banks and the English Enlightenment.* Cambridge: Cambridge University Press, 1994.

Gates, Henry Louis Jr. *The Signifying Monkey: A Theory of African American Literary Criticism.* New York and London: Oxford University Press, 1986.

———. Introduction. *Writing "Race," and the Difference It Makes.* Ed. Henry Louis Gates. Chicago: University of Chicago Press, 1996. 1–20.

Gautier, Gary. "Slavery and the Fashioning of Race in *Oronooko, Robinson Crusoe,* and Equiano's *Life." The Eighteenth Century: Theory and Interpretation* 42: 2 (2001): 161–79.

Geggus, David P. *The Impact of the Haitian Revolution in the Atlantic World.* Columbia: University of South Carolina Press, 2001.

Gelber, Harry G. *The Dragon and the Foreign Devils.* London: Bloomsbury, 2007.

Gilbert Sandra M. and Susan Gubar. *The Madwoman in the Attic: The Woman Writer and the Nineteenth-Century Literary Imagination.* 2nd ed. New Haven: Yale University Press, 2000.

Gilman, Sander L. "Black Bodies, White Bodies: Toward an Iconography of Female Sexuality in Late Nineteenth-Century Art, Medicine, and Literature." In Henry Louis Gates. Ed. *"Race," Writing, and Difference.* Chicago and London: University of Chicago Press, 1985. 223–61.

Goldberg, David Theo. Introduction. In David Theo Goldberg. Ed. *Anatomy of Racism.* Minnesota: University of Minnesota Press, 1990.

———. *Racist Culture: Philosophy and the Politics of Meaning.* Oxford: Blackwell, 1993.

Goodfield-Toulmin, June. "Some Aspects of English Physiology." *Journal of the History of Biology* 2 (1969): 283–320.

Gossett, Thomas F. *Race: The History of an Idea in America.* Dallas: Southern Methodist University Press, 1960.

Gould, Philip. *Barbaric Traffic: Commerce and Antislavery in the Eighteenth-Century Atlantic World.* Cambridge MA: Harvard University Press, 2003.

Gould, Stephen Jay. "Bound by the Great Chain." *The Flamingo's Smile: Reflections in Natural History.* New York: W.W. Norton, 1985. 281–90.

———. *Bully for Brontosaurus: Reflections in Natural History.* New York: W.W. Norton, 1991.

———. "Chimp on the Chain." *Natural History* 92 (1983): 18–25.

———. "The Hottentot Venus." *Natural History* 91 (1982): 20–27.

———. *The Mismeasure of Man.* Harmondsworth: Penguin, 1981.

———. *Ontogeny and Phylogeny.* Cambridge MA: Harvard University Press, 1977.

Grabo, Carl A. *Newton among the Poets: Shelley's Use of Science in Prometheus Unbound.* Chapel Hill: University of North Carolina Press, 1930.

Griggs, E.L. *Thomas Clarkson: The Friend of Slaves.* London: Allen and Unwin, 1936.

Guy, R. Kent. "Who Were the Manchus? A Review Essay." *Journal of Asian Studies* 61:2 (2002): 151–64.

Haegar, J.H. "Coleridge's Speculations on Race." *Studies in Romanticism* 13 (1974): 333–57.

Hair, P.E.H. "Attitudes to Africans in English Primary Sources on Guinea up to 1650." *History in Africa* 26 (1999): 223–90.

Hall, Kim F. *Things of Darkness: Economies of Race and Gender in Early Modern England.* Ithaca: Cornell University Press, 1995.

Hall, Stuart. "The Spectacle of the Other." In Stuart Hall. Ed. *Representations: Cultural Representations and Signifying Practices.* London: Sage Publications, 1997.

Hammond, Dorothy and Alta Jablow. *The Africa That Never Was: Four Centuries of British Writing about Africa.* New York: Twayne Publishers, 1970.

Hannaford, Ivan. *Race: the History of an Idea in the West.* Baltimore: Johns Hopkins University Press, 1996.

Hartigan, John. "Establishing the Fact of Whiteness." Eds. Torres, Mirón, and Xavier Inda. 1999. 43–68.

Hevia, James L. *Cherishing Men from Afar: Qing Guest Ritual and the Macartney Embassy of 1793.* Durham and London: Duke University Press, 1995.

———. *English Lessons: The Pedagogy of Imperialism in Nineteenth-Century China.* Durham and London: Duke University Press, 2004.

Hibbert, Christopher. *The Dragon Wakes: China and the West 1793–1911.* Harlow: Longman, 1970.

Hill, Mike. Ed. *Whiteness: A Critical Reader.* New York: New York University Press, 1997.

Hill, Thomas E. and Bernard Boxhill. "Kant and Race." In Boxhill. Ed. *Race and Racism.* 2003. 448–71.

Hiney, Tom. *On the Missionary Trail.* London: Chatto & Windus, 2000.

Hoare, Michael E. *The Tactless Philosopher: Johann Reinhold Forster (1729–98).* Melbourne: Hawthorne Press, 1976.

Hobhouse, Henry. *Seeds of Change: Six Plants that Transformed the World.* London: Sidgwick and Jackson, 1985.

Hochschild, Adam. *Bury the Chains: The British Struggle to Abolish Slavery.* London: Macmillan, 2005.

Hodgen, Margaret T. *Early Anthropology in the Sixteenth and Seventeenth Centuries.* Pennsylvania: University of Pennsylvania Press, 1964.

Hofkosh, Sonia. "Tradition and the Interesting Narrative: Capitalism, Abolitionism, and the Romantic Individual." In Richardson and Hofkosh. Eds. *Romanticism, Race and Imperial Culture, 1780–1834.* 1996. 330–43.

Hogg, Gary. *Cannibalism and Human Sacrifice.* London: Robert Hale, 1990.

Holmes, Richard. *Shelley: the Pursuit.* London: Flamingo, 1995.

Hsia, Adrian. *Chinesia: The European Construction of China in the Literature of the 17th and 18th Centuries.* Tubingen: Max Niemeyer Verlag, 1998.

———. Ed. *The Vision of China in the English Literature of the Seventeenth and Eighteenth Centuries.* Hong Kong: Chinese University Press, 1998.

Hsü, Immanuel C.Y. *The Rise of Modern China.* Oxford: Oxford University Press, 1970.

Hudson, Nicholas. "From 'Nation' to 'Race': The Origins of Racial Classification in Eighteenth-Century Thought." *Eighteenth-Century Studies* 29 (1996): 247–64.

Hulme, Peter. *Colonial Encounters: Europe and the Native Caribbean 1492–1797.* London and New York: Routledge, 1986.

———. *Remnants of Conquest: The Island Caribs and their Visitors, 1877–1998.* Oxford: Oxford University Press, 2000.

———. "Black, Yellow, and White on St. Vincent: Moreau de Jonnès's Carib Ethnography." In Nussbaum. Ed. *The Global Eighteenth Century.* 182–94.

Immerwahr, John. "Hume's Revised Racism." *Journal of the History of Ideas* 53 (1992): 481–86.

Izhboldin, Boris S. *Essays on Tatar History.* New Delhi: New Book Society of India, 1963.

Jackson, Mark. "Changing Depictions of Disease: Race, Representation and the History of Mongolism." In Ernst and Harris. Eds. *Race, Science and Medicine.* 166–88.

Jacyna, L.S. "Immanence or Transcendence: Theories of Organization in Britain, 1790–1835." *Isis* 74 (1983): 311–29.

JanMohammed, Abdul R. "The Economy of the Manichaean Allegory: The Function of Racial Difference in Colonialist Literature." In Gates. Ed. *"Race," Writing and the Difference It Makes.* 78–106.

Jordan, Winthrop D. Introduction. In Samuel Stanhope Smith. *An Essay on the Causes of the Variety of Complexion and Figure in the Human Species.* Ed. Winthrop D. Jordan. Cambridge, MA: The Belknap Press of Harvard University Press, 1965. vi–lvi.

———. *White Over Black: American Attitudes Toward the Negro, 1550–1812.* Chapel Hill: University of North Carolina Press, 1986.

Jordanova, Ludmilla. *Sexual Visions: Images of Gender in Science and Medicine between the Eighteenth and Twentieth Centuries.* Madison: University of Wisconsin Press, 1989.

Juengel, Scott. "Countenancing History: Mary Wollstonecraft, Samuel Stanhope Smith, and Enlightenment Racial Science." *ELH* 68 (2001): 897–927.

Junker, Thomas. "Blumenbach's Racial Geometry." *Isis* 89 (1998): 498–501.

Kaul, Suvir. *Poems of Nation, Anthems of Empire: English Verse in the Long Eighteenth Century.* Charlottesville and London: University Press of Virginia, 2000.

Keane, Patrick J. *Coleridge's Submerged Politics: The Ancient Mariner and Robinson Crusoe.* Columbia and London: University of Minnesota Press, 1994.

Keith, Arthur. "A Discourse on the Portraits and Personality of John Hunter." *British Medical Journal* 1 (1928): 1–15.

Kemp, M. *Dr. William Hunter at the Royal Academy of Arts.* Glasgow: Glasgow University Press, 1975.

Kenyon-Jones, Christine. *Kindred Brutes: Animals in Romantic Period Writing.* London: Ashgate, 2001.

King-Hele, Desmond. *Erasmus Darwin: A Life of Unequalled Achievement.* London: Giles de la Mare, 1999.

King, Richard C. "The (Mis) Uses of Cannibalism in Contemporary Cultural Critique." *Diacritics* 30 (2000): 106–23.

Kitson, J. Peter. Ed. *Placing and Displacing Romanticism.* London: Ashgate, 2001.

———. *The Abolition Debate.* Vol. 2. *Slavery, Abolition and Emancipation.* London: Pickering and Chatto 1999.

———. "Romantic Displacements: Representing Cannibalism." In Peter Kitson. Ed. *Placing and Displacing Romanticism.* Aldershot: Ashgate, 2001. 204–25.

———. Ed. *Theories of Race.* Vol. 8. *Slavery, Abolition and Emancipation.* London: Pickering and Chatto, 1999.

———. and Debbie Lee. Eds. *Slavery, Abolition and Emancipation: Writings from the British Romantic Period.* 8 vols. London: Pickering and Chatto, 1999.

Knight, Charles A. "Ironic Loneliness: The Case of Goldsmith's Chinaman." *JEGP* 82 (1983): 347–64.

Knight, David. *Ordering the World: A History of Classifying Man.* London: Andre Deutsch, 1981.

Knox-Shaw, Peter. "Fanny Price Refuses to Kowtow." *The Review of English Studies,* New Series 47 (1996): 212–21.

Kobler, John. *The Reluctant Surgeon: A Biography of John Hunter.* London: Doubleday, 1960.

Koerner, Lisbet. *Linnaeus: Nature and Nation.* Harvard: Harvard University Press, 1999.

Kowalski-Wallace Elizabeth. *Consuming Subjects: Women, Shopping and Business in the Eighteenth Century.* New York: Columbia University Press, 1997.

Krise, Thomas W. Ed. *Caribbeana: An Anthology of English Literature of the West Indies, 1657–1777.* Chicago: University of Chicago Press, 1999.

Lach, Donald F. *Asia in the Making of Europe,* 3 vols. Chicago: University of Chicago Press, 1965–93.

———. "China and the Era of Enlightenment." *Journal of Modern History* 14 (1942): 209–23.

———. *China in the Eyes of Europe: The Sixteenth Century.* Chicago: University of Chicago Press, 1965.

Lamb, Jonathan, Vanessa Smith, and Nicholas Thomas. Eds. *Exploration & Exchange: A South Seas Anthology 1680–1900.* Chicago: University of Chicago Press, 2000.

———. *Preserving the Self in the South Seas 1680–1840.* Chicago: University of Chicago Press, 2001.

Larrimore, Mark. "Race, Freedom and the Fall in Steffens and Kant." In Ed. Eigen and Larrimore. 2006. 91–120.

———. "Sublime Waste: Kant on the Destiny of the Races." *Canadian Journal of Philosophy. Supplementary Volume* (1999): 99–125.

Larson, James L. *Reason and Experience: The Representation of Natural Order in the Work of Carl von Linné.* Berkeley: University of California Press, 1971.

———. *Interpreting Nature: The Science of Living Form from Linnaeus to Kant.* Baltimore and London: Johns Hopkins University Press, 1974.

Leask, Nigel. *British Romantic Writers and the East: Anxieties of Empire.* Cambridge: Cambridge University Press, 1992.

———. *Curiosity and the Aesthetics of Travel Writing 1770-1840.* Oxford: Oxford University Press, 2002.

———. "Kubla Khan and Orientalism: The Road to Xanadu Revisited." *Romanticism* 4 (1998): 1–21.

Lee, Debbie. *Slavery and the Romantic Imagination.* Philadelphia: University of Pennsylvania Press, 2002.

Le Guyader, Herve. *Geoffroy Saint-Hilaire: A Visionary Naturalist.* Chicago: University of Chicago Press, 2004.

Lestringant, Frank. *Cannibals: The Discovery and Representation of the Cannibal from Columbus to Jules Verne.* Trans. Rosemary Morris. London: Polity Press, 1997.

Levere, Trevor H. *Poetry Realized in Nature: Samuel Taylor Coleridge and Early Nineteenth Century Science.* Cambridge: Cambridge University Press, 1981.

Linebaugh, Peter. "The Tyburn Riot against the Surgeons." In Douglas Hay. Ed. *Albion's Fatal Tree: Crime and Society in Eighteenth-Century England.* New York: Pantheon, 1975.

Lively, Adam. *Masks.* London: Chatto and Windus, 1998.

Livingstone, Frank B. "On the Nonexistence of Human Races." In Sandra G. Harding. Ed. *The Racial Economy of Science: Towards a Democratic Future.* Bloomington: Indiana University Press, 1992.

Lloyd, David. "Race under Representation." *Oxford Literary Review* 13 (1991): 62–94.

Lovejoy, Arthur O. *The Great Chain of Being: A Study of the History of an Idea.* 1936. Cambridge, MA: Harvard University Press, 1964.

Lovett, Richard. *The History of the London Missionary Society, 1795–1895.* 2 vols. London: Henry Frowde, 1899.

Lowes, John Livingston. *The Road to Xanadu: A Study in the Ways of the Imagination.* 1927. London: Pan Books, 1978.

Luke, Hugh Jr. "Sir William Lawrence, Physician to Shelley and Mary." *Papers on English Language and Literature* I (1965): 141–52.

Lynskey, William. "The Scientific Sources of Goldsmith's Animated Nature." *Studies in Philology* 40 (1943): 33–57.

Lyon, Charles H. *To Wash an Aethiop White: British Ideas about Black African Educability 1530–1969.* New York: Teachers College Press, 1975.

Macdonald, D.L. *Poor Polidori: A Critical Biography of the Author of The Vampyre.* Toronto and London: University of Toronto Press, 1991.

MacDonald, Helen. *Human Remains: Dissection and Its Histories.* New Haven and London: Yale University Press, 2005.

MacDougall, Hugh A. *Racial Myth in English History.* Hanover and London: University of New England Press, 1982.

Mackerras, Colin. *Western Images of China.* Hong Kong and Oxford: Oxford University Press, 1989.

Makdisi, Saree. *Romantic Imperialism: Universal Empire and the Culture of Modernity.* Cambridge: Cambridge University Press, 1992.

Malchow H.L. *Gothic Images of Race in Nineteenth-Century Britain.* Stanford: Stanford University Press, 1996.

Man, John. *Kublai Khan: The Mongol King Who Remade China.* London: Random House, 2006.

Markely, Robert. *The Far East and the English Imagination, 1600–1730.* Cambridge: Cambridge University Press, 2006.

Marozzi, Justin. *Tamerlane: Sword of Islam, Conqueror of the World.* London: HarperCollins, 2004.

Marren, Susan. "Between Slavery and Freedom: The Transgressive Self in Olaudah Equiano's Autobiography." *PMLA* 108.1 (1993): 94–105.

Marshall, P.J. and Glyndwr Williams. *The Great Map of Mankind: British Perceptions of the World in the Age of Enlightenment.* London: Dent, 1982.

Marshall, Tim. *Murdering to Dissect: Grave-Robbing Frankenstein and the Anatomy Literature.* Manchester: Manchester University Press, 1995.

McClintock, Anne. *Imperial Leather: Race, Gender and Sexuality in the Colonial Contest.* New York and London: Routledge, 1995.

McKusick, James. "Coleridge and the Politics of Pantisocracy." In Fulford and Kitson. Eds. *Romanticism and Colonialism*. Cambridge: Cambridge University Press, 1998. 107–28.

———. "The Politics of Language in Byron's *The Island*." *ELH* 59 (1992): 839–56.

———. " 'That Silent Sea': Coleridge, Pantisocracy, and the Exploration of the South Pacific." *The Wordsworth Circle* 24 (1993): 102–6.

Meijer, Miriam Claude. *Race and Aesthetics in the Anthropology of Petrus Camper (1722–1789)*. Amsterdam: Rodopi, 1999.

Mellor, Anne K. "The Female in *Frankenstein*." In Anne K. Mellor. Ed. *Romanticism and Feminism*. Bloomington and Indianapolis: Indiana University Press, 1998. 220–32.

———. "Frankenstein, Racial Science, and the Yellow Peril." *Nineteenth-Century Contexts* 23 (2001): 1–28.

———. *Mary Shelley: her Life, Her Fictions, Her Monsters*. London and New York: Routledge, 1988.

Memmi, Albert. *Racism*. Editons Gallimard, 1982. Trans. Steve Martinot. Minnesota: University of Minnesota Press, 2000.

Meyer, A.W. "Some Historical Aspects of the Recapitulation Idea." *Quarterly Review of Biology* 10 (1935): 379–96.

Millward, James A., Ruth W. Dunnell, Mark C. Elliot, and Philipe Forêt. Eds. *New Qing Imperial History: The Making of Inner Asian Empire at Qing Chengde*. London: RoutledgeCurzon, 2004. 91–106.

———. "Qing Inner Asia and the Return of the Torghuts." In James A. Millward, Ruth W. Dunnell, Mark C. Elliot and Philipe Forêt. Eds. *New Qing Imperial History: The Making of Inner Asian Empire at Qing Chengde*. London: RoutledgeCurzon, 2004. 91–106.

Montagu, Ashley M.F. *Edward Tyson, M.D. F.R.S 1650–1708 and the Rise of Human and Comparative Anatomy in England*. Philadelphia: The American Philosophical Society, 1943.

Moore, Wendy. *The Knife Man: Blood, Body-Snatching and the Birth of Modern Surgery*. London: Bantam Books, 2005.

Moran, Francis III. "Between Primates and Primitives: Natural Man as the Missing Link in Rousseau's *Second Discourse*." In Ward and Lott. Eds. *Philosophers on Race*. 2002. 125–44.

Morgan, David. *The Mongols*. Oxford: Blackwell, 1986.

Morretti, Franco. *Signs Taken for Wonders: Essays on the Sociology of Literary Form*. London: Verso Books, 1988.

Morton, Timothy. "Blood Sugar." Eds. Fulford and Kitson. 1998. 87–106.

———. *The Poetics of Spice: Romantic Consumerism and the Exotic*. Cambridge: Cambridge University Press, 2000.

———. *Shelley and the Revolution in Taste: The Body and the Natural World*. Cambridge: Cambridge University Press, 1994.

Mosse, George L. *Towards the Final Solution: A History of European Racism*. Madison: University of Wisconsin Press, 1985.

Mote, F. W. *Imperial China 900–1800*. Cambridge MA: Harvard University Press, 1999.

Mudford, Peter G. "William Lawrence and the Natural History of Man." *Journal of the History of Ideas* 29 (1968): 430–36.

Mungello, D.E. *Curious Land: Jesuit Accommodation and the Origins of Sinology*. Honolulu: The University of Hawai'i Press, 1985.

Muthu, Sankar. *Enlightenment against Empire*. Princeton: Princeton University Press, 2003.

Neill, Stephen. *A History of Christian Missions*. Harmondsworth: Penguin, 1964; Reprinted, 1980.

Niro, Brian. *Race*. Basingstoke: Palgrave, 2003.

Nussbaum, Felicity A. Ed. *The Global Eighteenth Century*. Baltimore: Johns Hopkins University Press, 2003.

———. *The Limits of the Human: Fictions of Anomaly, Race, and Gender in the Long Eighteenth Century*. Cambridge: Cambridge University Press, 2003.

———. *Torrid Zones: Maternity, Sexuality, and Empire in Eighteenth-Century English Narratives*. Baltimore: John Hopkins University Press, 1995.

Obeyesekere, Gananath. *The Apotheosis of Captain Cook: European Mythmaking in the Pacific, with a New Afterword*. Princeton: Princeton University Press, 1997.

———. "'British Cannibals': Contemplation of an Event in the Death and Resurrection of James Cook, Explorer." *Critical Inquiry* 18 (1992): 630–54.

Ogude, S.E. "Facts into Fiction: Equiano's Narrative Reconsidered." *Research in African Literatures* 13 (1982): 31–43.

Outram, Dorinda. *Georges Cuvier, Vocation, Science and Authority in Post-Revolutionary France*. Manchester: Manchester University Press. 1984.

Parker, Edward Harper. *Thousand Years of the Tartars*. London: Kegan Paul, 1924.

Perdue, Peter C. *China Marches West: The Qing Conquest of Central Eurasia*. Cambridge MA: Belknap Press of Harvard University Press, 2005.

Peterson, Thomas Virgil. *Ham and Japheth: The Mythic World of Whites in the Antebellum South*. London: Scarecrow Press, 1978.

Peyrefitte, Alain. *The Collison of Two Civilisations: The British Expedition to China 1792–4*. London: Harvill (HarperCollins), 1993.

Pickerstone, John V. and Steven V. F. Butler. "The Politics of Medicine in Manchester, 1788–1792: Hospital Reform and Public Health Services in the Early Industrial City." *Medical History* 28 (1984): 227–49.

Poliakov, Léon. *The Aryan Myth: A History of Racist and Nationalistic Ideas in Europe*. London and New York: Barnes & Noble, 1974.

Pomeranz, Kenneth. *The Great Divergence: China, Europe and the Making of the Modern World Economy*. Princeton: Princeton University Press, 2000.

Popkin, Richard H. *Isaac La Peyrère (1596–1676): His Life, Work and Influence*. Leiden: E.J. Brill, 1987.

———. "The Philosophical Basis of Eighteenth-Century Racism." Ed. Harold E. Pagliaro. *Racism in the Eighteenth Century: Studies in*

Eighteenth Century Culture. Vol. 2. Cleveland and London: The Press of Case Western University. 1973. 245–62.

Porter, David. *Ideographia: The Chinese Cipher in Early Modern Europe.* Stanford: Stanford University Press, 2001.

Potkay, Adam. "Olaudah Equiano and the Art of Spiritual Autobiography." *Eighteenth-Century Studies* 27.4 (1994): 677–92.

Pratt, Mary Louise. *Imperial Eyes: Travel Writing and Transculturation.* New York and London, 1992.

Prawdin, Michael. *The Mongol Empire: Its Rise and Legacy.* London: Allen and Unwin, 1941.

Pritchard, Earl H. *The Crucial Years of Early Anglo-Chinese Relations, 1750–1800.* Washington: Pullman, 1936.

Qian, Zhongshu. "China in the Literature of the Seventeenth Century." In Hsia. Ed. *Vision of China.* 1998. 29–68.

Rae, Isobel. *Knox the Anatomist.* Edinburgh and London: Oliver and Boyd, 1964.

Rainger, Ronald. "Race, Politics, and Science: The Anthropological Society of London in the 1880s." *Victorian Studies* 22 (1978): 51–70.

Rawski, Evelyn. *The Last Emperors: A Social History of the Qing Imperial Institutions.* Berkeley and Los Angeles: University of California Press, 1998.

———. "The 'Prosperous Age': China in the Kangxi, Yongzheng and Qianlong Reigns." In Rawski and Rawson. Eds. *China: The Three Emperors, 1662–1795.* 2006. 178–207. 22–40.

Rawski, Evelyn and Jessica Rawson. Eds. *China: The Three Emperors, 1662–1795,* London: Royal Academy of Arts, 2006.

Rawson, Claude. "Savages Noble and Ignoble: Natives, Cannibals and Others in South-Pacific Narratives by Gulliver, Bougainville, and Diderot, with Notes of the Encyclopaedia and on Voltaire." *Eighteenth-Century Life* 18 (1994): 168–97.

Reill, Peter Hanns. *Vitalizing Nature in the Enlightenment.* Berkeley and London: University of California Press, 2005.

Rennie, Neil. *Far-Fetched Facts; Literature and the Idea of the South Seas.* Oxford: Oxford University Press, 1995.

Richardson, Alan. *Literature, Education and Romanticism.* Cambridge: Cambridge University Press, 1994.

———. " 'The Sorrows of Yamba' by Eaglesfield Smith and Hannah More: Authorship, Ideology, and the Fractures of Antislavery Discourse." *Romanticism on the Net* 28 (2002). February 10, 2007 at http://www.erudit.org/revue/ron/2002/v/n28/007209ar.html.

Richardson, Alan and Sonia Hofkosh. Eds. *Romanticism, Race, and Imperial Culture, 1780–1834.* Bloomington: Indiana University Press, 1996.

Richardson, David. "The British Empire and the Atlantic Slave Trade, 1660–1807." In *The Oxford History of the British Empire.* Vol. 2. *The Eighteenth Century.* Ed. P.J. Marshall. Oxford and New York: Oxford University Press. 1998. 440–63.

Richardson, Ruth. *Death, Dissection and the Destitute.* Chicago: University of Chicago Press, 2001.

Rieger, James. "Dr Polidori and the Genesis of *Frankenstein*." *Studies in English Literature* 3 (1963): 461–72.

Roger, Jacques and Sarah Lucille Bonnefoi. *Buffon*. Ithaca: Cornell University Press, 1999.

Rolfe, Ian W.D. "William and John Hunter: Breaking the Great Chain of Being." In *William Hunter and the Eighteenth-Century Medical World*. Ed. W.F. Bynum and Roy Porter. Cambridge: Cambridge University Press, 1985. 297–322.

Rupp-Eisendreich, Britta. *Choses occultes en histoire des sciences humaines: le destin de la "science nouvelle" de Christophe Meiners*. *Ethnographie* (1983): 90–91, 131–83.

Russell, E.S. *Form and Function: A Contribution to the History of Animal Morphology*. London: John Murray, 1916.

Ruston, Sharon. *Shelley and Vitality*. Basingstoke: Palgrave, 2005.

Saakwa-Mante, Norris. "Western Medicine and Racial Constitutions: Surgeon John Atkins' Theory of Polygenism and Sleepy Distemper in the 1730s." In Ernst and Harris. Ed. *Race, Science and Medicine*. London and New York: Routledge. 1999. 28–57.

Said, Edward W. *Culture and Imperialism* 1993. London: Vintage, 1994.

———. *Orientalism* 1978. Harmondsworth, Penguin, 1978.

Salmond, Anne. *The Trial of the Cannibal Dog: The Remarkable Story of Captain Cook's Encounters in the South Seas*. New Haven: Yale University Press, 2003.

———. *Two Worlds: First Meetings between Maori and Europeans, 1642–1772*. Auckland: Viking, 1991.

Sanbourn, Geoffrey. *The Sign of the Cannibal: Melville and the Making of a Postcolonial Reader*. Durham and London: Duke University Press, 1998.

Sandiford, Keith. *Measuring the Moment: Strategies of Protest in Eighteenth-Century Afro-English Writing*. Selingsgrove, PA: Susquehanna University Press, 1988.

Sarafianos, A. "The Natural History of Man and the Politics of Medical Portraiture in Manchester." *Art Bulletin* 88 (2006): 102–18.

Saunders, J.J. "Matthew Paris and the Mongols." In T. A. Sandqist and M.R. Powicke. Eds. *Essays in Medieval History Presented to Bertie Wilkinson*. Toronto: University of Toronto Press, 1969. 116–33.

Schama, Simon. *Rough Crossings: Britain, the Slaves and the American Revolution*. London: BBC Books, 2005.

Schiebinger, Londa. "The Anatomy of Difference: Race and Sex in Eighteenth-Century Science." *Eighteenth-Century Studies* 23 (1990): 387–405.

———. *The Mind Has No Sex? Women in the Origins of Modern Science*. Cambridge MA: Harvard University Press, 1989.

———. *Nature's Body*. London: Pandora, 1994.

Schneider, Elisabeth Wintersteen. *Coleridge, Opium and Kubla Khan*. Chicago: University of Chicago Press, 1953.

Shaffer, E.S. *"Kubla Khan" and the Fall of Jerusalem: The Mythological School in Biblical Criticism and Secular Literature.* Cambridge: Cambridge University Press, 1975.

Shell, Susan M. "Kant's Concept of a Human Race." Eigen and Larrimore. Eds. 2006. 55–72.

Shyllon F.O. *Black Slaves in Britain.* London: Oxford University Press, 1974.

Singer, Aubrey. *The Lion & the Dragon: The Story of the First British Embassy to the Court of the Emperor Qianlong in Peking 1792–94.* London: Barrie and Jenkins, 1992.

Sloan, Phillip R. "Buffon, German Biology and the Historical Interpretation of Species." *British Journal of the History of Science* 12 (1979): 109–53.

———. "The Buffon-Linnaeus Controversy." *Isis* 67 (1976): 356–75.

———. "The Idea of Racial Degeneracy in Buffon's *Histoire Naturelle.*" In Harold E. Pagliaro. Ed. *Studies in Eighteenth-Century Culture.* Cleveland and London: Case of Western Reserve University, 1973. 293–321.

Smith, Hamilton Jewett. *Oliver Goldsmith's* The Citizen of the World. New Haven: Yale University Press, 1926.

Smith, Vanessa. *Literary Culture and the Pacific.* Cambridge: Cambridge University Press, 1998.

Solow, Barbara Lewis and Stanley L. Engerman. Eds. *British Capitalism and Caribbean Slavery: the Legacy of Eric Williams.* Cambridge: Cambridge University Press, 1987.

Spence, Jonathan D. *The Chan's Great Continent: China in Western Minds.* London: Allen Lane Penguin Press, 1999.

———. *The Search for Modern China.* New York: W.W. Norton, 1990.

Spivak, Gayatri Chakravorty. "Can the Subaltern Speak." In Cary Nelson and Lawrence Grossberg. Eds. *Marxism and the Interpretation of Culture.* Chicago: University of Illinois Press, 1988. 271–313.

St Clair, William. *The Grand Slave Emporium: Cape Coast Castle and the British Slave Trade.* Profile Books: London, 2006.

Stanton, William. *The Leopard's Spots: Scientific Attitudes towards Race in America 1815–59.* Chicago: University of Chicago Press, 1960.

Stepan, Nancy Leys. *The Idea of Race in Science: Great Britain.* London: Macmillan, 1982.

———. "Race and Gender: The Role of Analogy in Science." *Isis* 77 (1986): 261–77.

Stocking, George W. Jr. "What's in a Name? The Origins of the Royal Anthropological Institute (1837–71)." *Man* 6 (1973): 369–90.

Strahlenberg, Philip John von. *An Historico-Geographical Description of the North and Eastern Parts of Europe and Asia but more particularly of Russia, Siberia and Great Tartary.* London, 1788.

Sypher, Wylie. *Guinea's Captive Kings: British Antislavery Literature of the XVIII Century.* New York: Octagon Books, 1969.

Taylor, Selwyn. *John Hunter and His Painters.* London: Royal College of Surgeons, 1993.

Teltscher, Kate. *The High Road to China: George Bogle, the Panchen Lama and the First British Expedition to Tibet.* London: Bloomsbury, 2006.

Temkin, Owen. *The Double Face of Janus.* Baltimore: Johns Hopkins University Press, 1977.

Thomas, Helen. *Romanticism and Slave Narratives.* Cambridge: Cambridge University Press, 2000.

Thomas, Hugh. *The Slave Trade: The History of the Atlantic Slave Trade, 1440–1870.* New York and London: Picador, 1977.

Thomas, Nicholas. *Colonialism's Culture: Anthropology, Travel and Government.* London: Polity Press, 1994.

———. *Discoveries: the Voyages of Captain Cook.* London: Allen Lane, 2003.

———. *Entangled Objects: Exchange, Material Culture, and Colonialism in the Pacific.* Cambridge, MA: Harvard University Press, 1991.

———. "The Force of Ethnology: Origins and Significance of the Melanesia/Polynesia Division," *Cultural Anthropology* 30 (1989): 27–34.

———. *In Oceania: Visions, Artifacts, Histories.* Durham and London: Duke University Press, 1997.

Torres, Rodolfo D., Louis F. Mirón, and Jonathan Xavier Inda. Eds. *Race, Identity and Citizenship: A Reader.* Oxford: Blackwell, 1999.

Turnbull, Paul. "Enlightenment Anthropology and the Ancestral Remains of Australian Aboriginal People." Calder, Lamb, and Orr. Ed. *Voyages and Beaches: Pacific Encounters, 1769–1840.* Honolulu: University of Hawai'i Press, 1999. 202–25.

Van Den Berghe, Pierre L. "Does Race Matter?" In Boxhill. Ed. *Race and Racism.* 2003. 101–13.

Veeder, William R. *Mary Shelley & Frankenstein: The Fate of Androgyny.* Chicago: University of Chicago Press, 1989.

Voeglin, Eric. "The Growth of the Race Idea." *Review of Politics* 2 (1940): 283–317.

Wakeman Jr. Frederic. *The Great Enterprise: The Manchu Reconstruction of Imperial Order in Seventeenth-Century China.* 2 vols. Berkeley: University of California Press, 1985.

Waley-Cohen, Joanna. "Diplomats, Jesuits and Foreign Curiosities." In Rawski and Rawson. Eds. *China: The Three Emperors, 1662–1795.* 2006. 178–207.

Walvin, James. *Questioning Slavery.* London and New York: Routledge, 1996.

Ward, Julie and Tommy L. Lott. Eds. *Philosophers on Race.* Oxford: Blackwell, 2002.

Wells, Kentwood D. "Sir William Lawrence (1783–1867): A Study of Pre-Darwinian Ideas on Heredity and Variation." *Journal of the History of Biology* 4 (1971): 319–62.

Whale, John. "De Quincey, Landscape, and Spiritual History." *Worldviews* (2001) 2: 4–19.

Wheeler, Roxann. ' "Betrayed by Some of My Own Complexion:' Cugoano, Abolition, and the Contemporary Language of Racialism." In Vincent

Carretta and Philip Gould. Eds. *Genius in Bondage: Literature of the Early Black Atlantic*. Lexington: University Press of Kentucky, 1999. 17–38.

———. *The Complexion of Race: Categories of Difference in Eighteenth-Century British Culture*. Philadelphia: University of Pennsylvania Press, 2000.

White, Hayden. *Tropics of Discourse: Essays in Cultural Criticism*. Baltimore and London: Johns Hopkins University Press, 1978.

Wiegman, Robyn. *American Anatomies: Theorizing Race and Gender*. Durham, NC: Duke University Press, 1995.

Williams, Eric. *Capitalism and Slavery*. Chapel Hill: University of North Carolina Press, 1944.

Williams, Glyndwr. *The Prize of All the Oceans*. London: HarperCollins, 1999.

Wilson, Ellen Gibson. *Thomas Clarkson: A Biography*. London: Macmillan, 1989.

Wilson, Kathleen. Ed. *A New Imperial History: Culture, Identity and Modernity in Britain and the Empire 1660–1840*. Cambridge: Cambridge University Press, 2003.

———. *This Island Race: Englishness, Empire and Gender in the Eighteenth Century*. London and New York: Routledge, 2003.

Wise, Sarah. *The Italian Boy: Murder and Grave-Robbery in 1830s London*. London: Jonathan Cape. 2004.

Wise, Stephen M. *Though the Heavens May Fall: The Landmark Trial that Led to the End of Human Slavery*. Pimlico: London, 2006.

Wokler, Robert. "Perfectible Apes in Decadent Cultures: Rousseau's Anthropology Revisited." *Daedalus* 107 (1978): 107–34.

———. "The Ape Debates in Enlightenment Anthropology." *Studies on Voltaire and the Eighteenth Century* 192 (1980): 1164–75.

Wood, Marcus. *Slavery, Empathy and Pornography*. Oxford: Oxford University Press, 2002.

———. Ed. *The Poetry of Slavery: An Anglo-American Anthology*. Oxford: Oxford University Press, 2003.

Woodard, Helena. *African-British Writings in the Eighteenth Century: The Politics of Reason and Race*. Westport: Greenwood Press, 1999.

Young, Robert J.C. *Colonial Desire: Hybridity in Theory, Culture and Race*. London and New York: Routledge, 1995.

Youngquist, Paul. *Monstrosities: Bodies and British Romanticism*. Minneapolis: University of Minnesota Press, 2003.

Zammito John H. *Kant, Herder and the Birth of Anthropology*. Chicago: University of Chicago Press, 2002.

Zantop, Suzanne. "The Beautiful, the Ugly, and the German: Race, Gender, and Nationality in Eighteenth-Century Anthropological Discourse." In P. Herminghouse and M. Mueller. Eds. *Gender and Germanness: Cultural Productions of Nation*. Providence, RI: Berghahn Books, 1997. 21–35.

————. *Colonial Fantasies: Conquest, Family, and Nation in Precolonial Germany, 1770–1870*. Durham and London: Duke University Press, 1997.

Zammito, John H. "Policing Polygeneticism in Germany, 1775: (Kames) Kant, and Blumenbach." In Eigen and Larrimore. Eds. *German Invention of Race*. 2006. 35–54.

Zhang, Shunhong. "The Qing Court's Perception of and Reaction to the Macartney Embassy." In Bickers. Ed. *Ritual and Diplomacy*. 1993. 31–43

INDEX

Printed in the United States
131274LV00003B/21/P

9 781403 976451